P9-AOI-058

IMAGE COMICS PRESENTS

ROCHE LIMIT

VOL. ONE ANOMALOUS

ROCHE LIMIT VOL.1. FIRST PRINTING, MARCH, 2015. PUBLISHED BY IMAGE COMICS, INC. OFFICE OF PUBLICATION: 2001 CENTER ST. SIXTH FLOOR, BERKELEY, CA 94704. COPYRIGHT © 2015 MICHAEL MORECI. ORIGINALLY PUBLISHED IN SINGLE MAGAZINE FORM ROCHE LIMIT 1-5. ALL RIGHTS RESERVED. ROCHE LIMIT™ (INCLUDING ALL PROMINENT CHARACTERS FEATURED HEREIN), ITS LOGO AND ALL CHARACTER LIKENESSES ARE TRADEMARKS OF MICHAEL MORECI, UNLESS OTHERWISE NOTED. IMAGE COMICS® AND ITS LOGOS ARE REGISTERED TRADEMARKS OF IMAGE COMICS, INC. NO PART OF THIS PUBLICATION MAY BE REPRODUCED OR TRANSMITTED, IN ANY FORM OR BY ANY MEANS (EXCEPT FOR SHORT EXCERPTS FOR REVIEW PURPOSES) WITHOUT THE EXPRESS WRITTEN PERMISSION OF IMAGE COMICS, INC. ALL NAMES, CHARACTERS, EVENTS AND LOCALES IN THIS PUBLICATION ARE ENTIRELY FICTIONAL. ANY RESEMBLANCE TO ACTUAL PERSONS (LIVING OR DEAD), EVENTS OR PLACES, WITHOUT SATIRIC INTENT, IS COINCIDENTAL. PRINTED IN THE USA. FOR INFORMATION REGARDING THE CPSIA ON THIS PRINTED MATERIAL CALL: 203-595-3636 AND PROVIDE REFERENCE
RICH – 609511.

ISBN: 978-1-63215-198-5
FOR INTERNATIONAL RIGHTS/FOREIGN LICENSING, CONTACT: FOREIGNLICENSING.IMAGECOMICS.COM

IMAGE COMICS, INC.
Robert Kirkman – Chief Operating Officer
Erik Larsen – Chief Financial Officer
Todd McFarlane – President
Marc Silvestri – Chief Executive Officer
Jim Valentino – Vice-President

Eric Stephenson – Publisher
Ron Richards – Director of Business Development
Jennifer de Guzman – Director of Trade Book Sales
Kat Salazar – Director of PR & Marketing
Corey Murphy – Director of Retail Sales
Jeremy Sullivan – Director of Digital Sales
Emilio Bautista – Sales Assistant
Branwyn Bigglestone – Senior Accounts Manager
Emily Miller – Accounts Manager
Jessica Ambriz – Administrative Assistant
Tyler Shainline – Events Coordinator
David Brothers – Content Manager
Jonathan Chan – Production Manager
Drew Gill – Art Director
Meredith Wallace – Print Manager
Addison Duke – Production Artist
Vincent Kukua – Production Artist
Tricia Ramos – Production Assistant
IMAGECOMICS.COM

Brookline Public Library

ONE

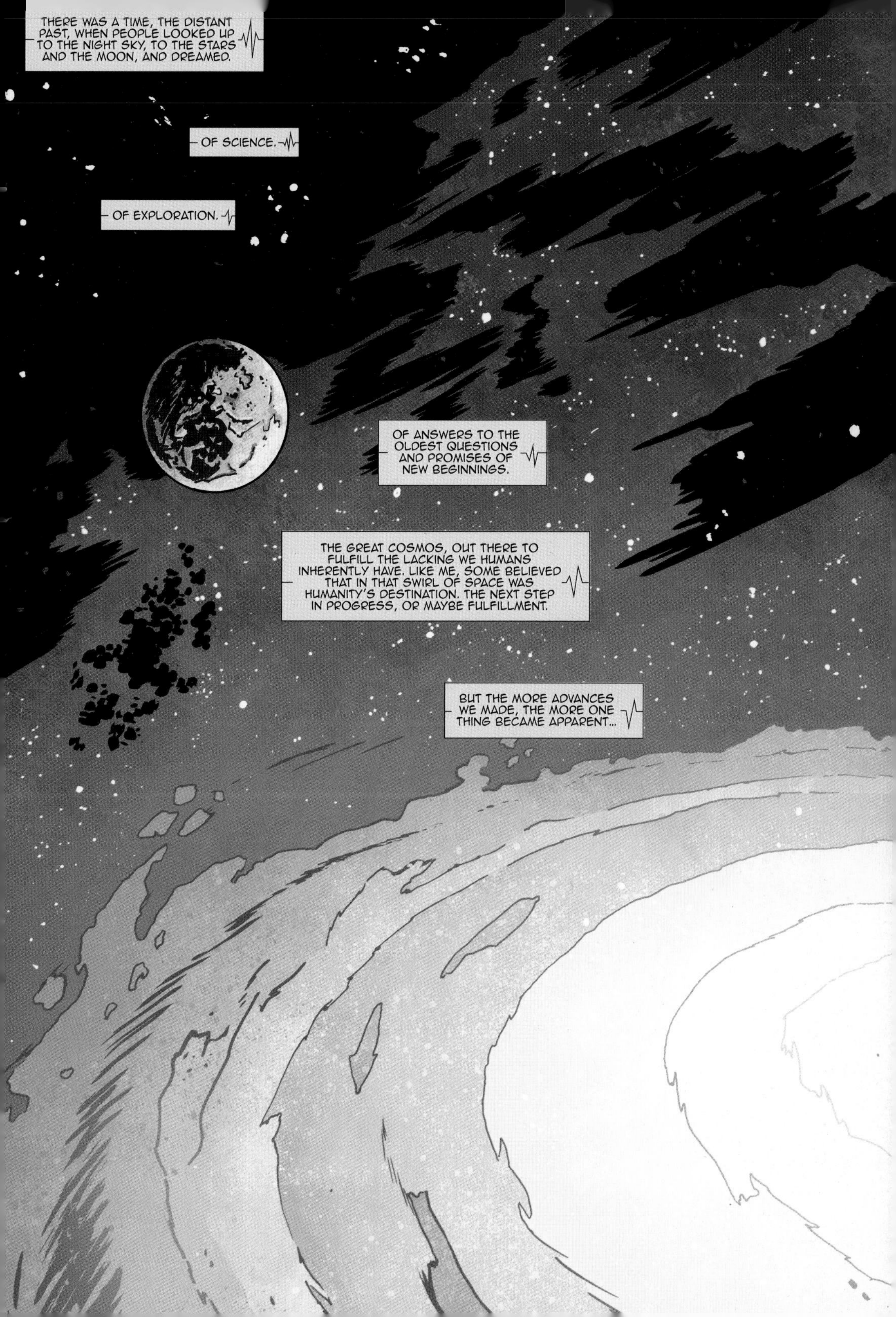
THERE WAS A TIME, THE DISTANT PAST, WHEN PEOPLE LOOKED UP TO THE NIGHT SKY, TO THE STARS AND THE MOON, AND DREAMED.
OF SCIENCE.
OF EXPLORATION.
OF ANSWERS TO THE OLDEST QUESTIONS AND PROMISES OF NEW BEGINNINGS.
THE GREAT COSMOS, OUT THERE TO FULFILL THE LACKING WE HUMANS INHERENTLY HAVE. LIKE ME, SOME BELIEVED THAT IN THAT SWIRL OF SPACE WAS HUMANITY'S DESTINATION. THE NEXT STEP IN PROGRESS, OR MAYBE FULFILLMENT.
BUT THE MORE ADVANCES WE MADE, THE MORE ONE THING BECAME APPARENT...

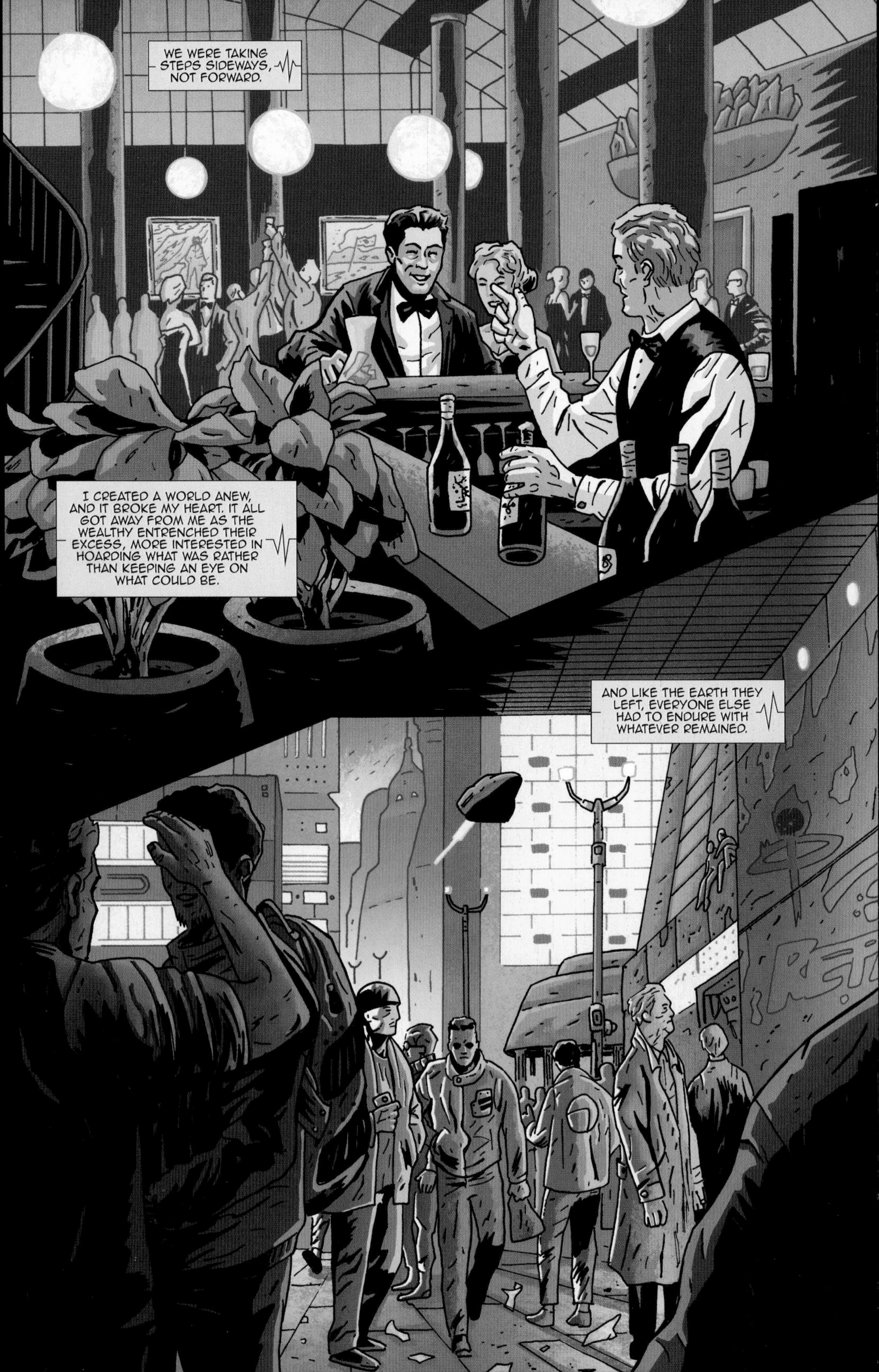

WE WERE TAKING STEPS SIDEWAYS, NOT FORWARD.
I CREATED A WORLD ANEW, AND IT BROKE MY HEART. IT ALL GOT AWAY FROM ME AS THE WEALTHY ENTRENCHED THEIR EXCESS, MORE INTERESTED IN HOARDING WHAT WAS RATHER THAN KEEPING AN EYE ON WHAT COULD BE.
AND LIKE THE EARTH THEY LEFT, EVERYONE ELSE HAD TO ENDURE WITH WHATEVER REMAINED.

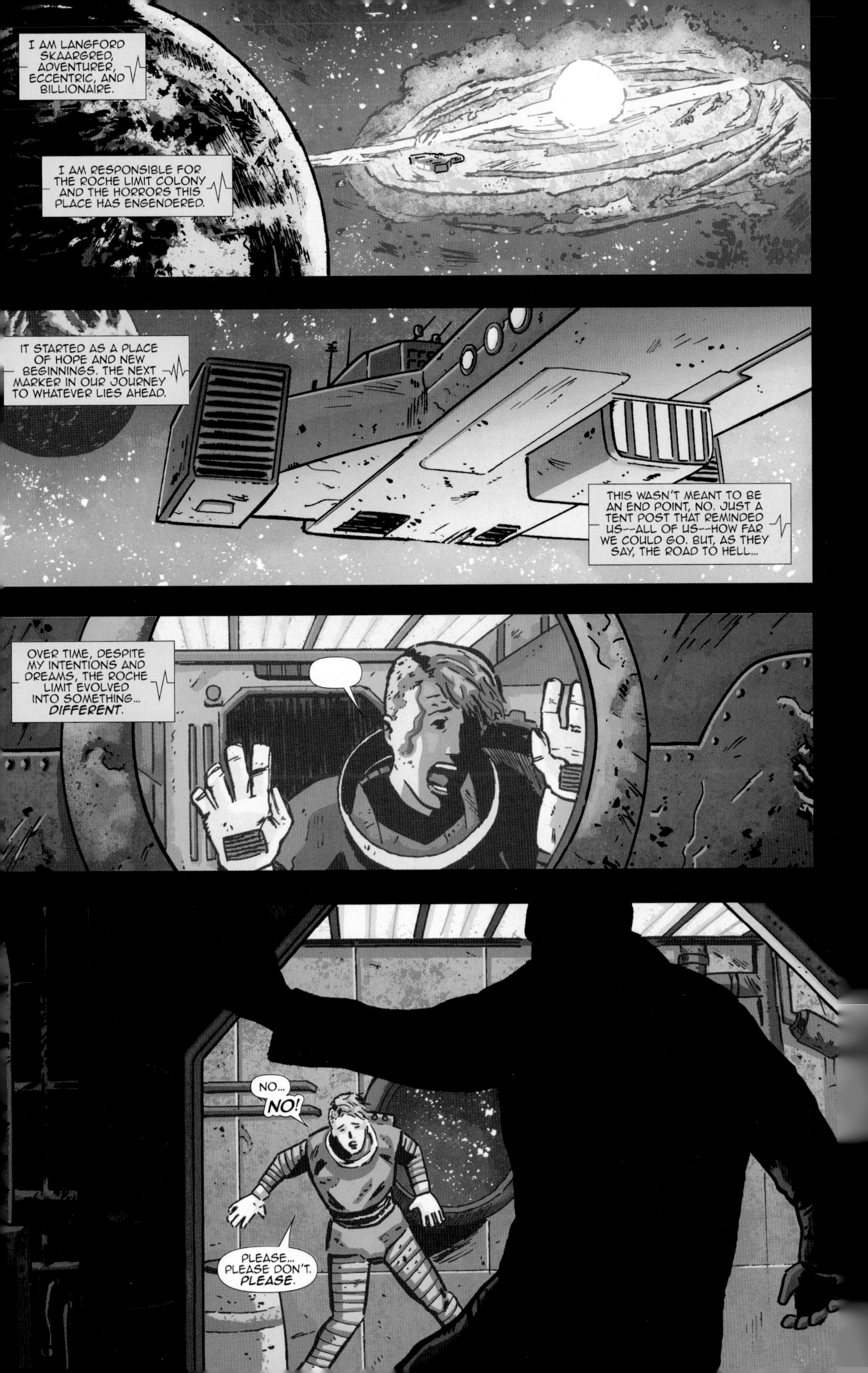
I AM LANGFORD SKAARGRED, ADVENTURER, ECCENTRIC, AND BILLIONAIRE.
I AM RESPONSIBLE FOR THE ROCHE LIMIT COLONY AND THE HORRORS THIS PLACE HAS ENGENDERED.
IT STARTED AS A PLACE OF HOPE AND NEW BEGINNINGS. THE NEXT MARKER IN OUR JOURNEY TO WHATEVER LIES AHEAD.
THIS WASN'T MEANT TO BE AN END POINT, NO. JUST A TENT POST THAT REMINDED US--ALL OF US--HOW FAR WE COULD GO. BUT, AS THEY SAY, THE ROAD TO HELL...
OVER TIME, DESPITE MY INTENTIONS AND DREAMS, THE ROCHE LIMIT EVOLVED INTO SOMETHING... *DIFFERENT*.
NO... ***NO!***
PLEASE... PLEASE DON'T. ***PLEASE***.

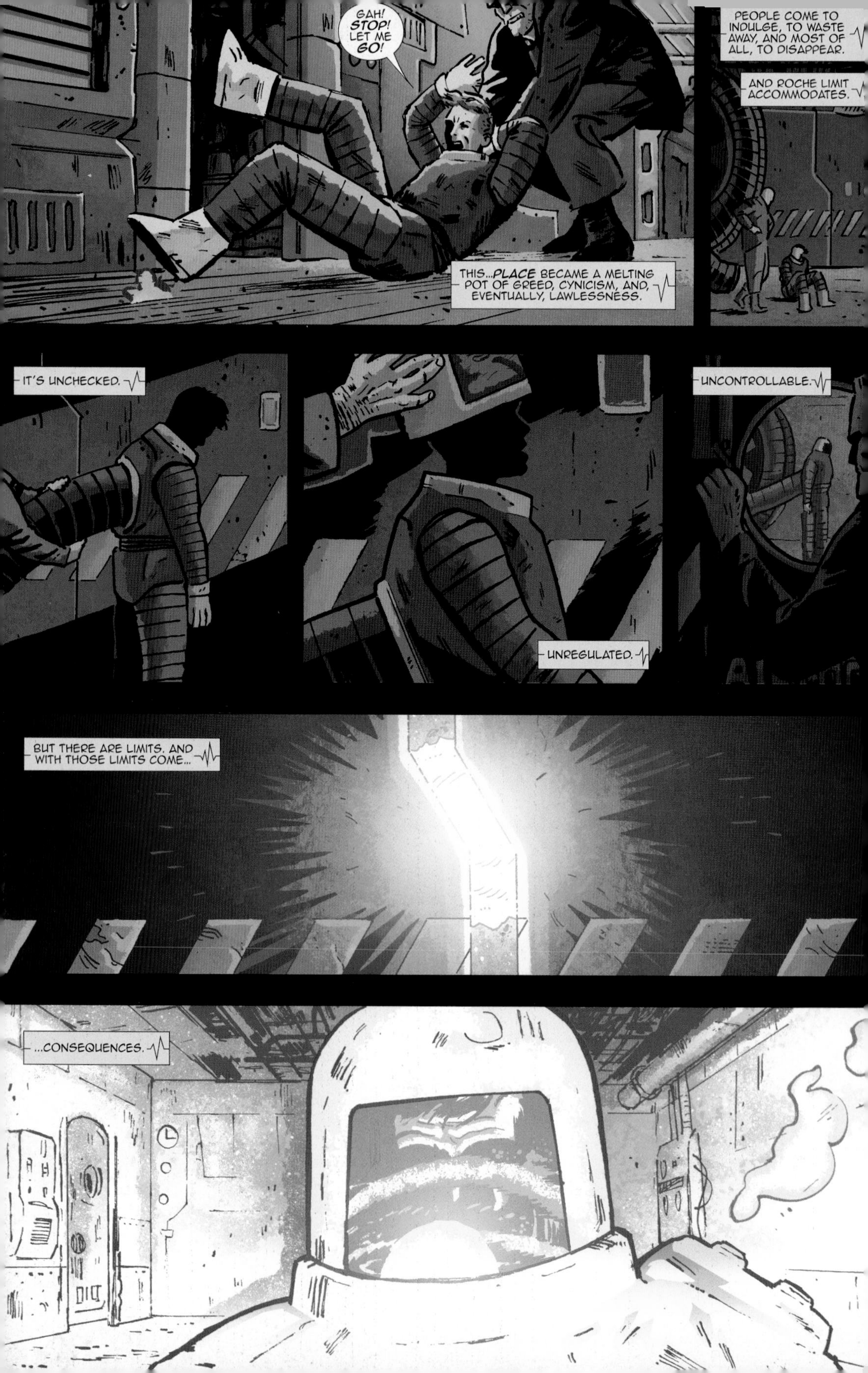
GAH! STOP! LET ME GO!
PEOPLE COME TO INDULGE, TO WASTE AWAY, AND MOST OF ALL, TO DISAPPEAR.
AND ROCHE LIMIT ACCOMMODATES.
THIS...PLACE BECAME A MELTING POT OF GREED, CYNICISM, AND, EVENTUALLY, LAWLESSNESS.
IT'S UNCHECKED.
UNREGULATED.
UNCONTROLLABLE.
BUT THERE ARE LIMITS. AND WITH THOSE LIMITS COME...
...CONSEQUENCES.

LD YOU FEEL THE
…ALY PULLING YOU
…AS SOME HAVE...

IF YOU MAKE THAT LEAP,
SHOULD YOU RETURN...

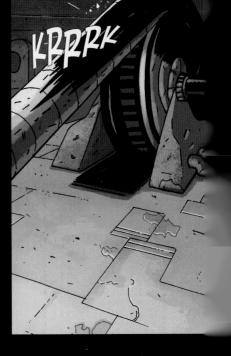

KRRRK

T MAY BE THE
…ATH OF US ALL.

ROCHE LIMIT COLONY

-Discovered by a joint United States/Russian terraforming expedition to Andromeda, little is known of this energy anomaly. The event behaves like a black hole without the crippling effects of gravity. It consumes light and energy, but its gravity isn't so dense that it collapses everything in its radius, nor does it prevent light from escaping.

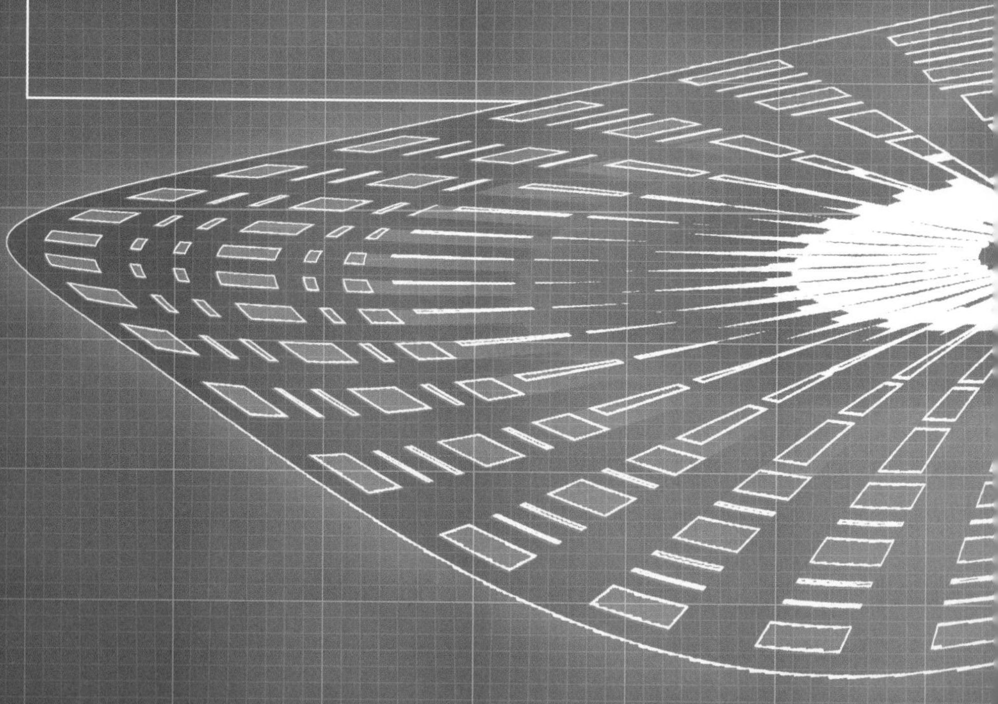

Roche Limit Colony

-A manmade space colony built in Dispater, a terrestrial dwarf planet, situated on the cusp of an energy anomaly in the Andromeda Galaxy.

-Population: Unknown. Estimations range from 10,000 to much more.

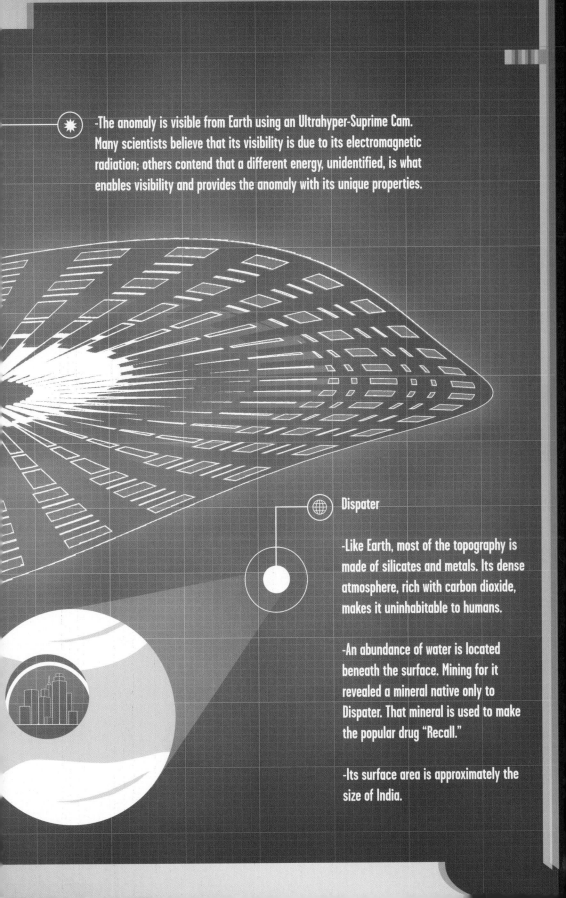

-The anomaly is visible from Earth using an Ultrahyper-Suprime Cam. Many scientists believe that its visibility is due to its electromagnetic radiation; others contend that a different energy, unidentified, is what enables visibility and provides the anomaly with its unique properties.

Dispater

-Like Earth, most of the topography is made of silicates and metals. Its dense atmosphere, rich with carbon dioxide, makes it uninhabitable to humans.

-An abundance of water is located beneath the surface. Mining for it revealed a mineral native only to Dispater. That mineral is used to make the popular drug "Recall."

-Its surface area is approximately the size of India.

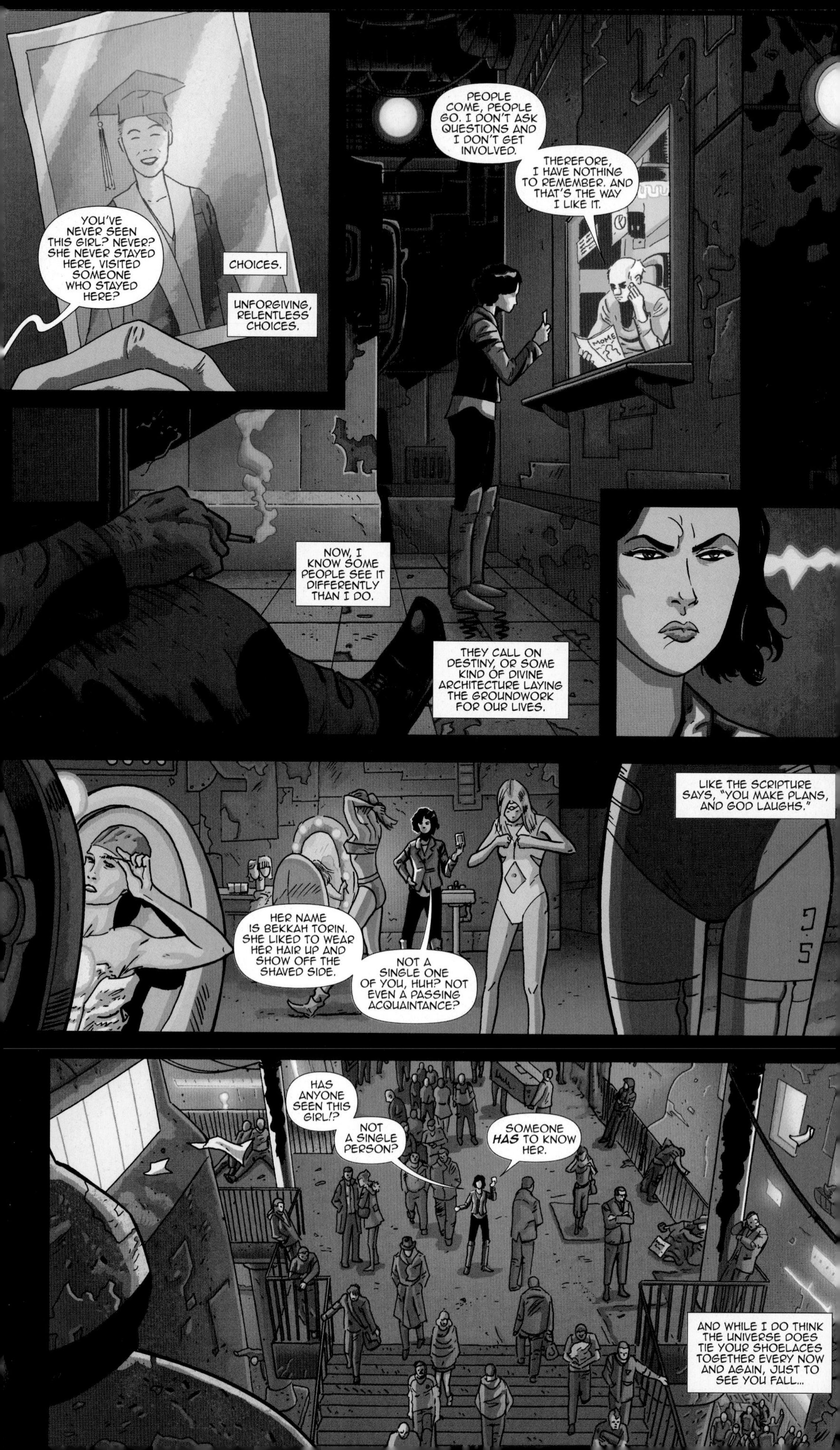
YOU'VE NEVER SEEN THIS GIRL? NEVER? SHE NEVER STAYED HERE, VISITED SOMEONE WHO STAYED HERE?
CHOICES.
UNFORGIVING, RELENTLESS CHOICES.
PEOPLE COME, PEOPLE GO. I DON'T ASK QUESTIONS AND I DON'T GET INVOLVED.
THEREFORE, I HAVE NOTHING TO REMEMBER. AND THAT'S THE WAY I LIKE IT.
NOW, I KNOW SOME PEOPLE SEE IT DIFFERENTLY THAN I DO.
THEY CALL ON DESTINY, OR SOME KIND OF DIVINE ARCHITECTURE LAYING THE GROUNDWORK FOR OUR LIVES.
LIKE THE SCRIPTURE SAYS, "YOU MAKE PLANS, AND GOD LAUGHS."
HER NAME IS BEKKAH TORIN. SHE LIKED TO WEAR HER HAIR UP AND SHOW OFF THE SHAVED SIDE.
NOT A SINGLE ONE OF YOU, HUH? NOT EVEN A PASSING ACQUAINTANCE?
HAS ANYONE SEEN THIS GIRL!?
NOT A SINGLE PERSON?
SOMEONE HAS TO KNOW HER.
AND WHILE I DO THINK THE UNIVERSE DOES TIE YOUR SHOELACES TOGETHER EVERY NOW AND AGAIN, JUST TO SEE YOU FALL...

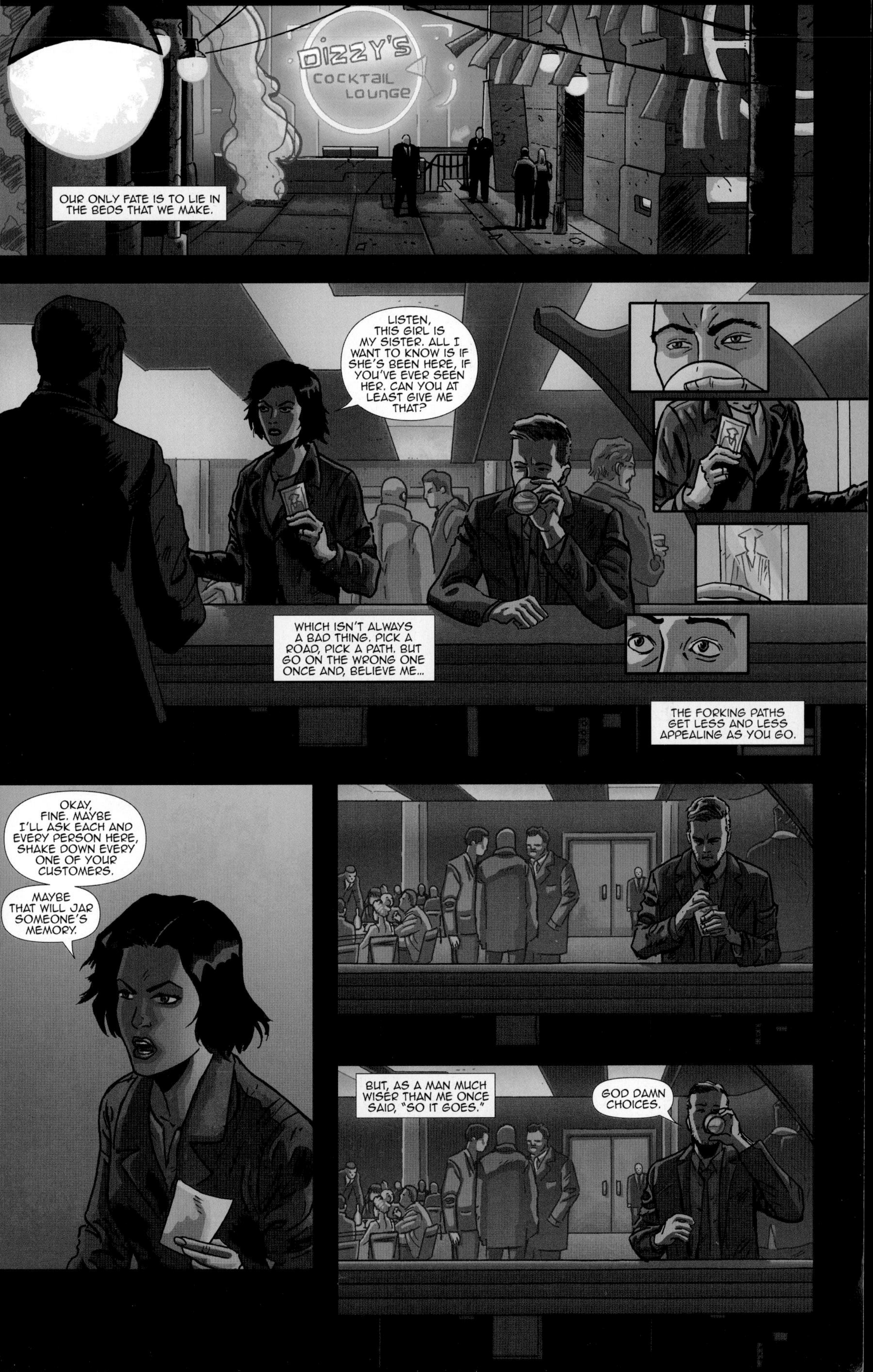
DIZZY'S
COCKTAIL LOUNGE
OUR ONLY FATE IS TO LIE IN THE BEDS THAT WE MAKE.
LISTEN, THIS GIRL IS MY SISTER. ALL I WANT TO KNOW IS IF SHE'S BEEN HERE, IF YOU'VE EVER SEEN HER. CAN YOU AT LEAST GIVE ME THAT?
WHICH ISN'T ALWAYS A BAD THING. PICK A ROAD, PICK A PATH. BUT GO ON THE WRONG ONE ONCE AND, BELIEVE ME...
THE FORKING PATHS GET LESS AND LESS APPEALING AS YOU GO.
OKAY, FINE. MAYBE I'LL ASK EACH AND EVERY PERSON HERE, SHAKE DOWN EVERY ONE OF YOUR CUSTOMERS.
MAYBE THAT WILL JAR SOMEONE'S MEMORY.
BUT, AS A MAN MUCH WISER THAN ME ONCE SAID, "SO IT GOES."
GOD DAMN CHOICES.

...AND THERE AIN'T NOBODY ON THIS DAMN ROCK DOESN'T KNOW YOU'RE TRYING TO RAISE YOUR KID SISTER.

MY BOSS, MAN BY THE NAME MR. MOSCOW, WOULD LIKE A WORD REGARDING YOUR--

I WONDER WHAT IT'LL BE.

THE WORD. IF HE HAS JUST THE ONE, I'D IMAGINE HE'LL HAVE TO CHOOSE VERY, VERY CAREFULLY.

HERE HE IS. IF THERE'S ONE PERSON WHO CAN TEACH AN HONORS COURSE IN WEARING OUT THEIR WELCOME, IT'S ALEX MOTHERFUCKING FORD.

GIRLIE, THIS CAT MAKES YOU SEEM ON THE LEVEL.

YEAH, WELL, YOUR MOTHER DRESSES YOU FUNNY.

HERE, HAVE A DRINK, WARREN. COOL OFF FOR A SECOND.

AS FOR THIS BUSINESS WITH MOSCOW AND THE GIRL, I THINK I'LL HANDLE IT FROM HERE.

HA.

HAHAHA!

WHAT, YOU THINK DOING THIS LITTLE THING FOR MOSCOW WILL GET YOU OUT OF THE SHADE SOME?

YOU'RE INTERFERING WITH MY BUSINESS HERE, ALEX. THAT MEANS YOU'RE INTERFERING WITH MOSCOW'S BUSINESS.

I THINK IT MIGHT BE BEST IF I TOOK THE GIRL AND YOU TO SEE MR. MOSCOW.

AH, THINKING. THAT'S WHAT YOU WERE DOING? I WAS WONDERING WHAT THAT GRUNTING SOUND WAS.

I THINK I HAVE A BETTER OFFER--MAYBE N FOR YOU, BUT FO YOUR FRIENDS HERE.

A MONTH SUPPLY OF RECALL FOR YOU TWO TO GET LOST.

THE STRONGEST BATCH I MAKE.

THE COMPANY YOU KEEP, WARREN.

FUN TRICK. AND WHAT ABOUT ME? I'M OFF RECALL. BEEN CLEAN THREE MONTHS NOW.

OH YEAH?

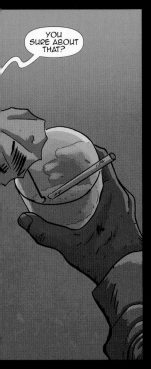

YOU SURE ABOUT THAT?

OH, WARREN, ONE THING...

THAT'S A SPECIAL BATCH YOU'RE ABOUT TO TRIP ON. RECALL MIXED WITH SOME HALLUCINOGENS.

IT'S GOING TO *SERIOUSLY* FUCK WITH YOUR BRAIN.

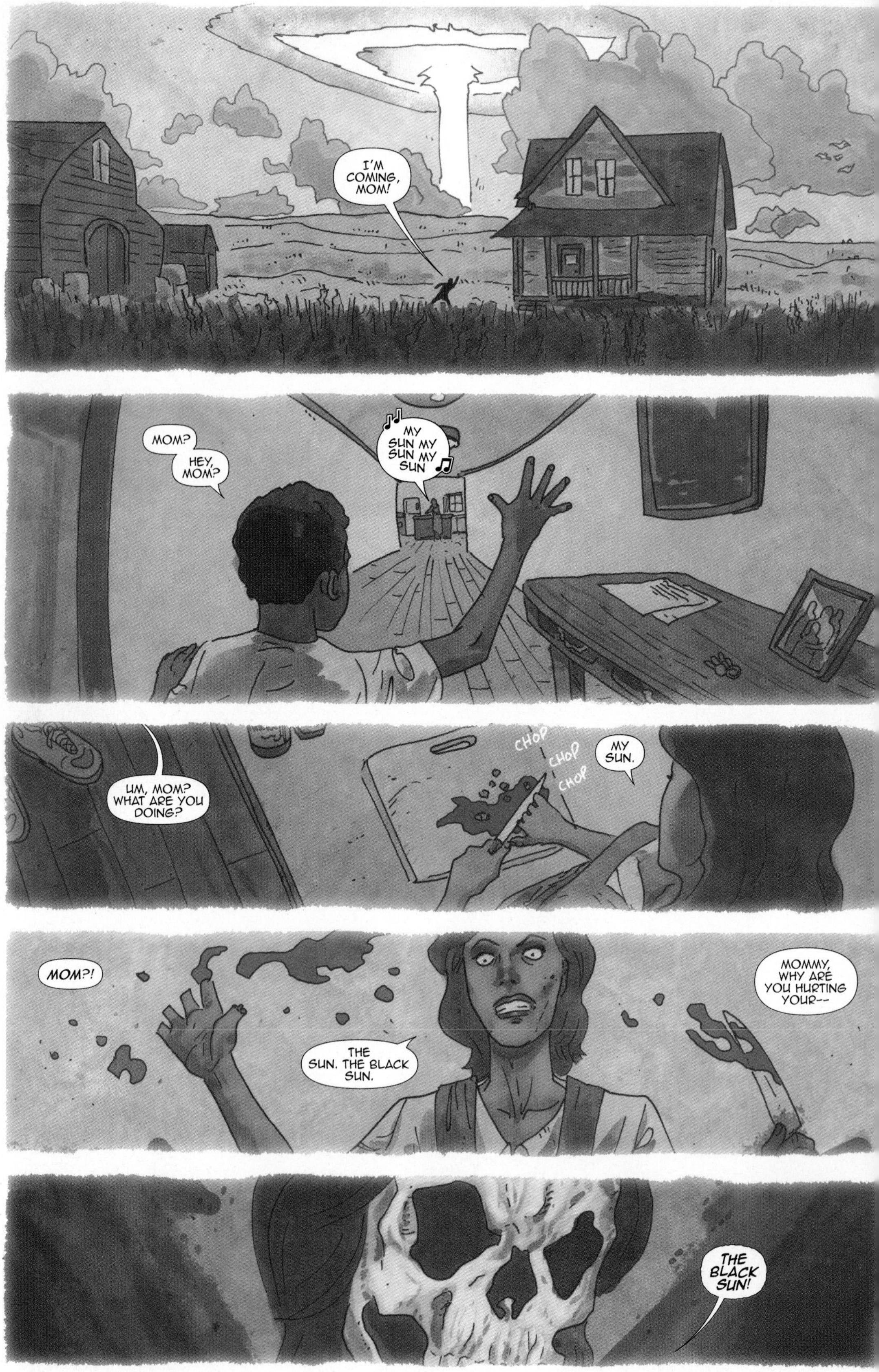
I'M COMING, MOM!
MOM?
HEY, MOM?
MY SUN MY SUN MY SUN
UM, MOM? WHAT ARE YOU DOING?
CHOP
CHOP
CHOP
MY SUN.
MOM?!
THE SUN. THE BLACK SUN.
MOMMY, WHY ARE YOU HURTING YOUR--
THE BLACK SUN!

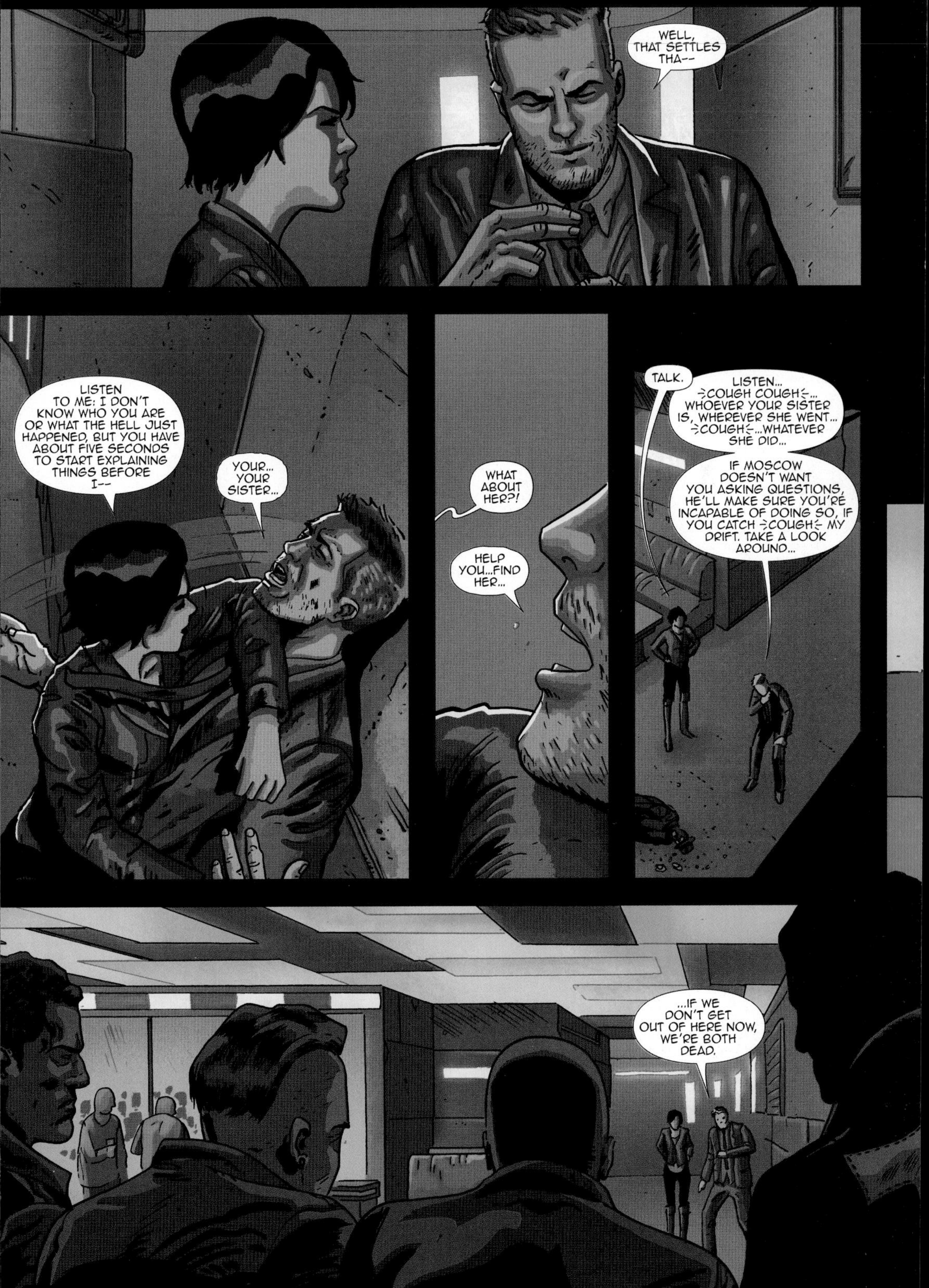
WELL, THAT SETTLES THA--
LISTEN TO ME: I DON'T KNOW WHO YOU ARE OR WHAT THE HELL JUST HAPPENED, BUT YOU HAVE ABOUT FIVE SECONDS TO START EXPLAINING THINGS BEFORE I--
YOUR... YOUR SISTER...
WHAT ABOUT HER?!
HELP YOU...FIND HER...
TALK.
LISTEN... >COUGH COUGH<... WHOEVER YOUR SISTER IS, WHEREVER SHE WENT... >COUGH<...WHATEVER SHE DID...
IF MOSCOW DOESN'T WANT YOU ASKING QUESTIONS, HE'LL MAKE SURE YOU'RE INCAPABLE OF DOING SO, IF YOU CATCH >COUGH< MY DRIFT. TAKE A LOOK AROUND...
...IF WE DON'T GET OUT OF HERE NOW, WE'RE BOTH DEAD.

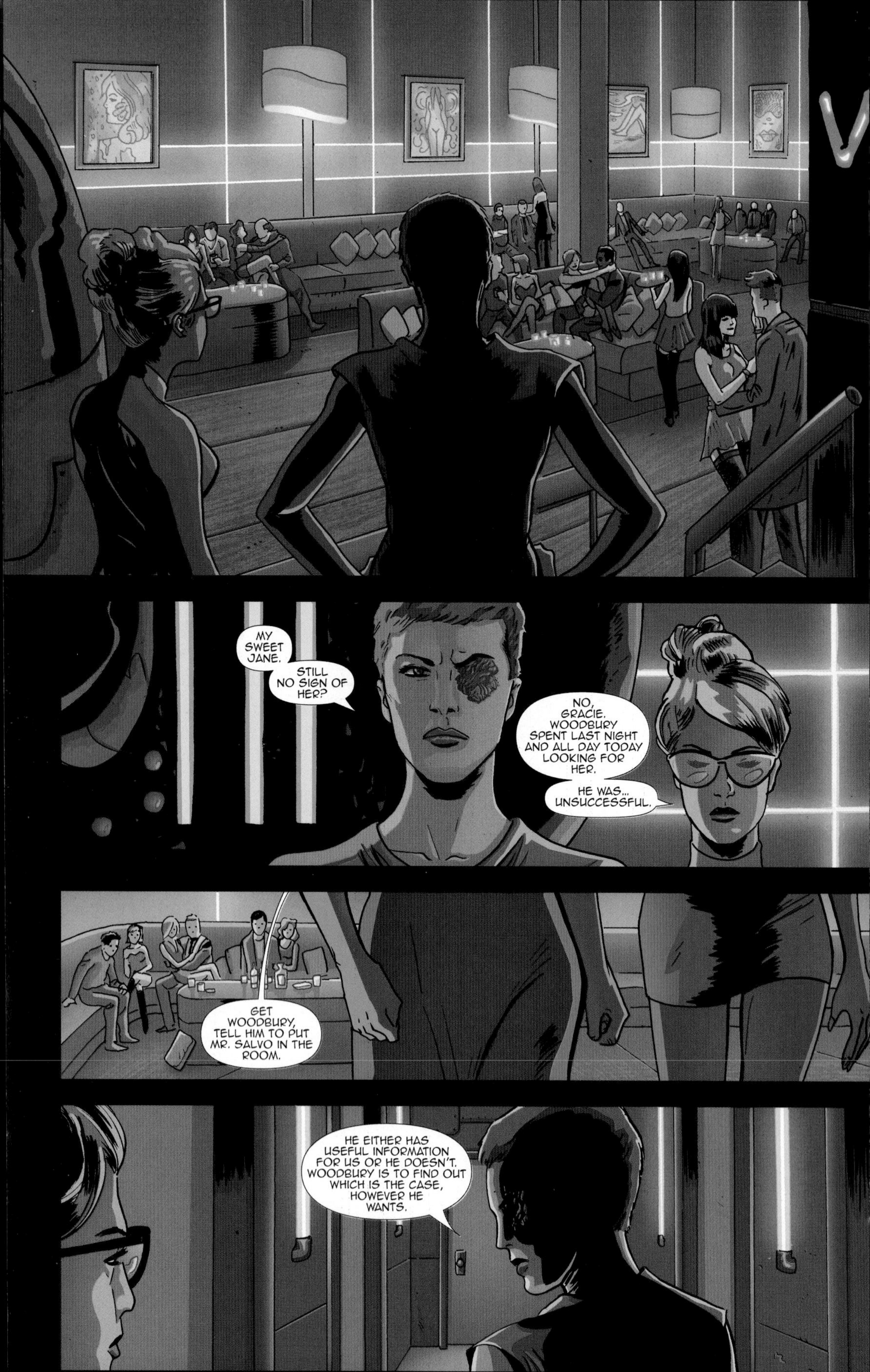
MY SWEET JANE.
STILL NO SIGN OF HER?
NO, GRACIE. WOODBURY SPENT LAST NIGHT AND ALL DAY TODAY LOOKING FOR HER.
HE WAS... UNSUCCESSFUL.
GET WOODBURY, TELL HIM TO PUT MR. SALVO IN THE ROOM.
HE EITHER HAS USEFUL INFORMATION FOR US OR HE DOESN'T. WOODBURY IS TO FIND OUT WHICH IS THE CASE, HOWEVER HE WANTS.

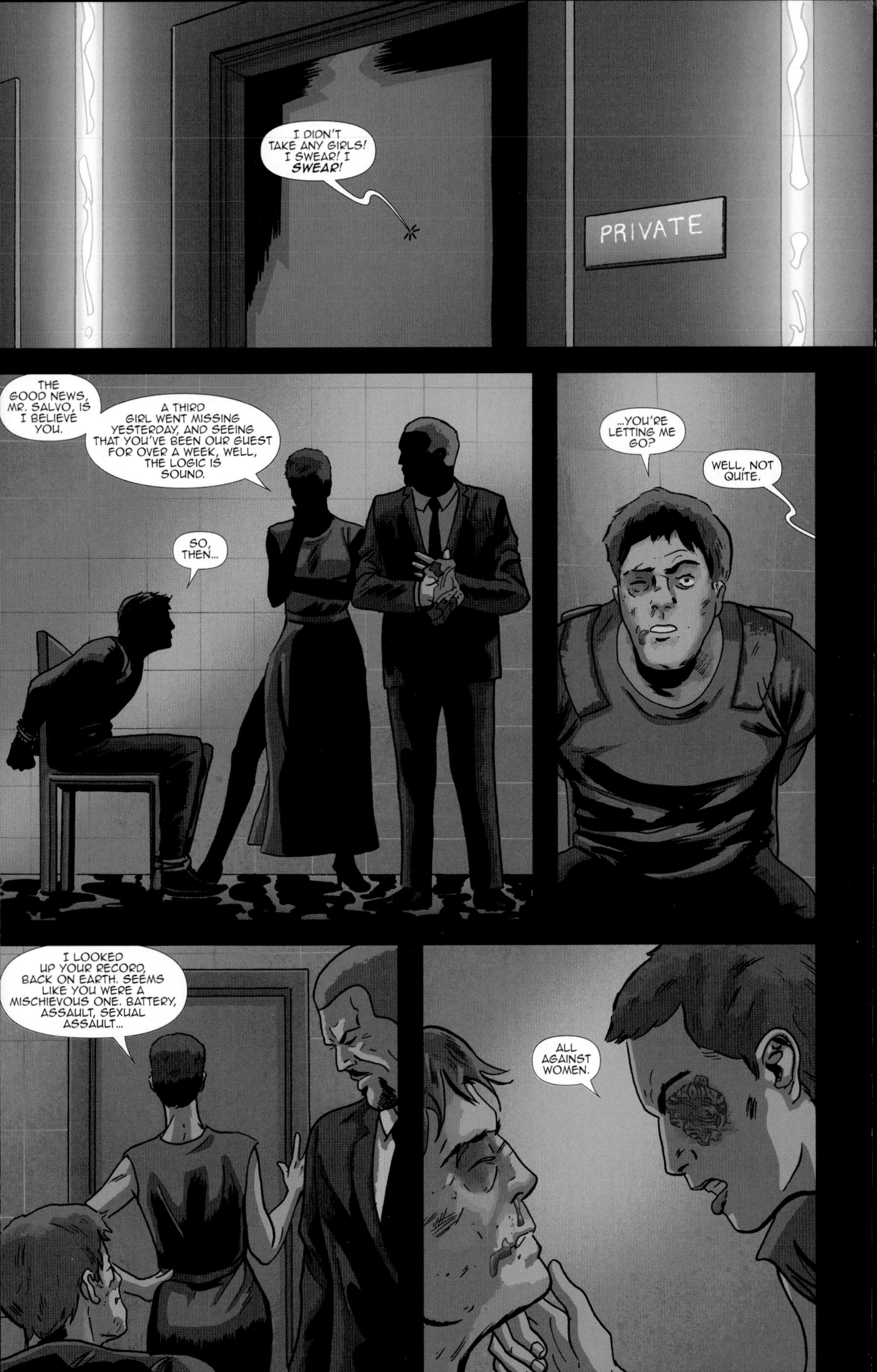
I DIDN'T TAKE ANY GIRLS! I SWEAR! I SWEAR!
PRIVATE
THE GOOD NEWS, MR. SALVO, IS I BELIEVE YOU.
A THIRD GIRL WENT MISSING YESTERDAY, AND SEEING THAT YOU'VE BEEN OUR GUEST FOR OVER A WEEK, WELL, THE LOGIC IS SOUND.
SO, THEN...
...YOU'RE LETTING ME GO?
WELL, NOT QUITE.
I LOOKED UP YOUR RECORD, BACK ON EARTH. SEEMS LIKE YOU WERE A MISCHIEVOUS ONE. BATTERY, ASSAULT, SEXUAL ASSAULT...
ALL AGAINST WOMEN.

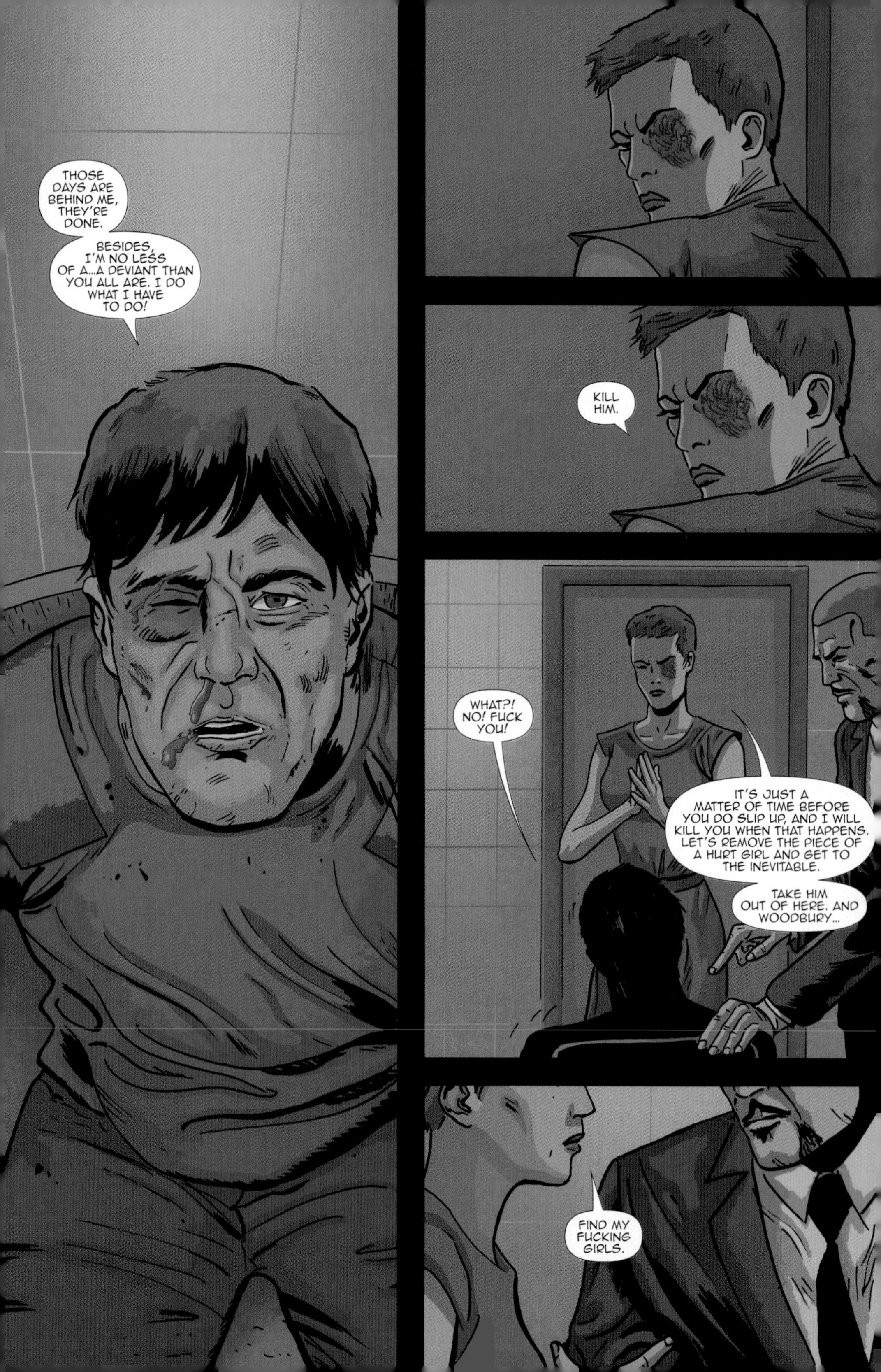
THOSE DAYS ARE BEHIND ME, THEY'RE DONE.
BESIDES, I'M NO LESS OF A...A DEVIANT THAN YOU ALL ARE. I DO WHAT I HAVE TO DO!
KILL HIM.
WHAT?! NO! FUCK YOU!
IT'S JUST A MATTER OF TIME BEFORE YOU DO SLIP UP, AND I WILL KILL YOU WHEN THAT HAPPENS. LET'S REMOVE THE PIECE OF A HURT GIRL AND GET TO THE INEVITABLE.
TAKE HIM OUT OF HERE. AND WOODBURY...
FIND MY FUCKING GIRLS.

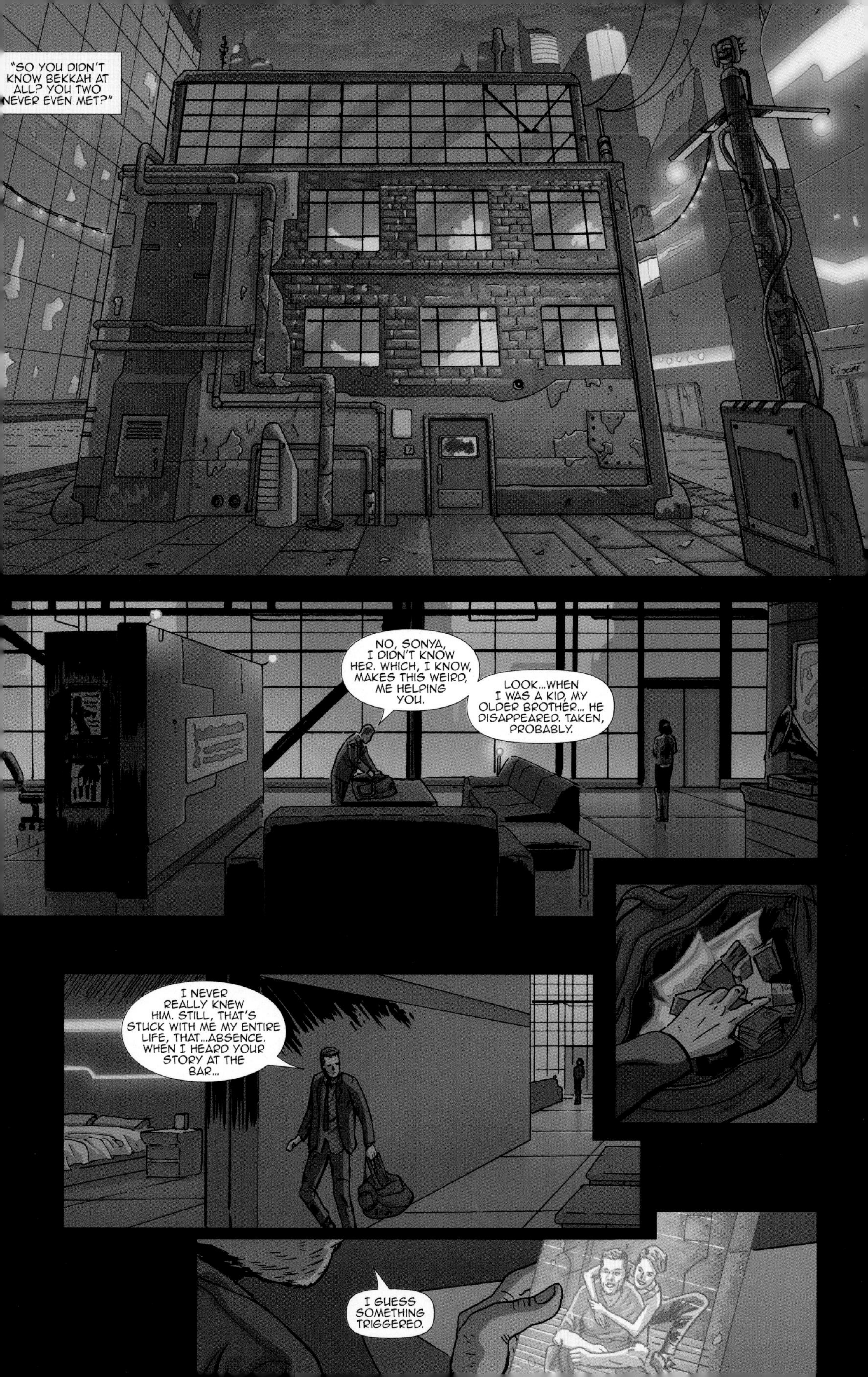
"SO YOU DIDN'T KNOW BEKKAH AT ALL? YOU TWO NEVER EVEN MET?"
NO, SONYA, I DIDN'T KNOW HER. WHICH, I KNOW, MAKES THIS WEIRD, ME HELPING YOU.
LOOK...WHEN I WAS A KID, MY OLDER BROTHER... HE DISAPPEARED. TAKEN, PROBABLY.
I NEVER REALLY KNEW HIM. STILL, THAT'S STUCK WITH ME MY ENTIRE LIFE, THAT...ABSENCE. WHEN I HEARD YOUR STORY AT THE BAR...
I GUESS SOMETHING TRIGGERED.

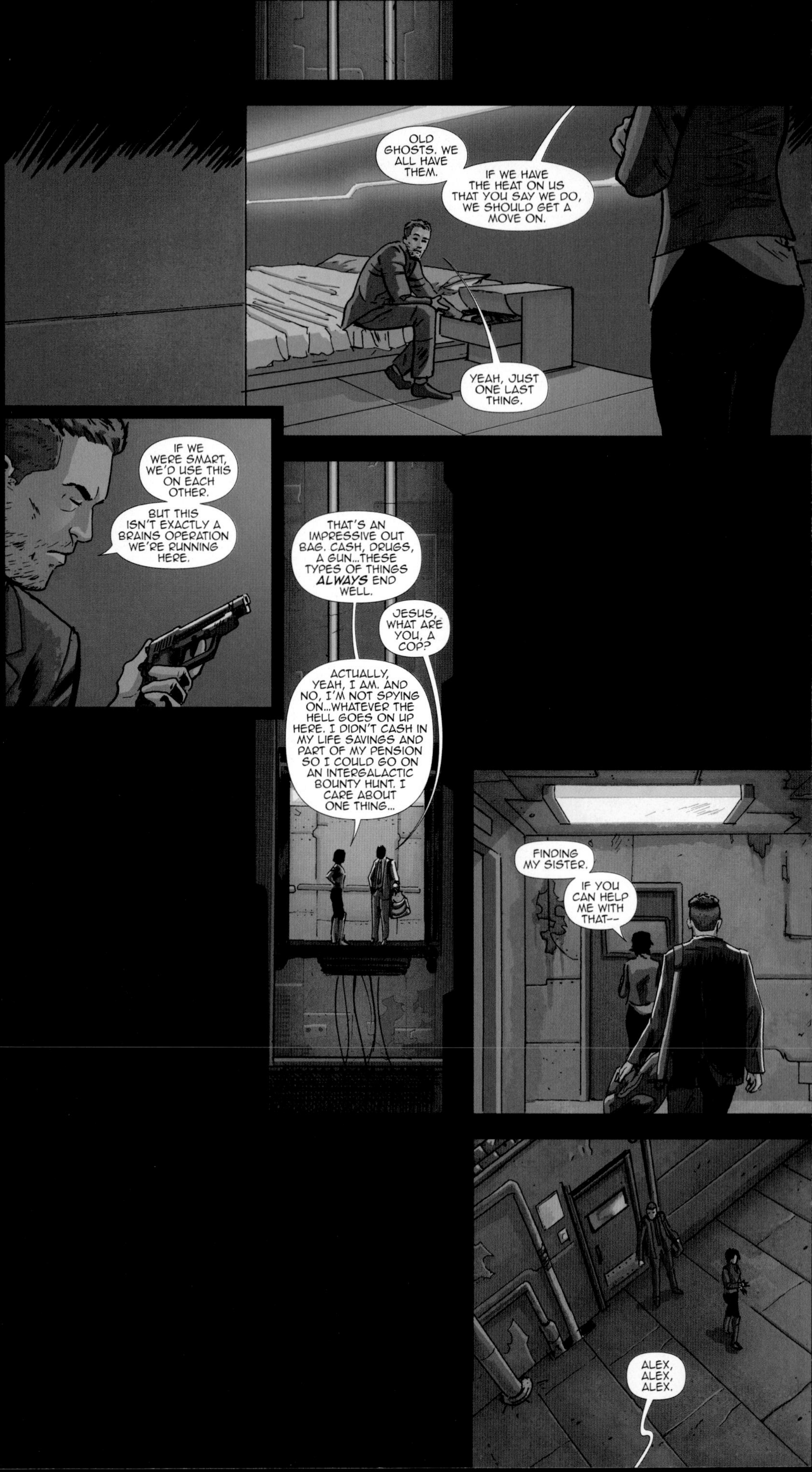
OLD GHOSTS. WE ALL HAVE THEM.
IF WE HAVE THE HEAT ON US THAT YOU SAY WE DO, WE SHOULD GET A MOVE ON.
YEAH, JUST ONE LAST THING.
IF WE WERE SMART, WE'D USE THIS ON EACH OTHER.
BUT THIS ISN'T EXACTLY A BRAINS OPERATION WE'RE RUNNING HERE.
THAT'S AN IMPRESSIVE OUT BAG. CASH, DRUGS, A GUN...THESE TYPES OF THINGS *ALWAYS* END WELL.
JESUS, WHAT ARE YOU, A COP?
ACTUALLY, YEAH, I AM. AND NO, I'M NOT SPYING ON...WHATEVER THE HELL GOES ON UP HERE. I DIDN'T CASH IN MY LIFE SAVINGS AND PART OF MY PENSION SO I COULD GO ON AN INTERGALACTIC BOUNTY HUNT. I CARE ABOUT ONE THING...
FINDING MY SISTER.
IF YOU CAN HELP ME WITH THAT--
ALEX, ALEX, ALEX.

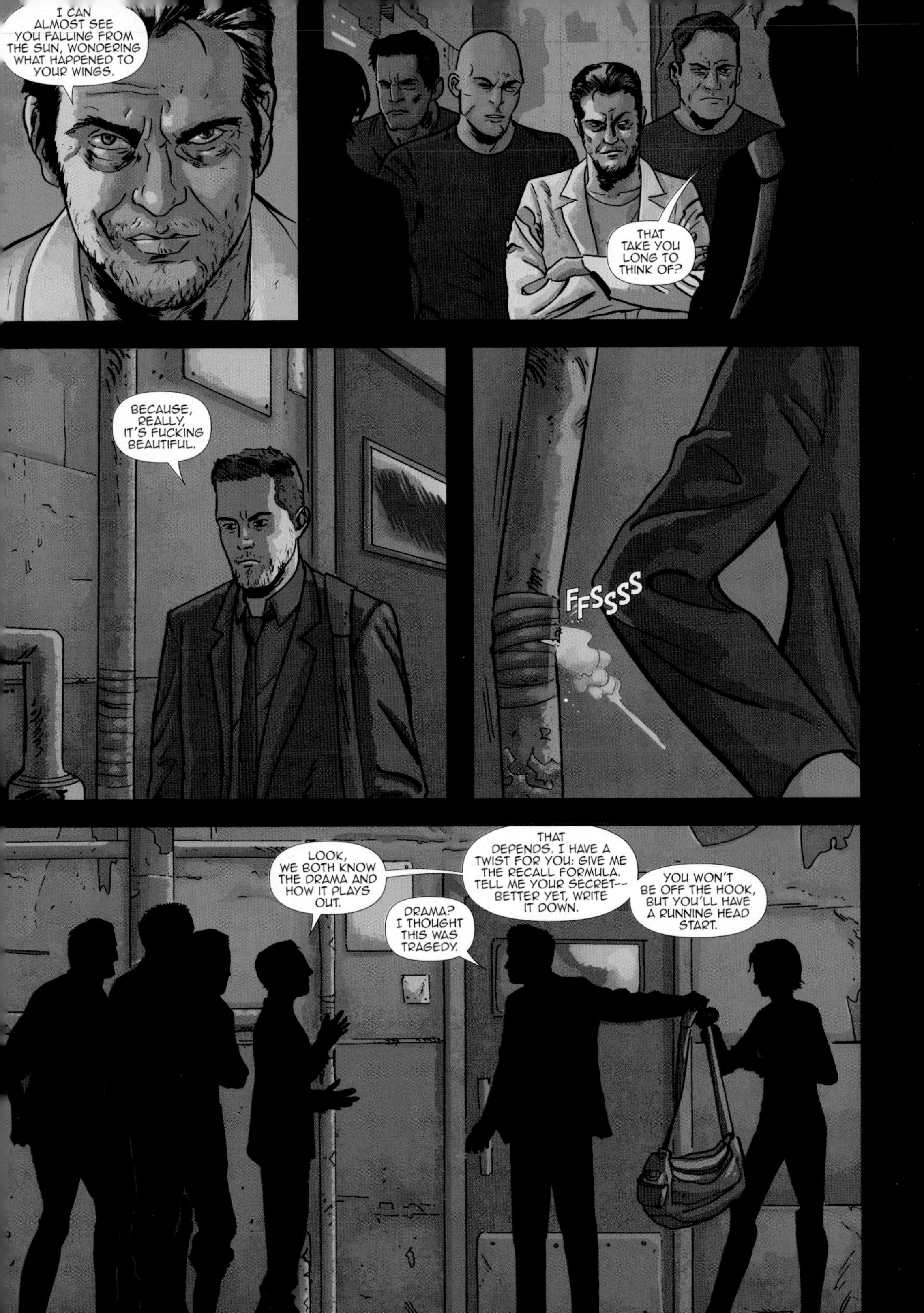
I CAN ALMOST SEE YOU FALLING FROM THE SUN, WONDERING WHAT HAPPENED TO YOUR WINGS.
THAT TAKE YOU LONG TO THINK OF?
BECAUSE, REALLY, IT'S FUCKING BEAUTIFUL.
FFSSSS
LOOK, WE BOTH KNOW THE DRAMA AND HOW IT PLAYS OUT.
DRAMA? I THOUGHT THIS WAS TRAGEDY.
THAT DEPENDS. I HAVE A TWIST FOR YOU: GIVE ME THE RECALL FORMULA. TELL ME YOUR SECRET-- BETTER YET, WRITE IT DOWN.
YOU WON'T BE OFF THE HOOK, BUT YOU'LL HAVE A RUNNING HEAD START.

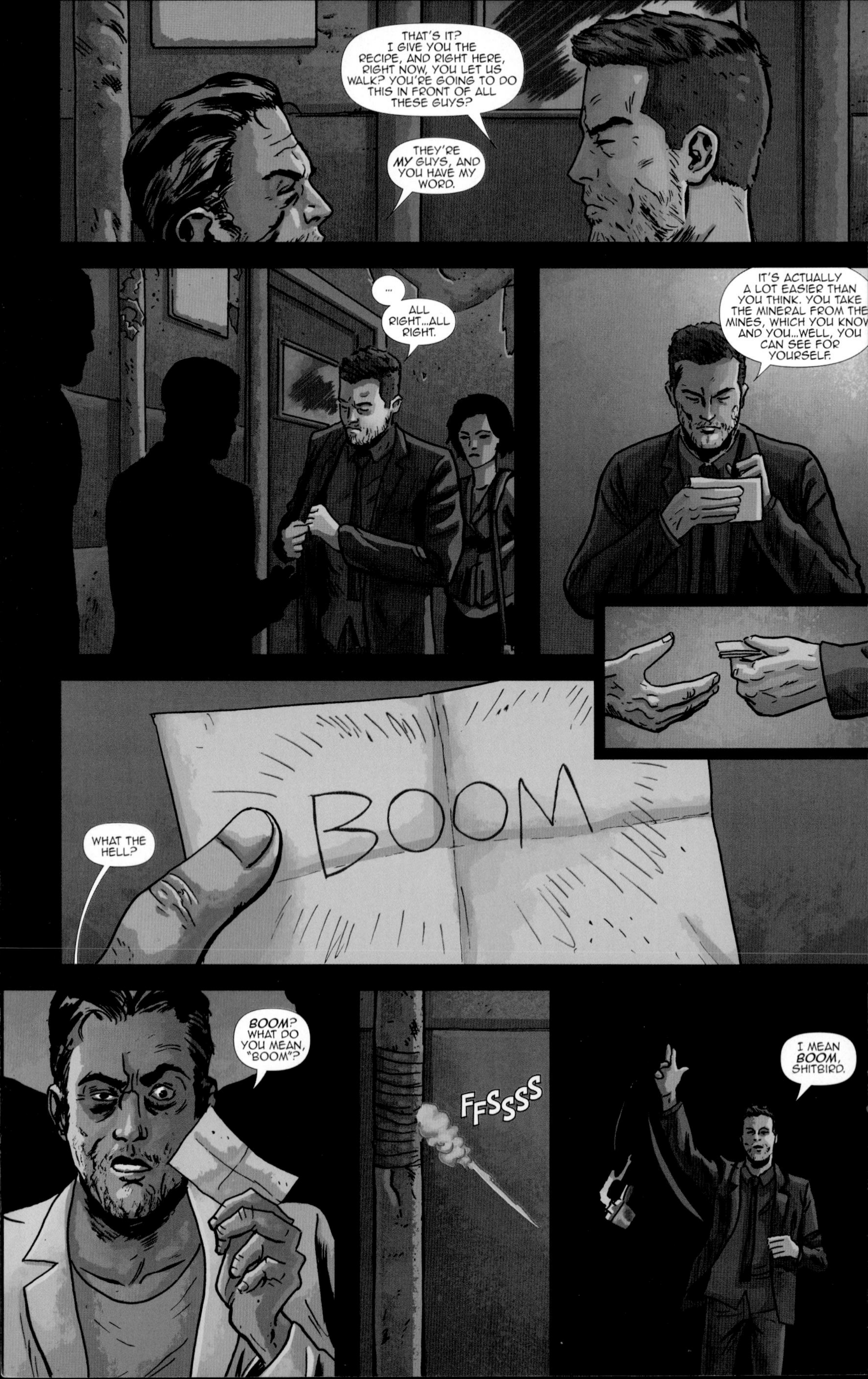
THAT'S IT? I GIVE YOU THE RECIPE, AND RIGHT HERE, RIGHT NOW, YOU LET US WALK? YOU'RE GOING TO DO THIS IN FRONT OF ALL THESE GUYS?
THEY'RE MY GUYS, AND YOU HAVE MY WORD.
...
ALL RIGHT...ALL RIGHT.
IT'S ACTUALLY A LOT EASIER THAN YOU THINK. YOU TAKE THE MINERAL FROM THE MINES, WHICH YOU KNOW AND YOU...WELL, YOU CAN SEE FOR YOURSELF.
BOOM
WHAT THE HELL?
BOOM? WHAT DO YOU MEAN, "BOOM"?
FFSSSS
I MEAN BOOM, SHITBIRD.

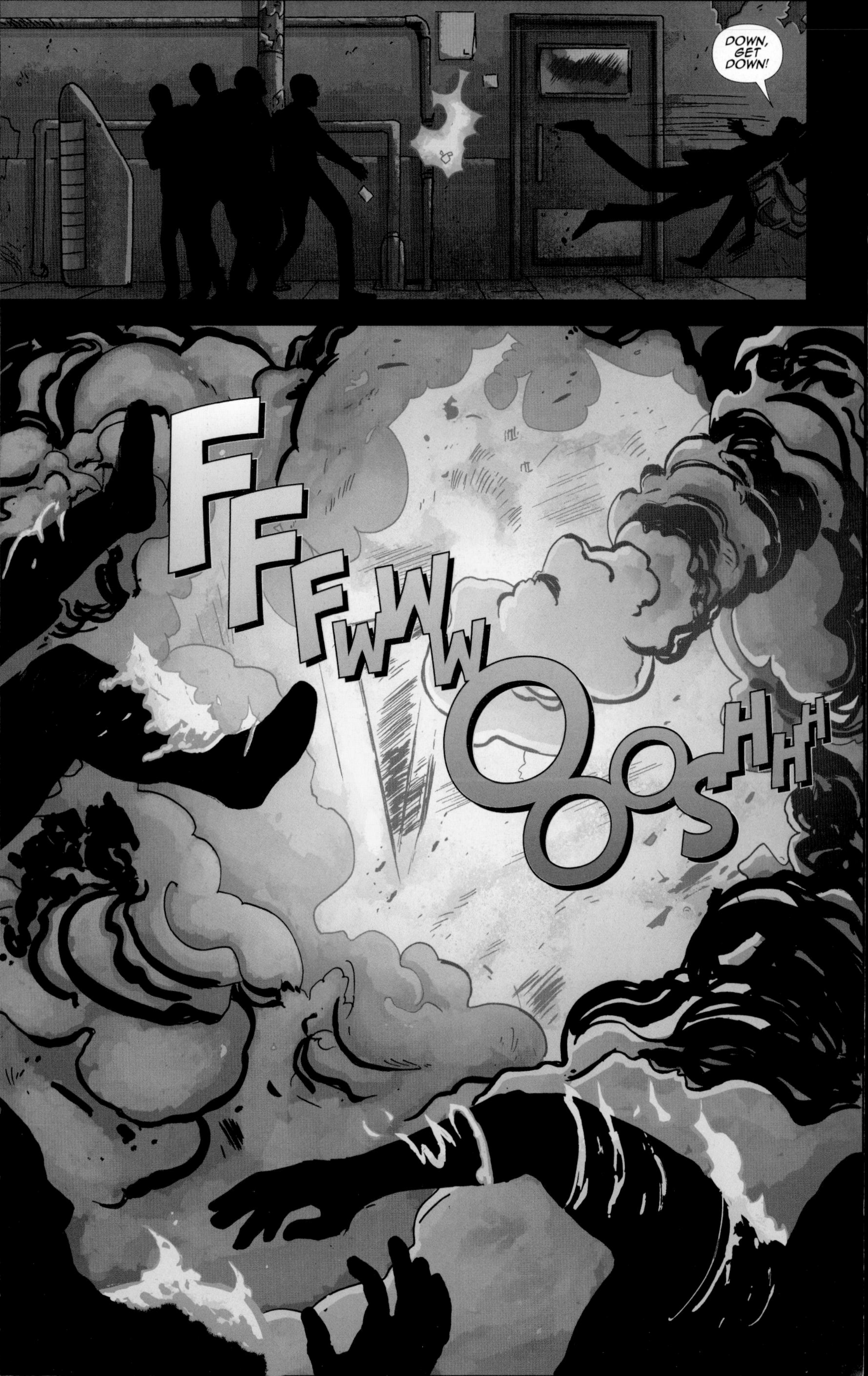
DOWN, GET DOWN!
FFFWWWOOOSHHH

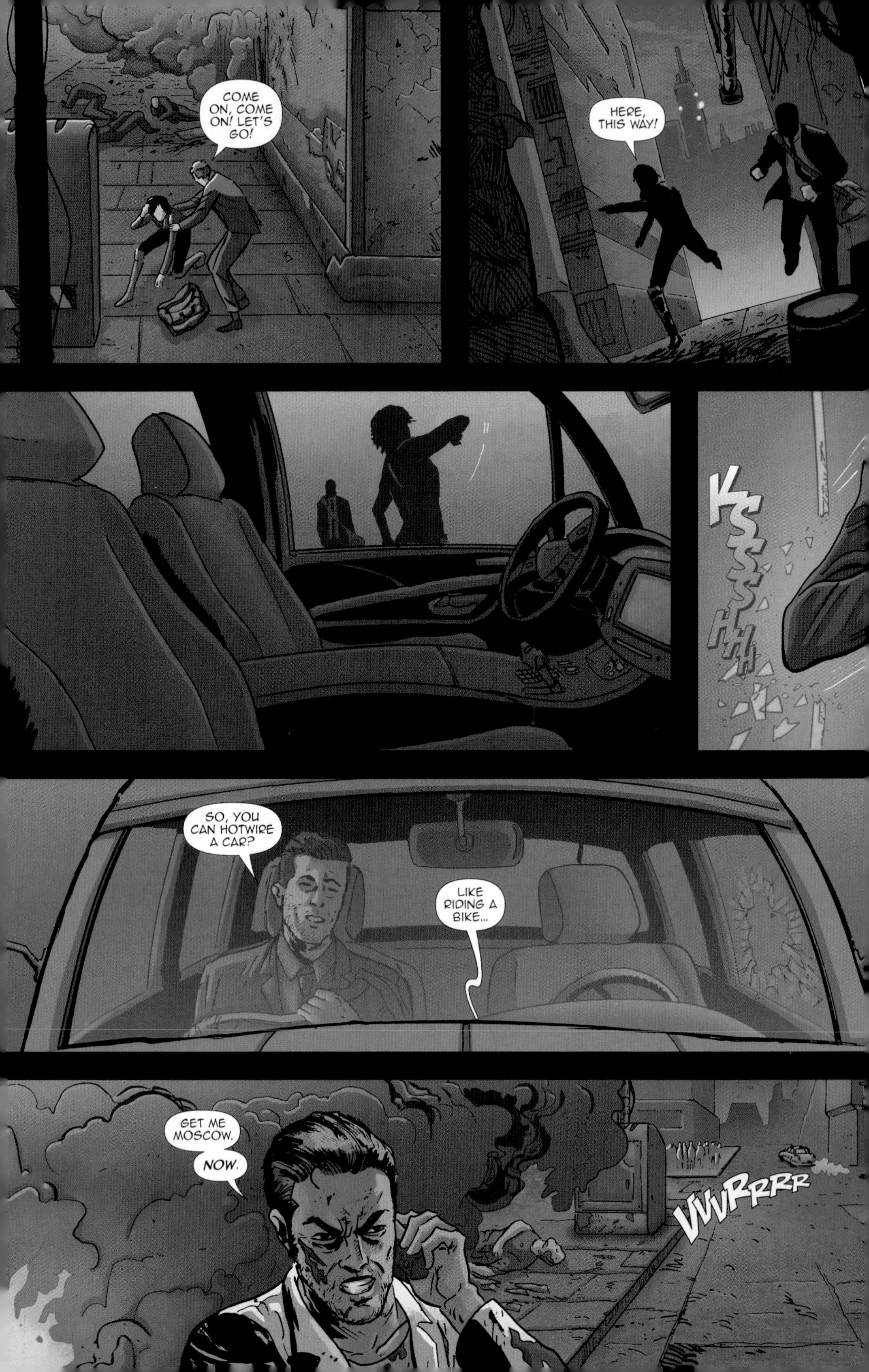

COME ON, COME ON! LET'S GO!
HERE, THIS WAY!
KSSSHH
SO, YOU CAN HOTWIRE A CAR?
LIKE RIDING A BIKE...
GET ME MOSCOW.
NOW.
VVVRRRR

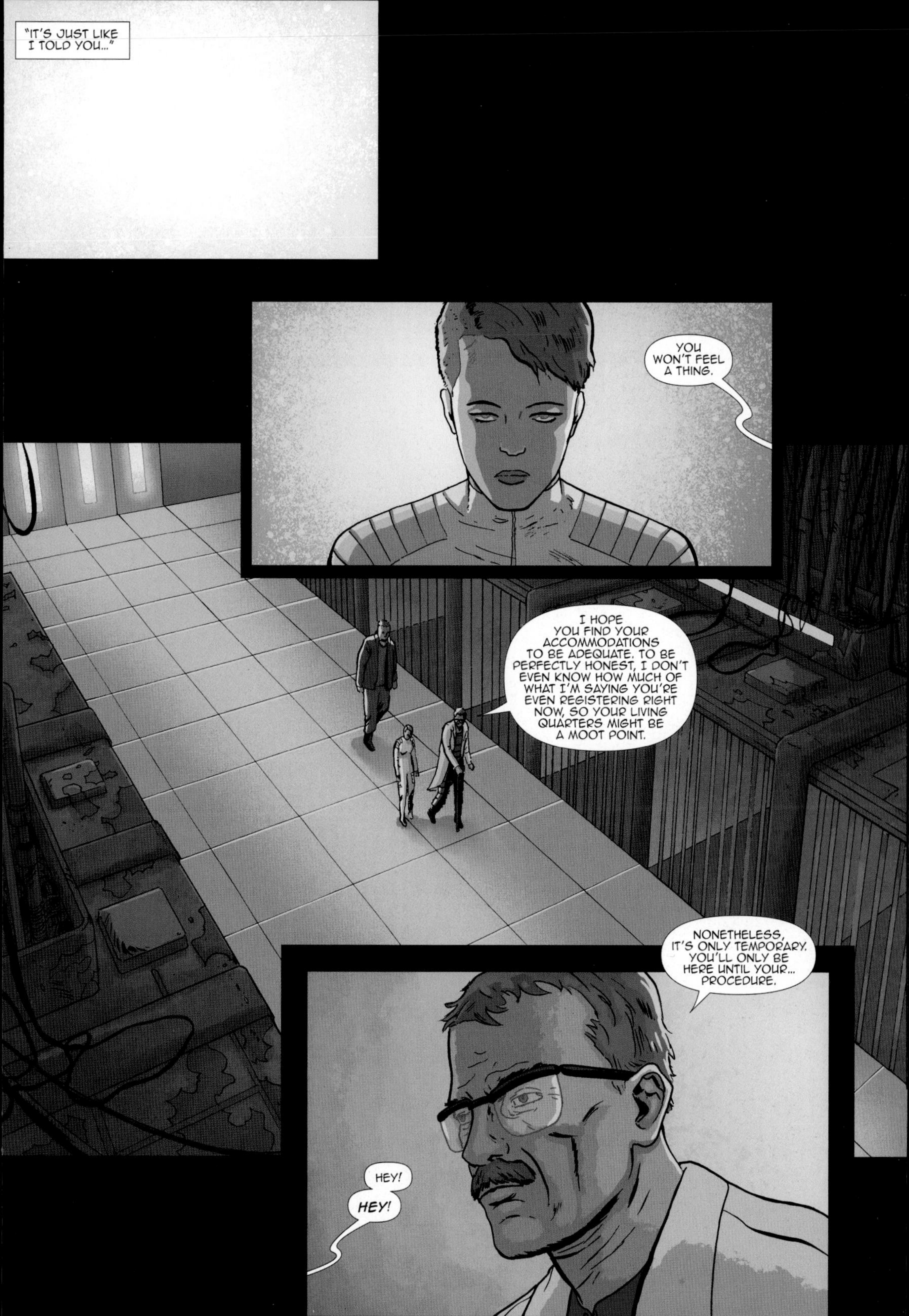
"IT'S JUST LIKE I TOLD YOU..."
YOU WON'T FEEL A THING.
I HOPE YOU FIND YOUR ACCOMMODATIONS TO BE ADEQUATE. TO BE PERFECTLY HONEST, I DON'T EVEN KNOW HOW MUCH OF WHAT I'M SAYING YOU'RE EVEN REGISTERING RIGHT NOW, SO YOUR LIVING QUARTERS MIGHT BE A MOOT POINT.
NONETHELESS, IT'S ONLY TEMPORARY. YOU'LL ONLY BE HERE UNTIL YOUR... PROCEDURE.
HEY!
HEY!

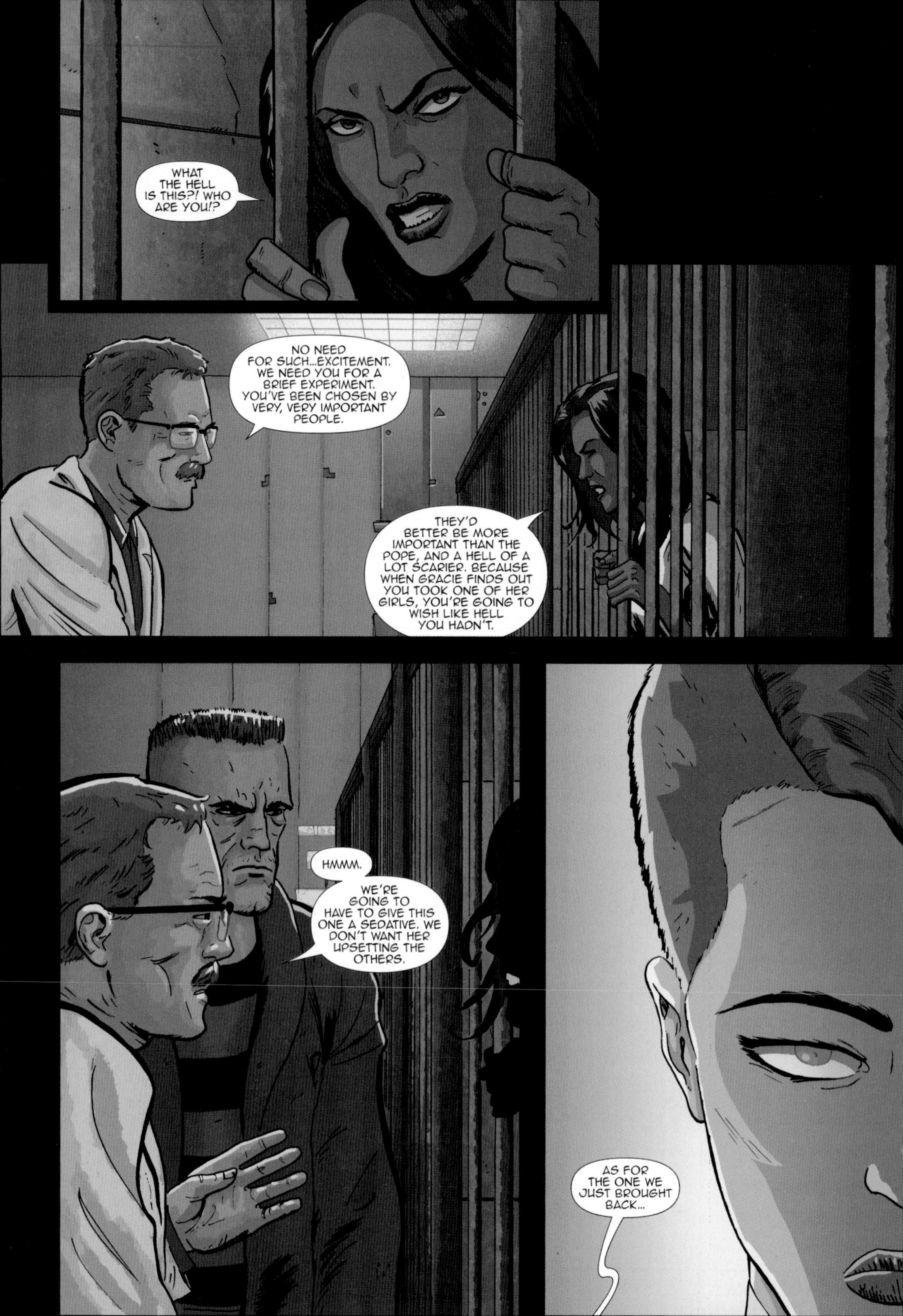
WHAT THE HELL IS THIS?! WHO ARE YOU!?
NO NEED FOR SUCH...EXCITEMENT. WE NEED YOU FOR A BRIEF EXPERIMENT. YOU'VE BEEN CHOSEN BY VERY, VERY IMPORTANT PEOPLE.
THEY'D BETTER BE MORE IMPORTANT THAN THE POPE, AND A HELL OF A LOT SCARIER. BECAUSE WHEN GRACIE FINDS OUT YOU TOOK ONE OF HER GIRLS, YOU'RE GOING TO WISH LIKE HELL YOU HADN'T.
HMMM.
WE'RE GOING TO HAVE TO GIVE THIS ONE A SEDATIVE. WE DON'T WANT HER UPSETTING THE OTHERS.
AS FOR THE ONE WE JUST BROUGHT BACK...

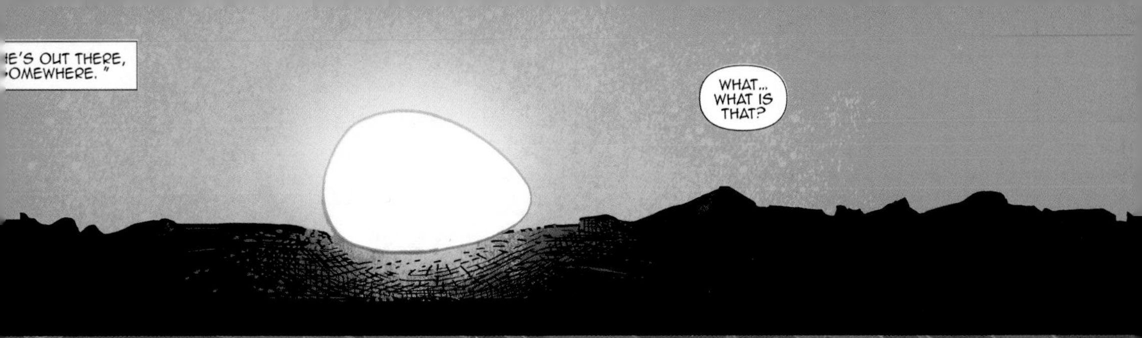

E'S OUT THERE,
OMEWHERE."
WHAT... WHAT IS THAT?

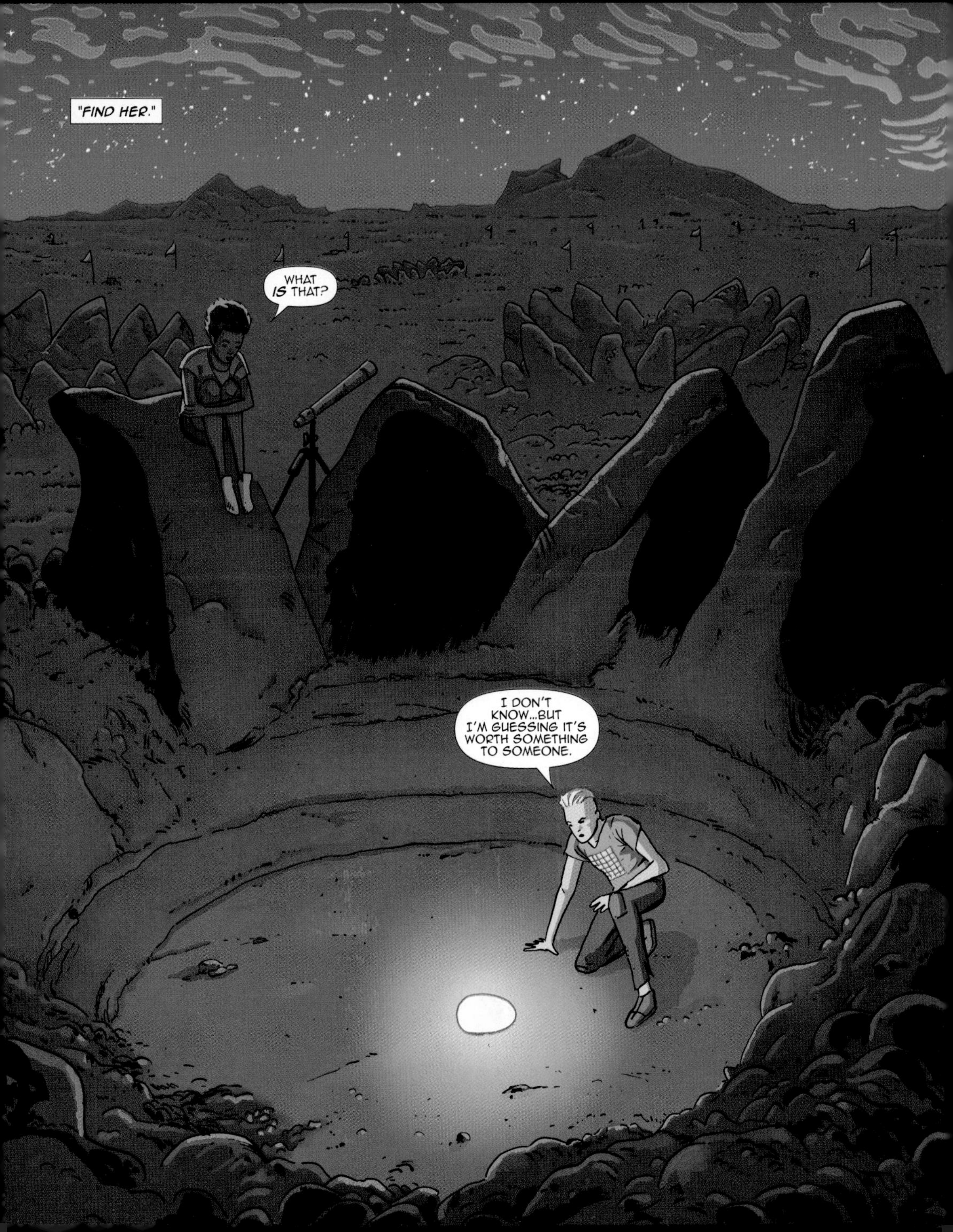

"FIND HER."
WHAT *IS* THAT?
I DON'T KNOW...BUT I'M GUESSING IT'S WORTH SOMETHING TO SOMEONE.

Langford Skaargred

In Memoriam 2010 - ?
By Stacia Loble

Langford Skaargred was not born of humble means. The son of Dominik Skaargred—an oil baron whose company, Brighton Briggs, made untold wealth in the Middle East—there was no opportunity, no resource, no dream that was beyond his grasp. Without ever having to lift a finger, he was on course to live a life most can hardly even fathom.

And then he burned it all to the ground.

Langford and I first met when he was on the verge of making, what I thought at the time, the worst mistake of his life. I told him that, and he laughed. Our paths first crossed at a fundraiser for Joe Rainey's bid for Texas governor at his home just outside of Austin. I was nervous about Langford being in attendance—I had written numerous scathing pieces about his father, who had just passed away a month prior to the event. My obituary op-ed, in fact, all but said "good riddance." I knew very little about Langford; his life was kept hidden from the press, and within moments of meeting him, I knew why. Langford was an idealist dreamer. He was the opposite of his father by virtue of having a soul, and a very warm one at that.

Here we were, at this formal event surrounded by uptight Texas oil and cattle barons, and Langford showed up in shorts and a faded polo. On the surface, it seems like rich-kid posturing, thumbing his nose at convention merely because he could. But the reality is, that's just who Langford was. His head was so far off in the clouds that social graces, to him, was a dog whistle frequency that he couldn't hear.

"I'm dismantling it."
Skaargred on the family business.

Langford approached me in the gallery of Rainey's massive home. With an easy smile he told me how much he admired my work exposing his father. "If only he could have bought some vision with all that money," he said. With a modicum of apprehension, I asked him what his plans were for the future of his father's business, which was now his as sole heir. "Oh," he said, casually, "I'm dismantling it."

Langford Skaargred

Morally, I truly admired his decision; but, thought he was an idiot.

NO LESS than five years later, I was wrong. After ceasing operations on the Br Briggs oilfields and letting his lu government contract expire, Langford in in a number of unique businesses development opportunities, all of somehow, made him even more wealth poured money into an urban farming s (that arguably saved Detroit), a private m association that made incredible ste innovations, and, of course, his most lu investment into marijuana agriculture newly-legalized Texas.

These projects—and more—were all init that Langford believed in, yet they didn't his ambition or passion. A student of Sagan—his collection of Sagan's writi extensive, to say the least—Langford ha true, singular passion: He wanted to go to More than that, actually—he wanted to pu boundaries of our galaxy, our imaginatio our very idea of existence.

Langford's motivations were always confu the general public. I can tell you that n Langford did was driven by capital Nothing. Every decision Langford made service to his passion and his instincts th trusted without question.

many people saw Langford's humanist side—he , on the surface, inscrutable, aloof, and inattentive. Langford was a man who believed in the nendous capacity for our race, and that belief rmed him of his implacable mindset that humans hardly scratched the surface of who were are, ıt we're capable of, and our place in the cosmos. gford wanted more, not for himself, but for us all.

; FIRST opportunity to satisfy his vision was a ıster and marked Langford's first brush with ıre. It was an event that changed his life.The idea establishing a colony on Mars, when it was first sented to Langford, was like fiction from a Ray dbury novel.

"Her death can't be for nothing."
Skaargred on Shelley Thirlby

ere were so many untaken steps between the rent technology available for Mars travel and what ; required for an actual colony that the leap was ımaginable. Whether Langford understood nething most people didn't or he was blinded by his ı desire is impossible to know; what is known is that poured considerable resources into this project, a ject that ended up taking the life of an astronaut the surface of Mars.

galactic
INDUSTRIES
WE WILL DREAM AGAIN.
WE WILL WONDER. WE WILL FEEL AWE.
THE UNIVERSE AWAITS.
COME EXPLORE WITH US.

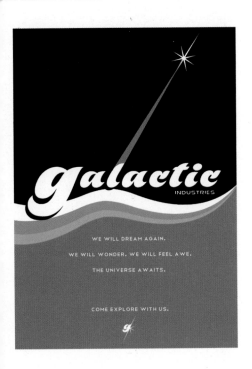

elley Thirlby's death devastated Langford, and it ıde him more determined. Where most people would ve cut ties with the far-fetched prospect of a colony Mars after such a tragedy, Langford invested more ıvily. He never spoke about Thirlby, save for one ıe. "Her death can't be for nothing."

Langford—via his company, Galactic—invested more than money into the colony, he invested himself. He vowed to be part of next expedition to Mars, that any other death would be his own. As preparations were made for the next voyage, Langford trained, rigorously, to become an astronaut. It wasn't easy, but Langford was impossible to deter, not when he's locked in on an idea. Resultant of that determination, he was on Mars when the first colony was being built, when history was made.

"I felt at home," Langford said of his journey. "And we've only just begun."

EVERYONE KNOWS the story of Dispater. Its discovery, its revelation as a semi-habitable planet. What's lost to all of us, myself included, is how it went so wrong so quickly.

"I felt at home, and we've only just begun."
Langford Skaargred

Langford invested everything he had into developing the Roche Limit Colony (an ominous name if there ever was one). It was meant to be a waypoint on our mission of discovering planets, life, and answers to the most profound questions. But a series of misfortunes, bad luck, and thinking driven by his heart and not his head left Langford broke and lost in his own colony. It's been two years, today, since anyone has heard from or seen him.

For Langford, understanding who we are, as people, was inexorably tied to our place in the universe. To understand our existence, we have to understand why we're here, we have to contextualize our role in the entirety of creation. Langford wasn't a scientist or a man of faith—he a humanistic dreamer who looked to the stars and believed something more was out there.

I hope he found what he was looking for.

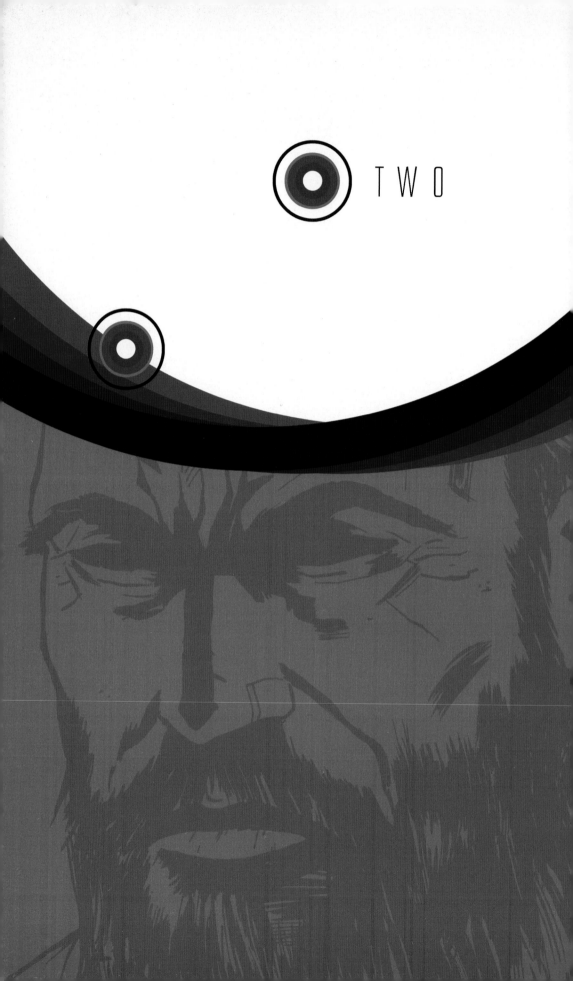

TWO

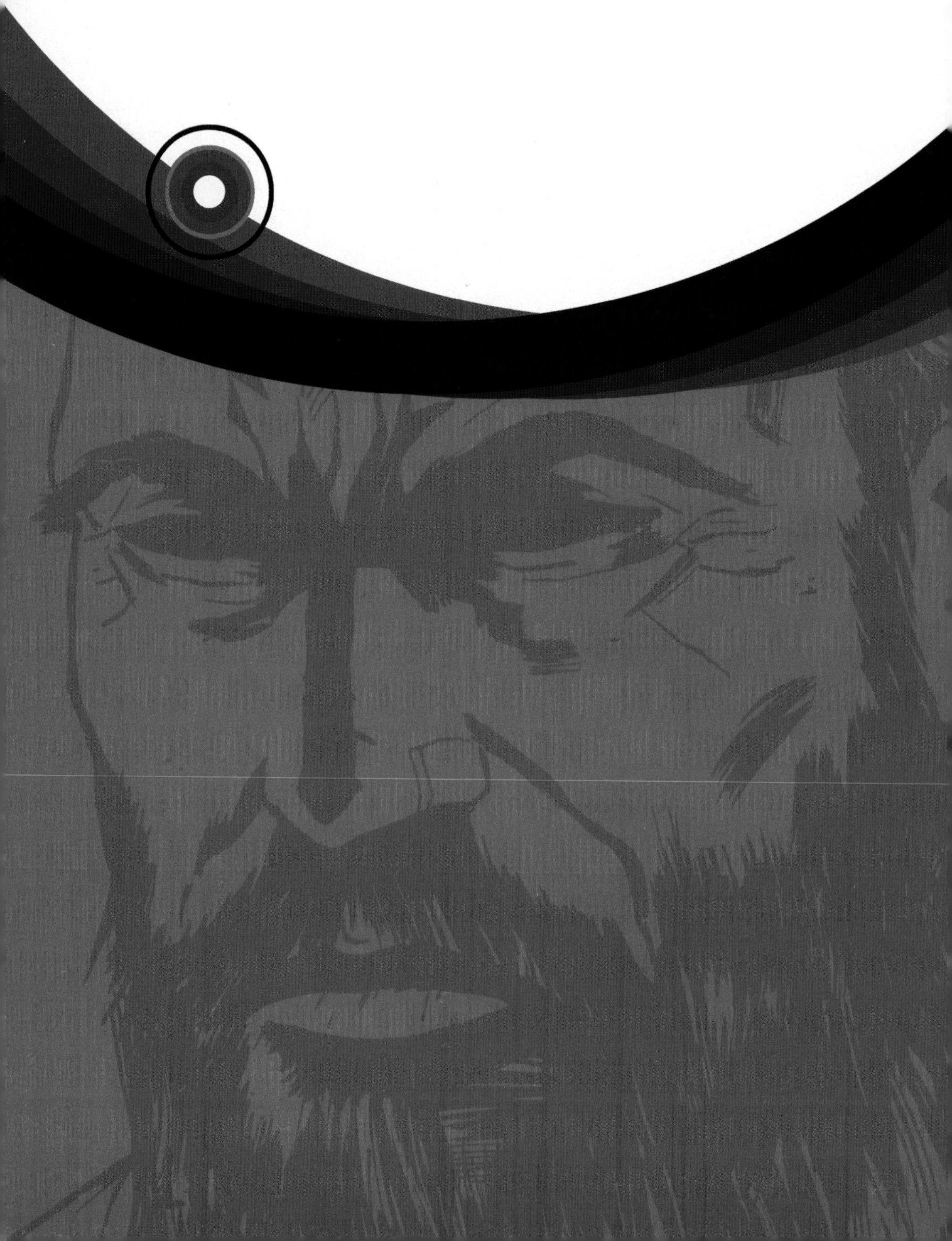

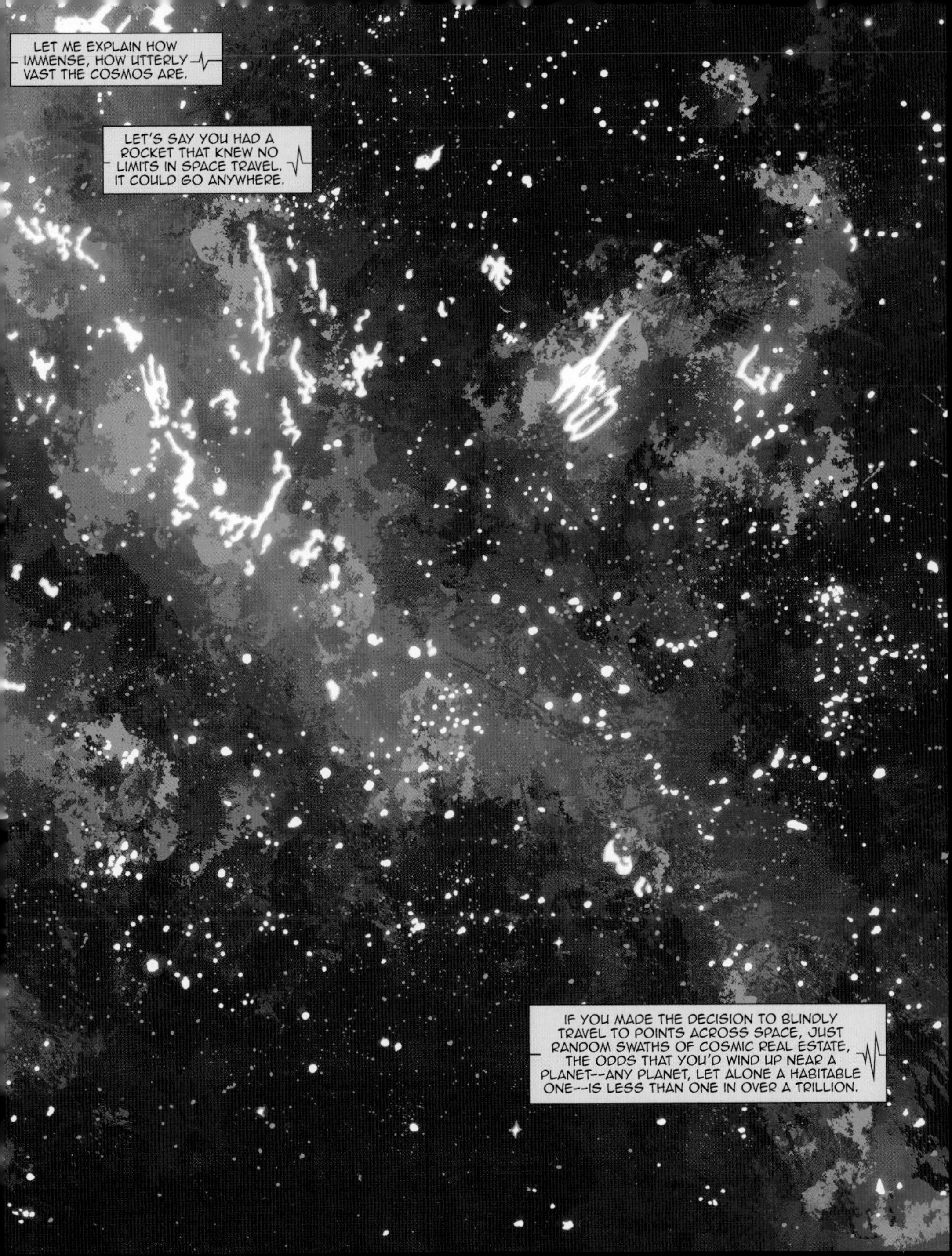
LET ME EXPLAIN HOW IMMENSE, HOW UTTERLY VAST THE COSMOS ARE.
LET'S SAY YOU HAD A ROCKET THAT KNEW NO LIMITS IN SPACE TRAVEL. IT COULD GO ANYWHERE.
IF YOU MADE THE DECISION TO BLINDLY TRAVEL TO POINTS ACROSS SPACE, JUST RANDOM SWATHS OF COSMIC REAL ESTATE, THE ODDS THAT YOU'D WIND UP NEAR A PLANET--ANY PLANET, LET ALONE A HABITABLE ONE--IS LESS THAN ONE IN OVER A TRILLION.
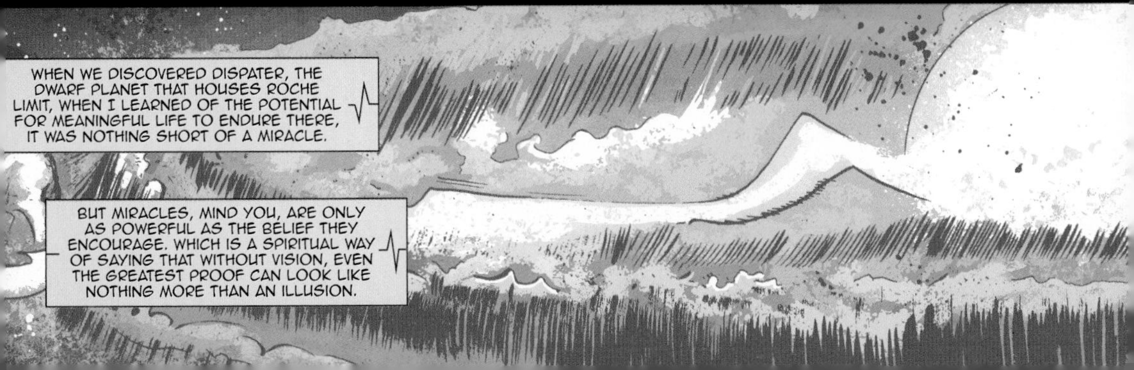
WHEN WE DISCOVERED DISPATER, THE DWARF PLANET THAT HOUSES ROCHE LIMIT, WHEN I LEARNED OF THE POTENTIAL FOR MEANINGFUL LIFE TO ENDURE THERE, IT WAS NOTHING SHORT OF A MIRACLE.
BUT MIRACLES, MIND YOU, ARE ONLY AS POWERFUL AS THE BELIEF THEY ENCOURAGE. WHICH IS A SPIRITUAL WAY OF SAYING THAT WITHOUT VISION, EVEN THE GREATEST PROOF CAN LOOK LIKE NOTHING MORE THAN AN ILLUSION.

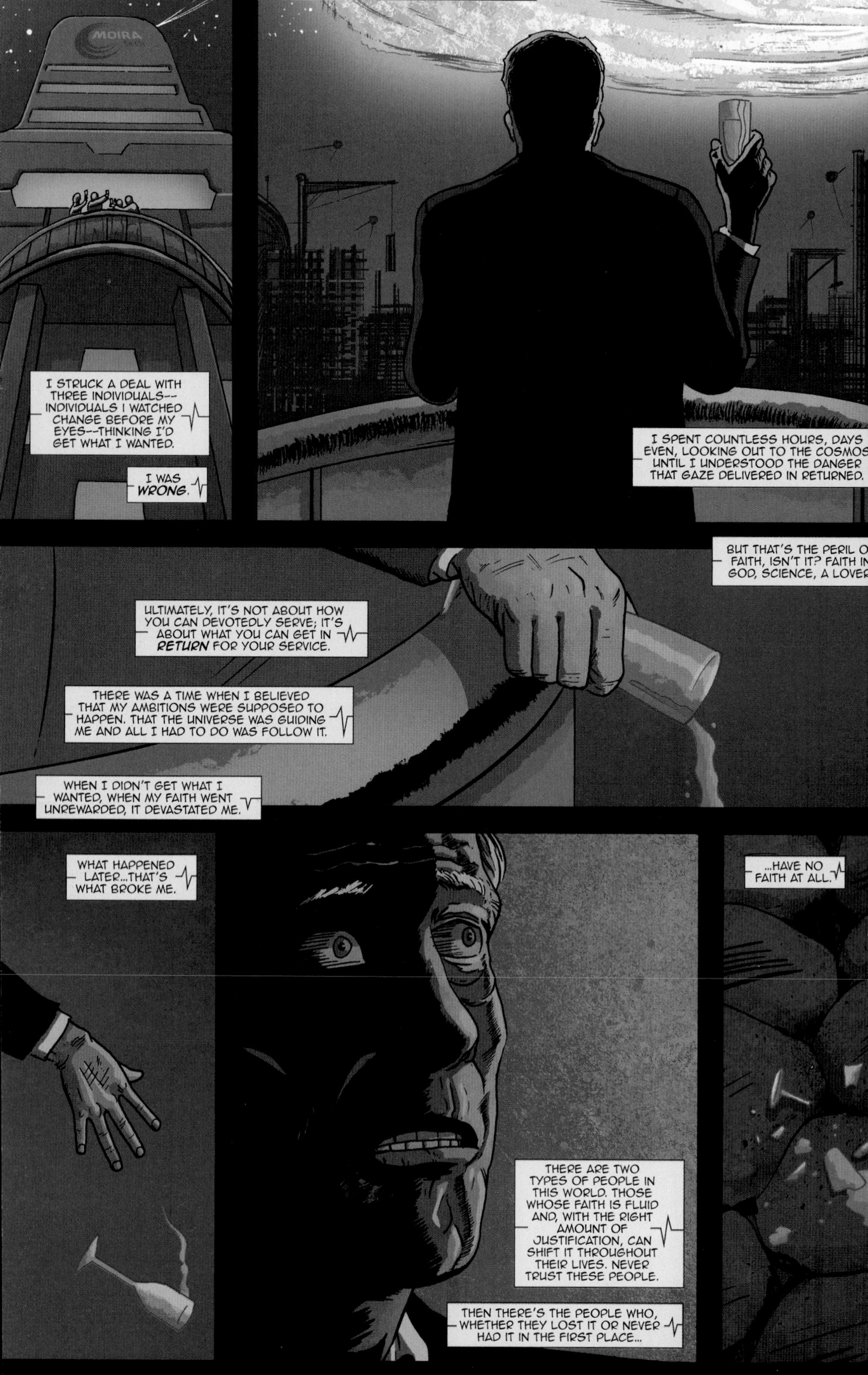
MOIRA
I STRUCK A DEAL WITH THREE INDIVIDUALS--INDIVIDUALS I WATCHED CHANGE BEFORE MY EYES--THINKING I'D GET WHAT I WANTED.
I WAS WRONG.
I SPENT COUNTLESS HOURS, DAYS EVEN, LOOKING OUT TO THE COSMOS UNTIL I UNDERSTOOD THE DANGER THAT GAZE DELIVERED IN RETURNED.
BUT THAT'S THE PERIL O FAITH, ISN'T IT? FAITH IN GOD, SCIENCE, A LOVER
ULTIMATELY, IT'S NOT ABOUT HOW YOU CAN DEVOTEDLY SERVE; IT'S ABOUT WHAT YOU CAN GET IN RETURN FOR YOUR SERVICE.
THERE WAS A TIME WHEN I BELIEVED THAT MY AMBITIONS WERE SUPPOSED TO HAPPEN. THAT THE UNIVERSE WAS GUIDING ME AND ALL I HAD TO DO WAS FOLLOW IT.
WHEN I DIDN'T GET WHAT I WANTED, WHEN MY FAITH WENT UNREWARDED, IT DEVASTATED ME.
WHAT HAPPENED LATER...THAT'S WHAT BROKE ME.
THERE ARE TWO TYPES OF PEOPLE IN THIS WORLD. THOSE WHOSE FAITH IS FLUID AND, WITH THE RIGHT AMOUNT OF JUSTIFICATION, CAN SHIFT IT THROUGHOUT THEIR LIVES. NEVER TRUST THESE PEOPLE.
THEN THERE'S THE PEOPLE WHO, WHETHER THEY LOST IT OR NEVER HAD IT IN THE FIRST PLACE...
...HAVE NO FAITH AT ALL.

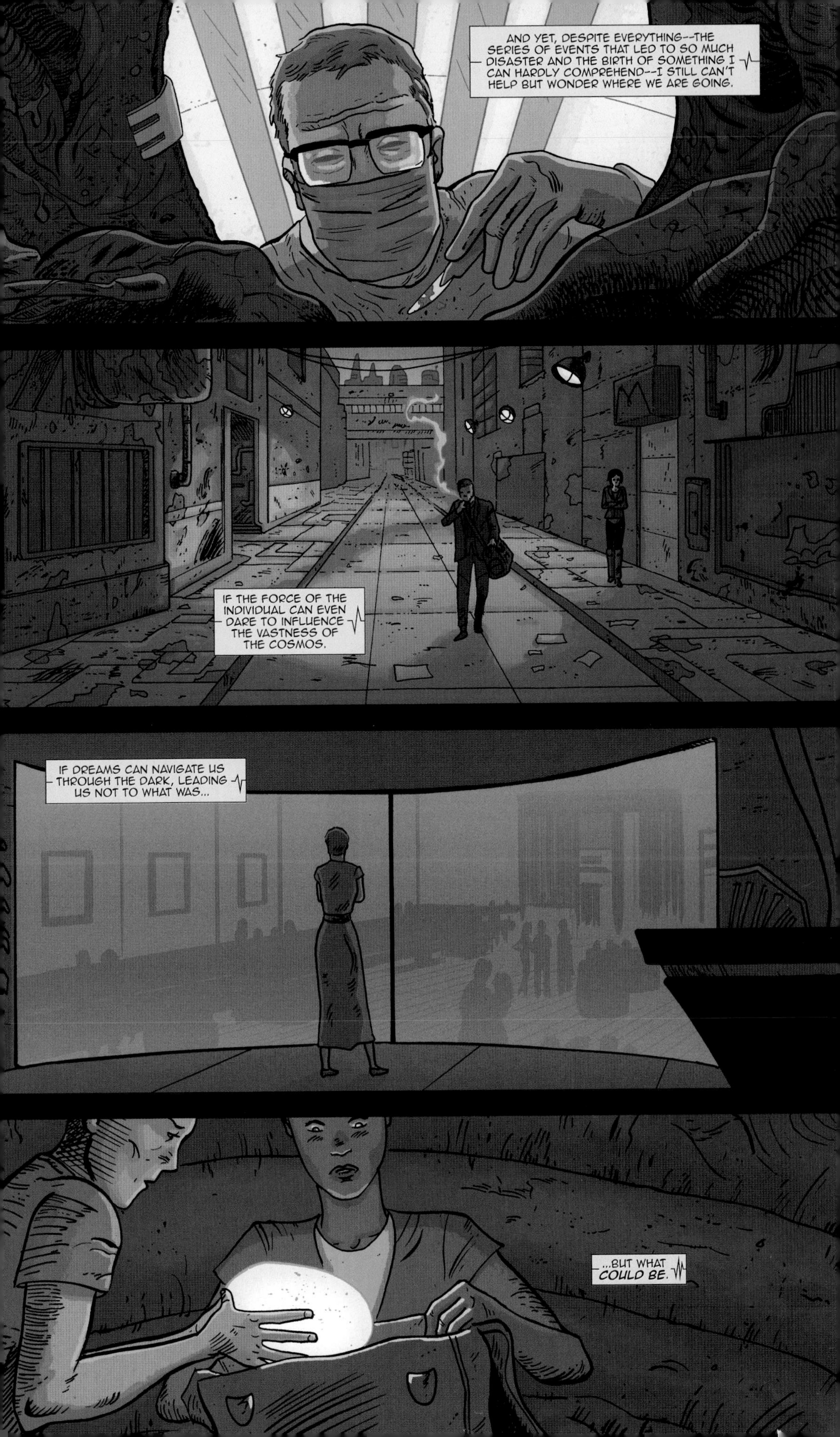
AND YET, DESPITE EVERYTHING--THE SERIES OF EVENTS THAT LED TO SO MUCH DISASTER AND THE BIRTH OF SOMETHING I CAN HARDLY COMPREHEND--I STILL CAN'T HELP BUT WONDER WHERE WE ARE GOING.
IF THE FORCE OF THE INDIVIDUAL CAN EVEN DARE TO INFLUENCE THE VASTNESS OF THE COSMOS.
IF DREAMS CAN NAVIGATE US THROUGH THE DARK, LEADING US NOT TO WHAT WAS...
...BUT WHAT *COULD BE.*

The Sun

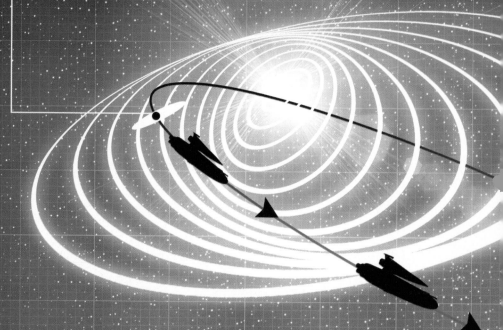

<< PREVIOUS SLIDE

Discovered by a joint United States/Russian terraforming expedition to Andromeda, little is known of this energy anomaly. The event behaves like a black hole without the crippling effects of gravity. It consumes light and energy, but its gravity isn't so dense that it collapses everything in its radius, nor does it prevent light from escaping.

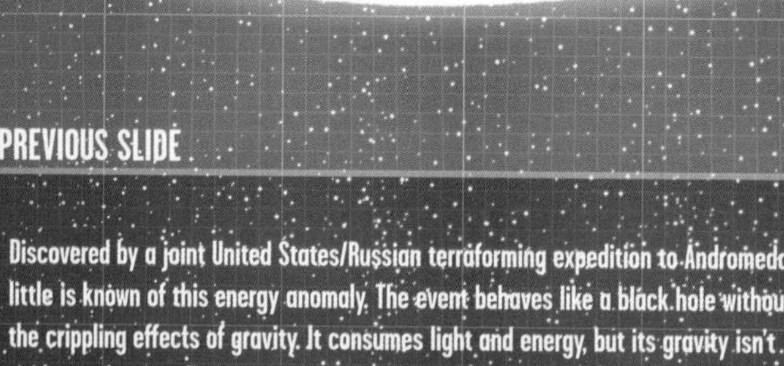

-The anomaly is visible from Earth using an Ultrahyper-Suprime Cam. Many scientists believe that its visibility is due to its electromagnetic radiation; others contend that a different energy, unidentified, is what enables visibility and provides the anomaly with its unique properties.

NEXT SLIDE >>

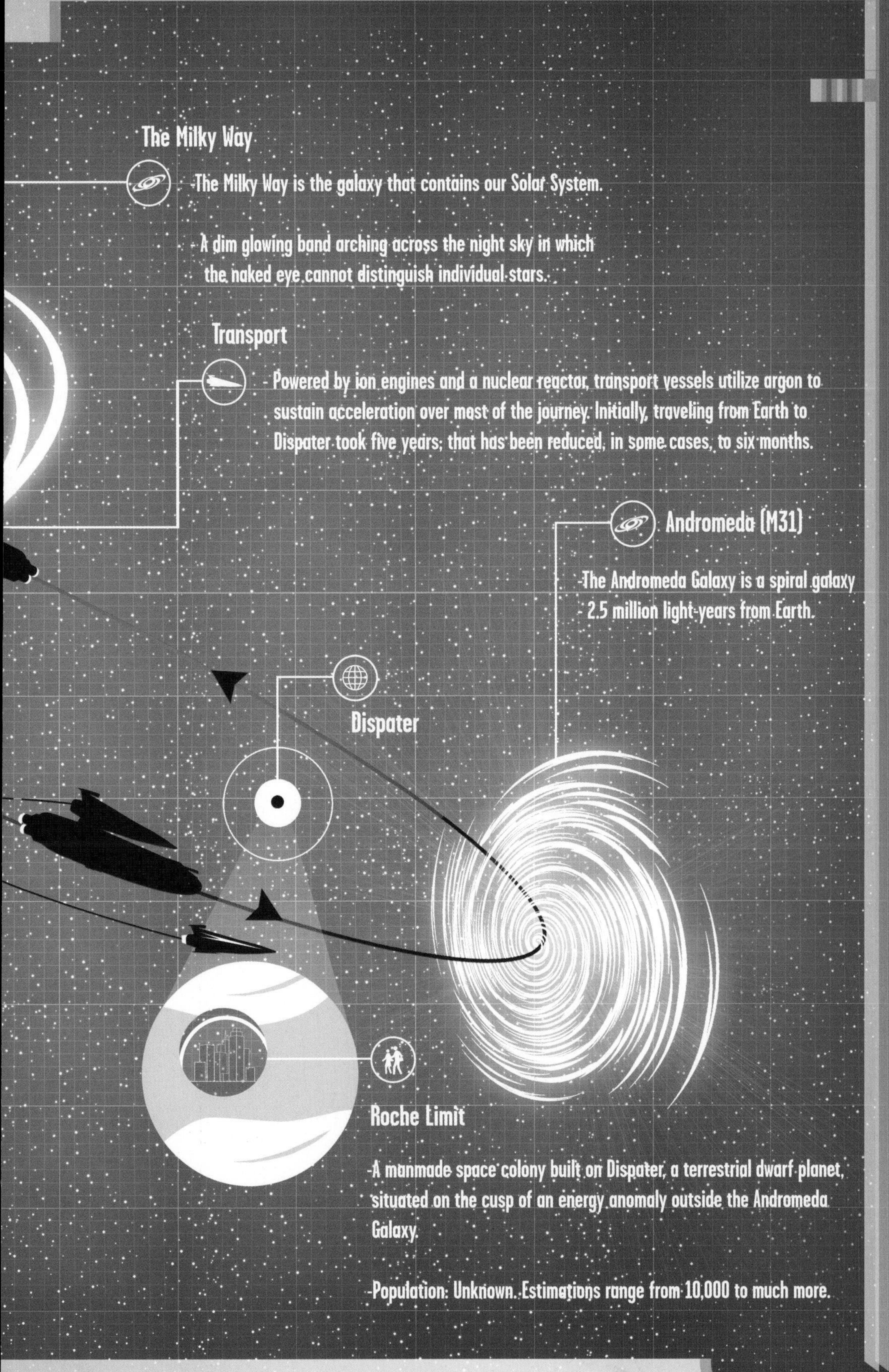
The Milky Way
-The Milky Way is the galaxy that contains our Solar System.
-A dim glowing band arching across the night sky in which the naked eye cannot distinguish individual stars.
Transport
-Powered by ion engines and a nuclear reactor, transport vessels utilize argon to sustain acceleration over most of the journey. Initially, traveling from Earth to Dispater took five years; that has been reduced, in some cases, to six months.
Andromeda (M31)
-The Andromeda Galaxy is a spiral galaxy
- 2.5 million light-years from Earth.
Dispater
Roche Limit
-A manmade space colony built on Dispater, a terrestrial dwarf planet, situated on the cusp of an energy anomaly outside the Andromeda Galaxy.
-Population: Unknown. Estimations range from 10,000 to much more.

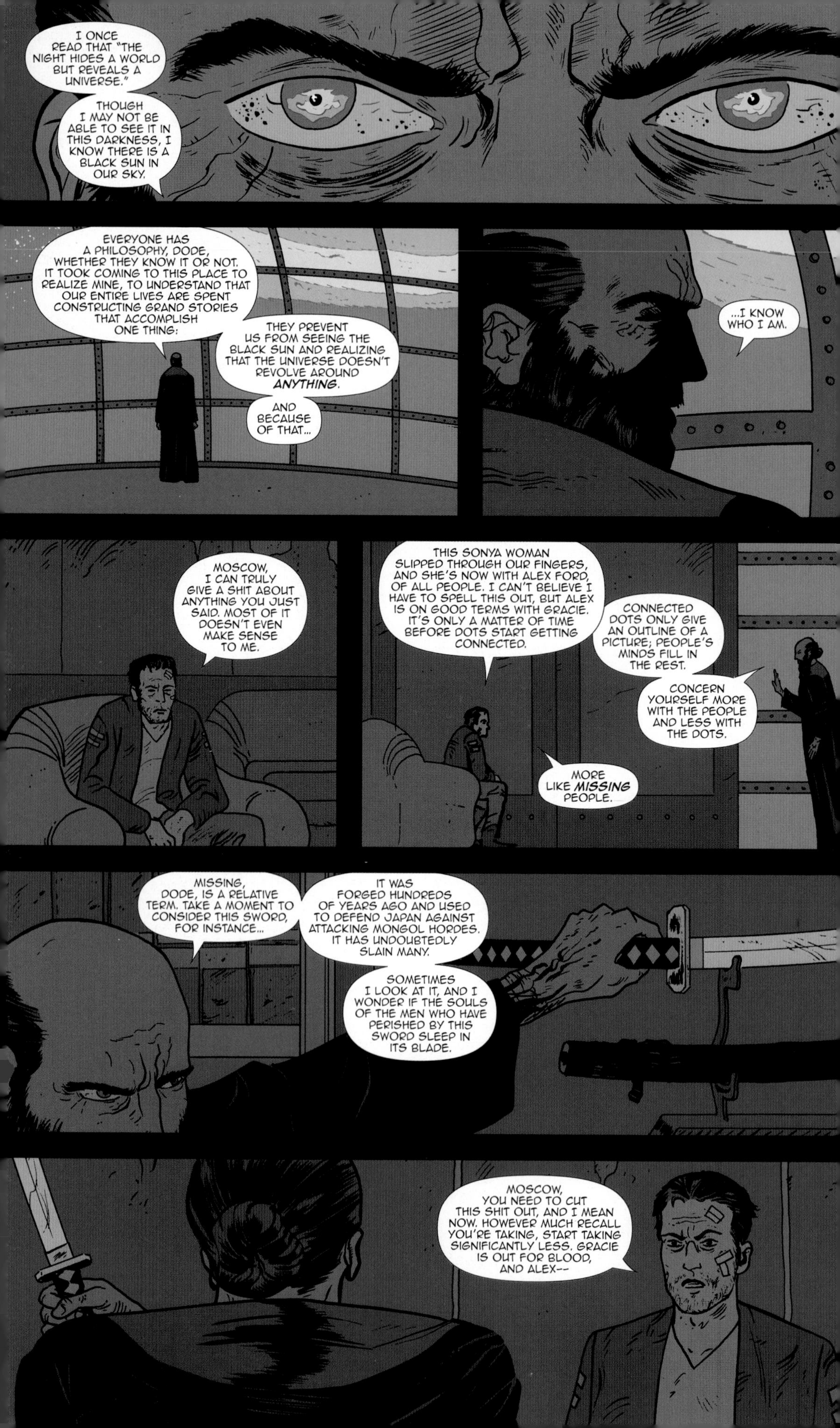
I ONCE READ THAT "THE NIGHT HIDES A WORLD BUT REVEALS A UNIVERSE."
THOUGH I MAY NOT BE ABLE TO SEE IT IN THIS DARKNESS, I KNOW THERE IS A BLACK SUN IN OUR SKY.
EVERYONE HAS A PHILOSOPHY, DODE, WHETHER THEY KNOW IT OR NOT. IT TOOK COMING TO THIS PLACE TO REALIZE MINE, TO UNDERSTAND THAT OUR ENTIRE LIVES ARE SPENT CONSTRUCTING GRAND STORIES THAT ACCOMPLISH ONE THING:
THEY PREVENT US FROM SEEING THE BLACK SUN AND REALIZING THAT THE UNIVERSE DOESN'T REVOLVE AROUND *ANYTHING*.
AND BECAUSE OF THAT...
...I KNOW WHO I AM.
MOSCOW, I CAN TRULY GIVE A SHIT ABOUT ANYTHING YOU JUST SAID. MOST OF IT DOESN'T EVEN MAKE SENSE TO ME.
THIS SONYA WOMAN SLIPPED THROUGH OUR FINGERS, AND SHE'S NOW WITH ALEX FORD, OF ALL PEOPLE. I CAN'T BELIEVE I HAVE TO SPELL THIS OUT, BUT ALEX IS ON GOOD TERMS WITH GRACIE. IT'S ONLY A MATTER OF TIME BEFORE DOTS START GETTING CONNECTED.
CONNECTED DOTS ONLY GIVE AN OUTLINE OF A PICTURE; PEOPLE'S MINDS FILL IN THE REST.
CONCERN YOURSELF MORE WITH THE PEOPLE AND LESS WITH THE DOTS.
MORE LIKE *MISSING* PEOPLE.
MISSING, DODE, IS A RELATIVE TERM. TAKE A MOMENT TO CONSIDER THIS SWORD, FOR INSTANCE...
IT WAS FORGED HUNDREDS OF YEARS AGO AND USED TO DEFEND JAPAN AGAINST ATTACKING MONGOL HORDES. IT HAS UNDOUBTEDLY SLAIN MANY.
SOMETIMES I LOOK AT IT, AND I WONDER IF THE SOULS OF THE MEN WHO HAVE PERISHED BY THIS SWORD SLEEP IN ITS BLADE.
MOSCOW, YOU NEED TO CUT THIS SHIT OUT, AND I MEAN NOW. HOWEVER MUCH RECALL YOU'RE TAKING, START TAKING SIGNIFICANTLY LESS. GRACIE IS OUT FOR BLOOD, AND ALEX--

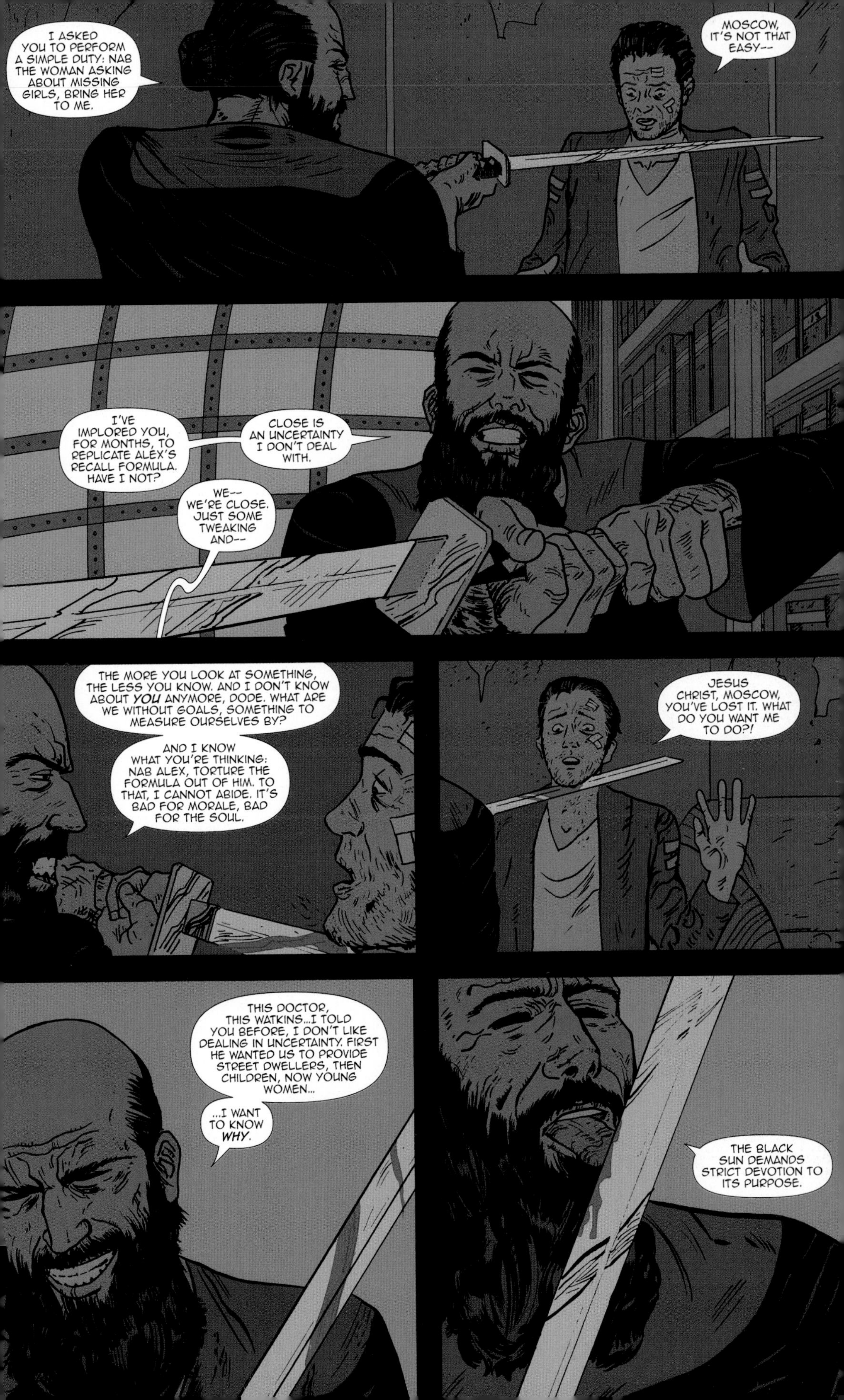
I ASKED YOU TO PERFORM A SIMPLE DUTY: NAB THE WOMAN ASKING ABOUT MISSING GIRLS, BRING HER TO ME.
MOSCOW, IT'S NOT THAT EASY--
I'VE IMPLORED YOU, FOR MONTHS, TO REPLICATE ALEX'S RECALL FORMULA. HAVE I NOT?
WE-- WE'RE CLOSE. JUST SOME TWEAKING AND--
CLOSE IS AN UNCERTAINTY I DON'T DEAL WITH.
THE MORE YOU LOOK AT SOMETHING, THE LESS YOU KNOW. AND I DON'T KNOW ABOUT YOU ANYMORE, DODE. WHAT ARE WE WITHOUT GOALS, SOMETHING TO MEASURE OURSELVES BY?
AND I KNOW WHAT YOU'RE THINKING: NAB ALEX, TORTURE THE FORMULA OUT OF HIM. TO THAT, I CANNOT ABIDE. IT'S BAD FOR MORALE, BAD FOR THE SOUL.
JESUS CHRIST, MOSCOW, YOU'VE LOST IT. WHAT DO YOU WANT ME TO DO?!
THIS DOCTOR, THIS WATKINS...I TOLD YOU BEFORE, I DON'T LIKE DEALING IN UNCERTAINTY. FIRST HE WANTED US TO PROVIDE STREET DWELLERS, THEN CHILDREN, NOW YOUNG WOMEN...
...I WANT TO KNOW WHY.
THE BLACK SUN DEMANDS STRICT DEVOTION TO ITS PURPOSE.

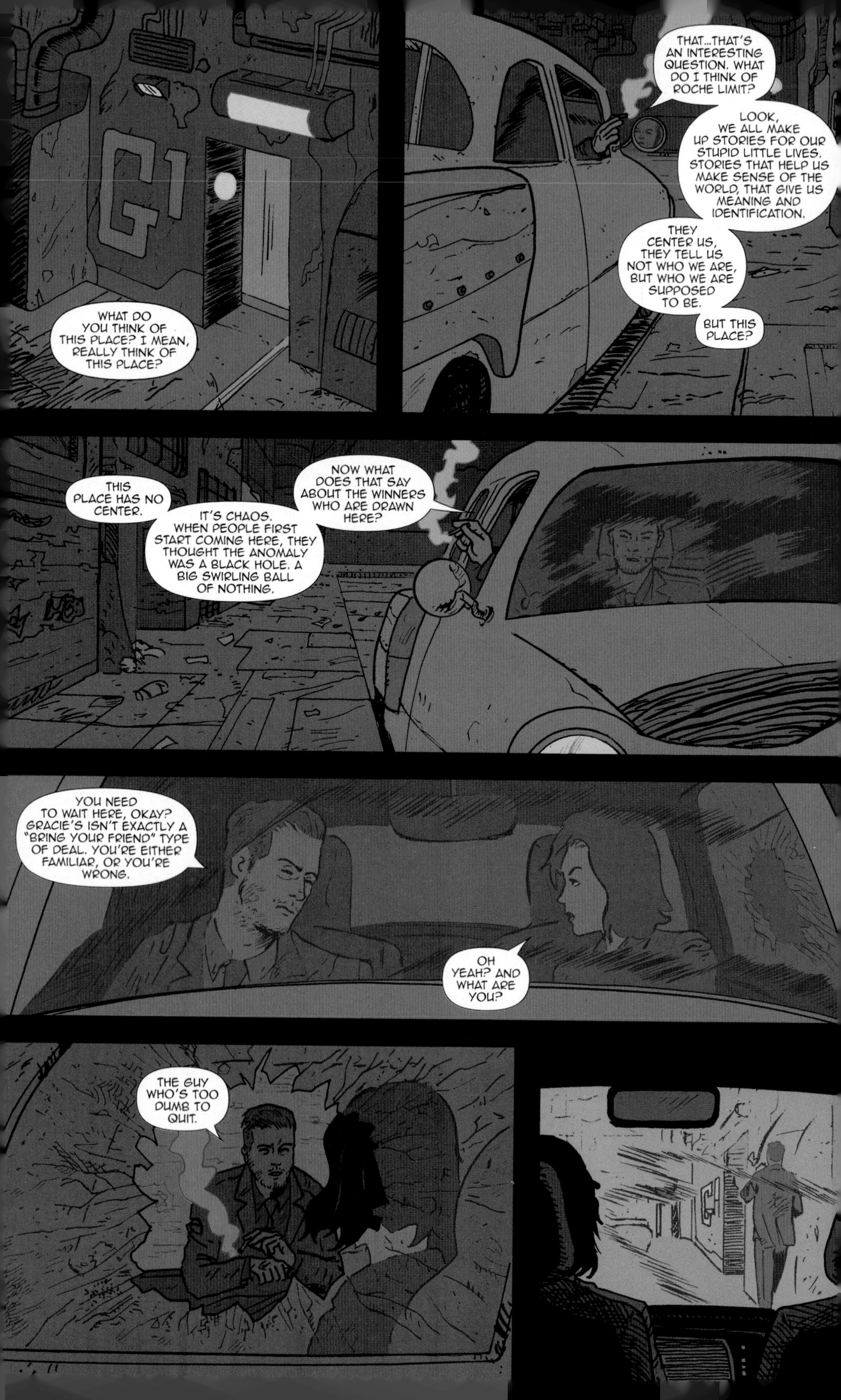
WHAT DO YOU THINK OF THIS PLACE? I MEAN, REALLY THINK OF THIS PLACE?
THAT...THAT'S AN INTERESTING QUESTION. WHAT DO I THINK OF ROCHE LIMIT?
LOOK, WE ALL MAKE UP STORIES FOR OUR STUPID LITTLE LIVES. STORIES THAT HELP US MAKE SENSE OF THE WORLD, THAT GIVE US MEANING AND IDENTIFICATION.
THEY CENTER US, THEY TELL US NOT WHO WE ARE, BUT WHO WE ARE SUPPOSED TO BE.
BUT THIS PLACE?
THIS PLACE HAS NO CENTER.
IT'S CHAOS. WHEN PEOPLE FIRST START COMING HERE, THEY THOUGHT THE ANOMALY WAS A BLACK HOLE. A BIG SWIRLING BALL OF NOTHING.
NOW WHAT DOES THAT SAY ABOUT THE WINNERS WHO ARE DRAWN HERE?
YOU NEED TO WAIT HERE, OKAY? GRACIE'S ISN'T EXACTLY A "BRING YOUR FRIEND" TYPE OF DEAL. YOU'RE EITHER FAMILIAR, OR YOU'RE WRONG.
OH YEAH? AND WHAT ARE YOU?
THE GUY WHO'S TOO DUMB TO QUIT.

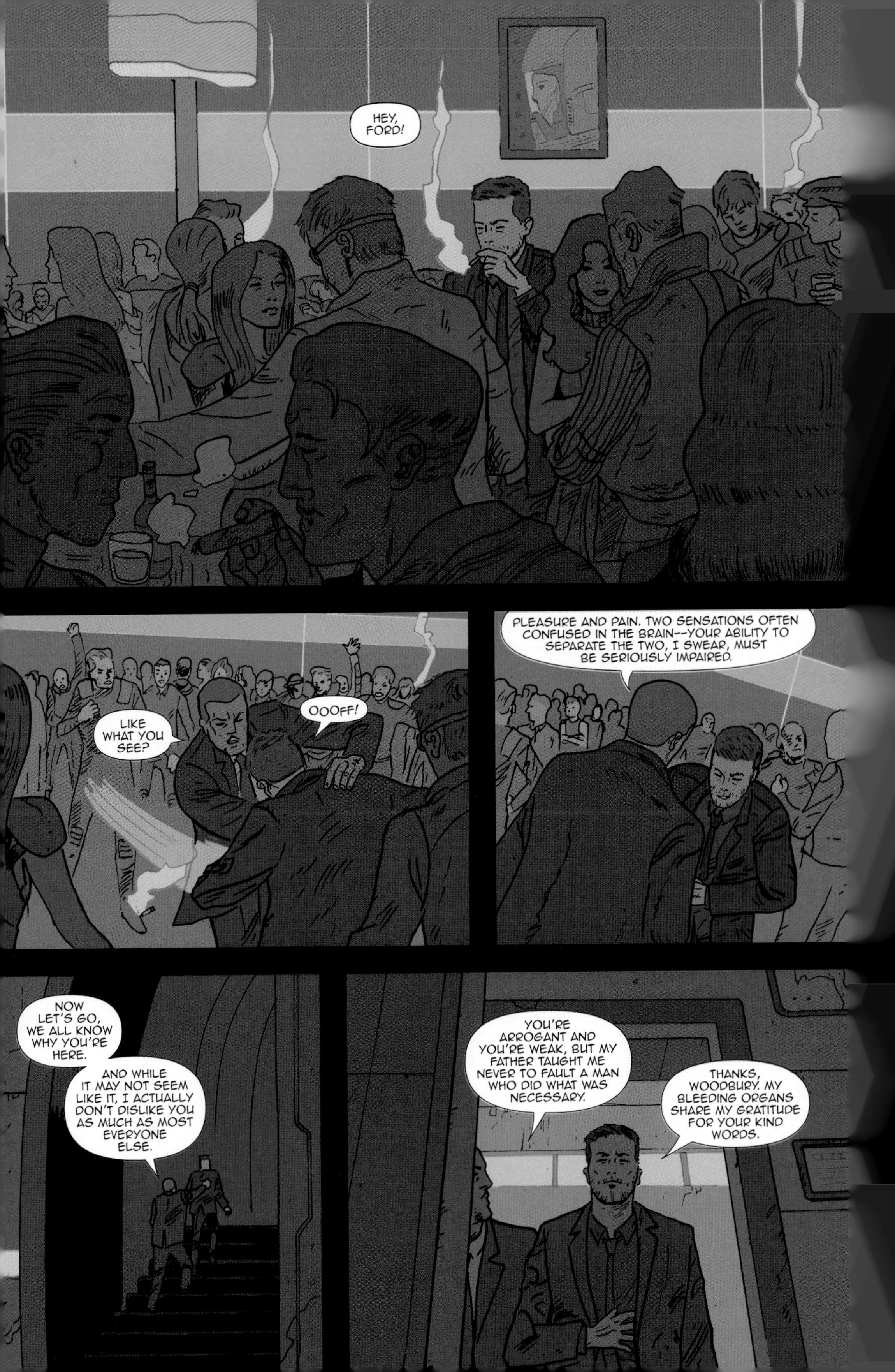
HEY, FORD!
LIKE WHAT YOU SEE?
OOOFF!
PLEASURE AND PAIN. TWO SENSATIONS OFTEN CONFUSED IN THE BRAIN--YOUR ABILITY TO SEPARATE THE TWO, I SWEAR, MUST BE SERIOUSLY IMPAIRED.
NOW LET'S GO, WE ALL KNOW WHY YOU'RE HERE.
AND WHILE IT MAY NOT SEEM LIKE IT, I ACTUALLY DON'T DISLIKE YOU AS MUCH AS MOST EVERYONE ELSE.
YOU'RE ARROGANT AND YOU'RE WEAK, BUT MY FATHER TAUGHT ME NEVER TO FAULT A MAN WHO DID WHAT WAS NECESSARY.
THANKS, WOODBURY. MY BLEEDING ORGANS SHARE MY GRATITUDE FOR YOUR KIND WORDS.

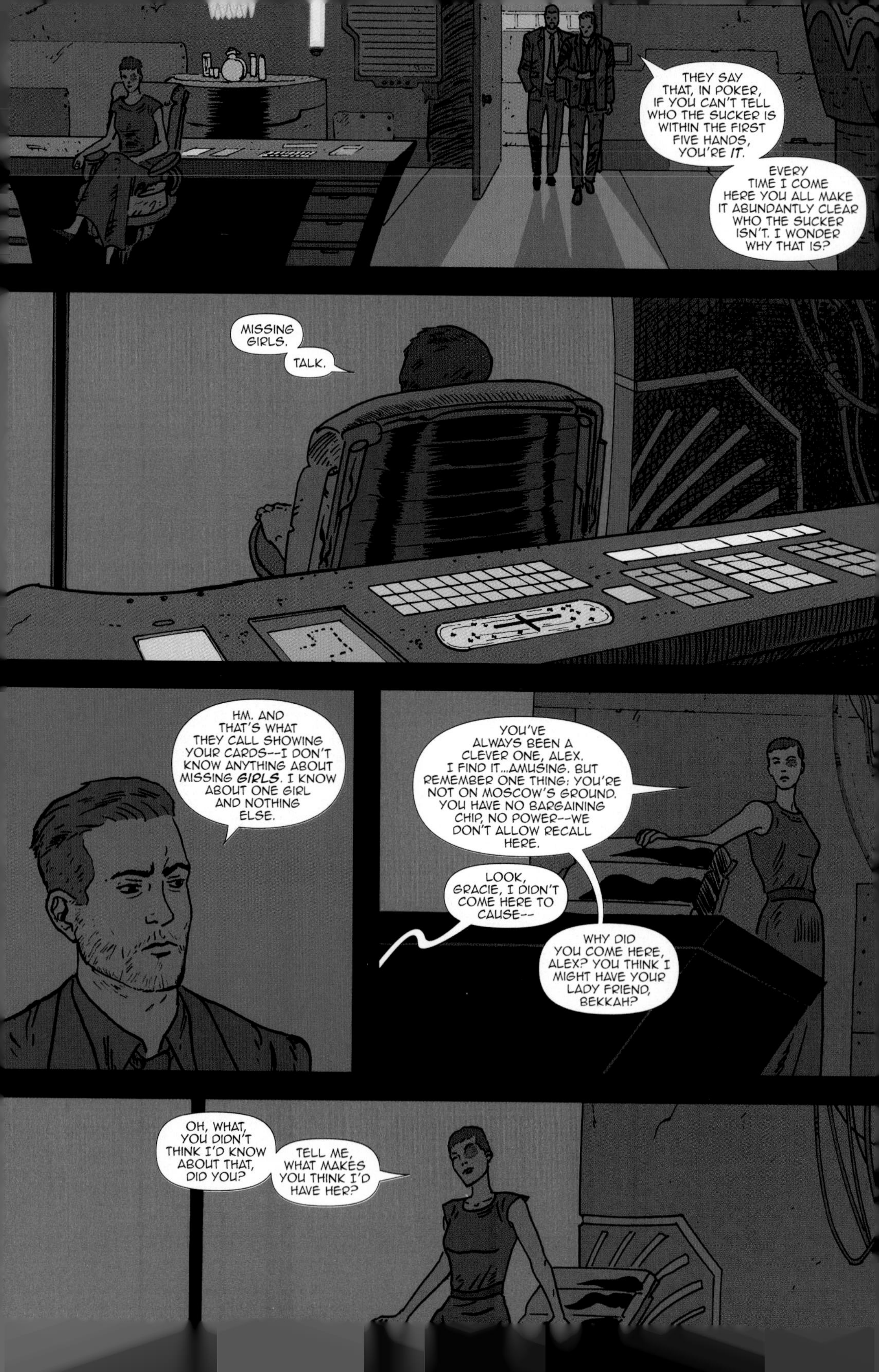
THEY SAY THAT, IN POKER, IF YOU CAN'T TELL WHO THE SUCKER IS WITHIN THE FIRST FIVE HANDS, YOU'RE *IT*.
EVERY TIME I COME HERE YOU ALL MAKE IT ABUNDANTLY CLEAR WHO THE SUCKER ISN'T. I WONDER WHY THAT IS?
MISSING GIRLS.
TALK.
HM. AND THAT'S WHAT THEY CALL SHOWING YOUR CARDS--I DON'T KNOW ANYTHING ABOUT MISSING *GIRLS*. I KNOW ABOUT ONE GIRL AND NOTHING ELSE.
YOU'VE ALWAYS BEEN A CLEVER ONE, ALEX. I FIND IT...AMUSING. BUT REMEMBER ONE THING: YOU'RE NOT ON MOSCOW'S GROUND. YOU HAVE NO BARGAINING CHIP, NO POWER--WE DON'T ALLOW RECALL HERE.
LOOK, GRACIE, I DIDN'T COME HERE TO CAUSE--
WHY DID YOU COME HERE, ALEX? YOU THINK I MIGHT HAVE YOUR LADY FRIEND, BEKKAH?
OH, WHAT, YOU DIDN'T THINK I'D KNOW ABOUT THAT, DID YOU?
TELL ME, WHAT MAKES YOU THINK I'D HAVE HER?

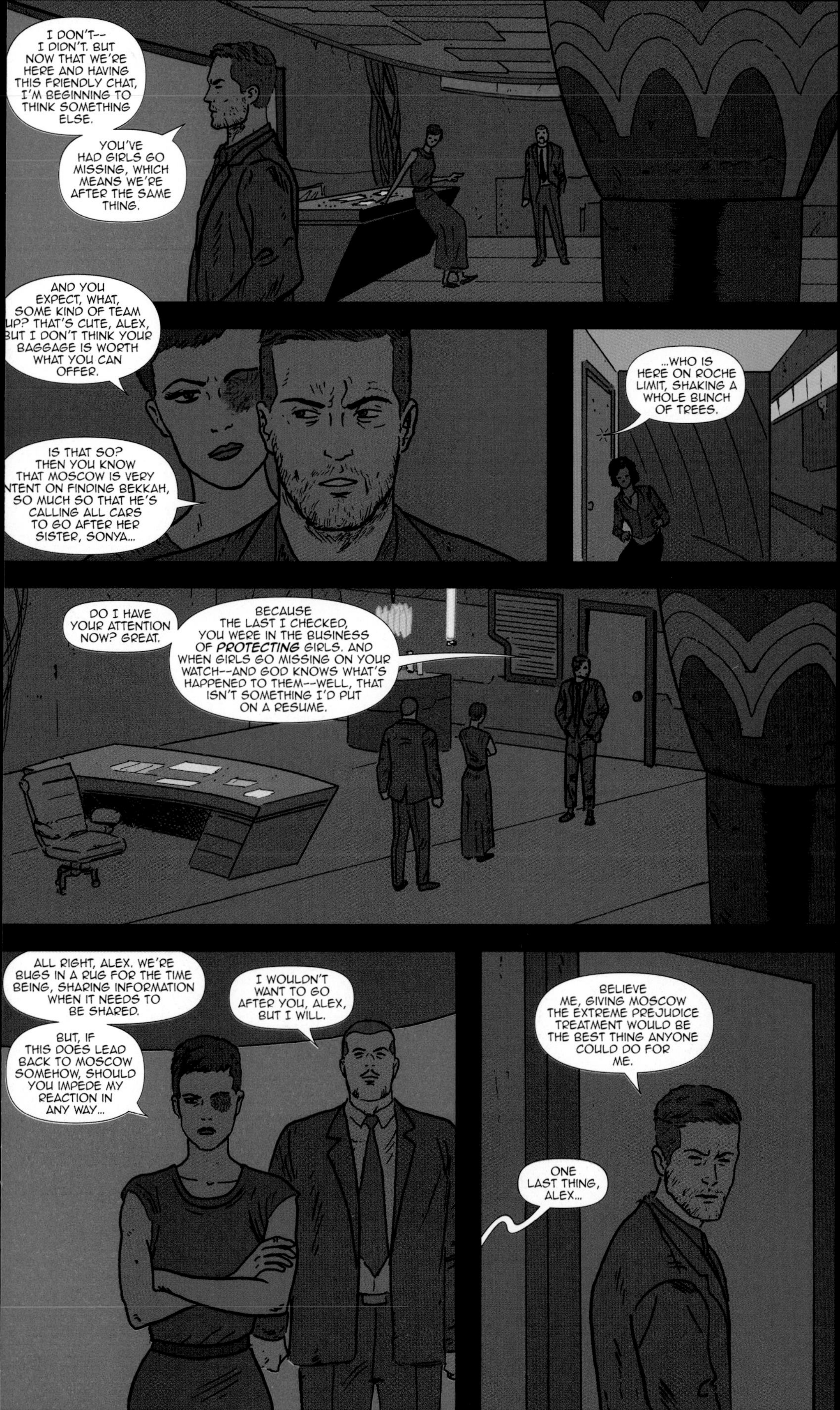
I DON'T-- I DIDN'T. BUT NOW THAT WE'RE HERE AND HAVING THIS FRIENDLY CHAT, I'M BEGINNING TO THINK SOMETHING ELSE.
YOU'VE HAD GIRLS GO MISSING, WHICH MEANS WE'RE AFTER THE SAME THING.
AND YOU EXPECT, WHAT, SOME KIND OF TEAM UP? THAT'S CUTE, ALEX, BUT I DON'T THINK YOUR BAGGAGE IS WORTH WHAT YOU CAN OFFER.
IS THAT SO? THEN YOU KNOW THAT MOSCOW IS VERY INTENT ON FINDING BEKKAH, SO MUCH SO THAT HE'S CALLING ALL CARS TO GO AFTER HER SISTER, SONYA...
...WHO IS HERE ON ROCHE LIMIT, SHAKING A WHOLE BUNCH OF TREES.
DO I HAVE YOUR ATTENTION NOW? GREAT.
BECAUSE THE LAST I CHECKED, YOU WERE IN THE BUSINESS OF *PROTECTING* GIRLS. AND WHEN GIRLS GO MISSING ON YOUR WATCH--AND GOD KNOWS WHAT'S HAPPENED TO THEM--WELL, THAT ISN'T SOMETHING I'D PUT ON A RESUME.
ALL RIGHT, ALEX. WE'RE BUGS IN A RUG FOR THE TIME BEING, SHARING INFORMATION WHEN IT NEEDS TO BE SHARED.
BUT, IF THIS DOES LEAD BACK TO MOSCOW SOMEHOW, SHOULD YOU IMPEDE MY REACTION IN ANY WAY...
I WOULDN'T WANT TO GO AFTER YOU, ALEX, BUT I WILL.
BELIEVE ME, GIVING MOSCOW THE EXTREME PREJUDICE TREATMENT WOULD BE THE BEST THING ANYONE COULD DO FOR ME.
ONE LAST THING, ALEX...

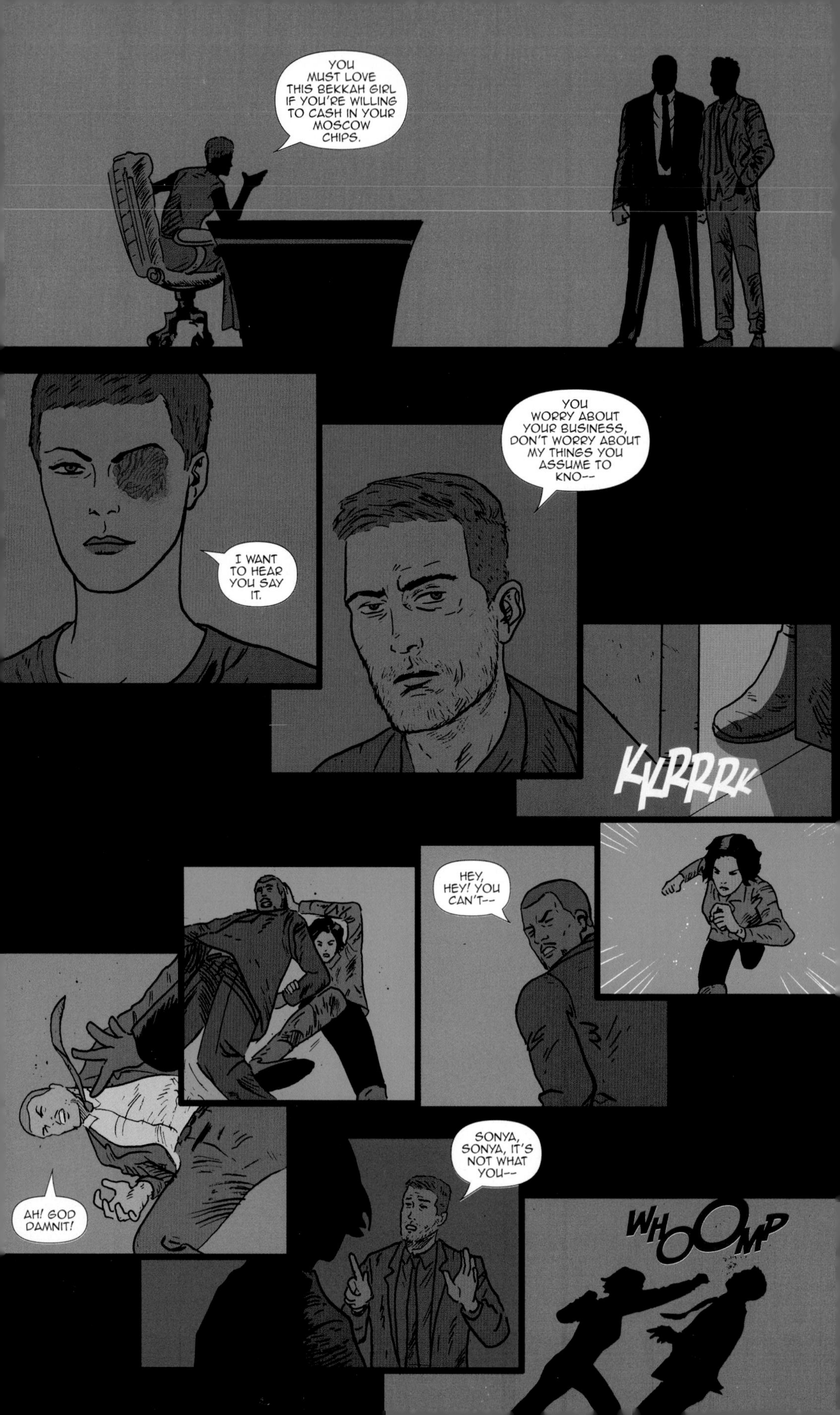
YOU MUST LOVE THIS BEKKAH GIRL IF YOU'RE WILLING TO CASH IN YOUR MOSCOW CHIPS.
I WANT TO HEAR YOU SAY IT.
YOU WORRY ABOUT YOUR BUSINESS, DON'T WORRY ABOUT MY THINGS YOU ASSUME TO KNO--
KVRRRK
HEY, HEY! YOU CAN'T--
AH! GOD DAMNIT!
SONYA, SONYA, IT'S NOT WHAT YOU--
WHOOMP

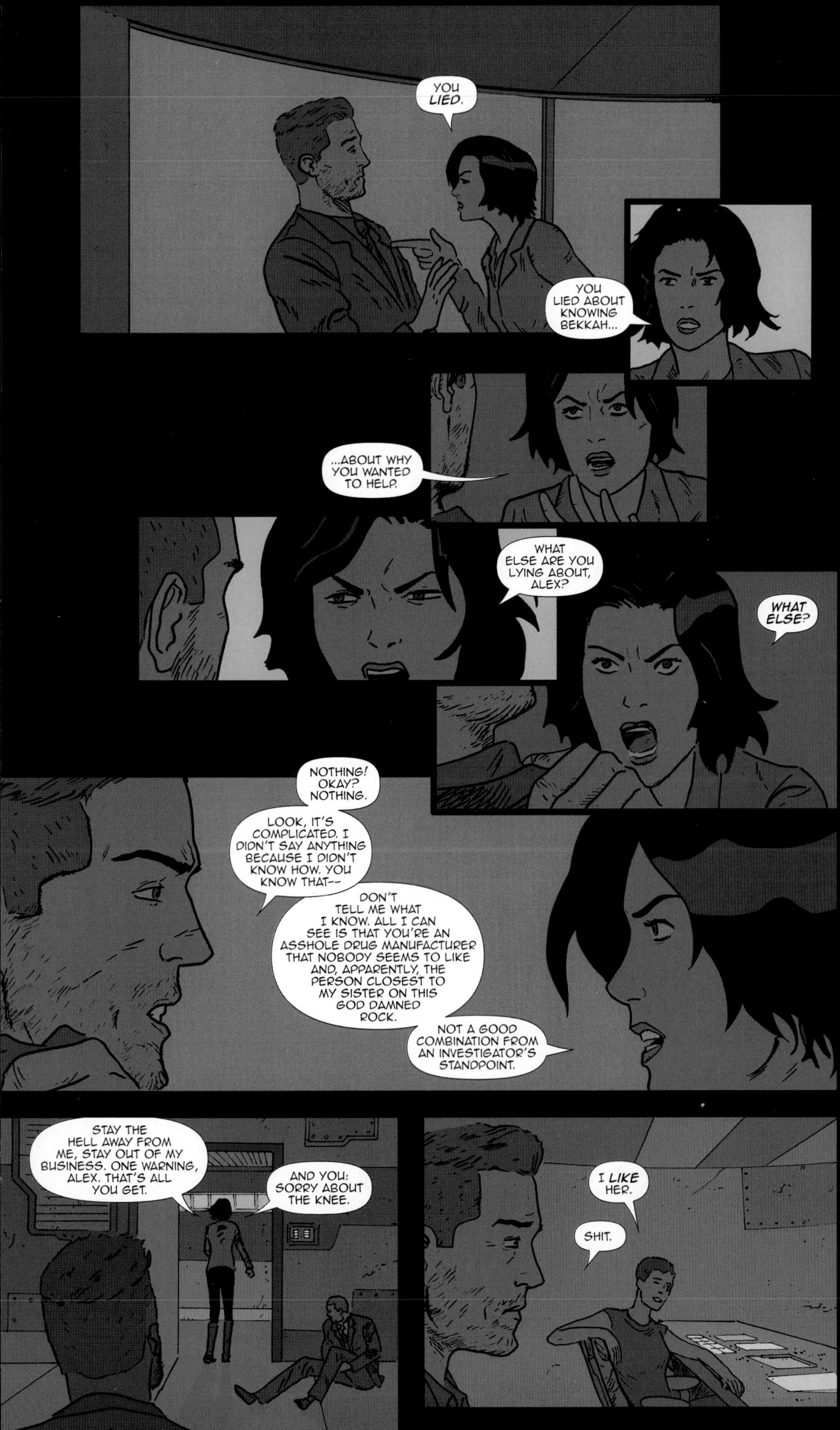
YOU LIED.
YOU LIED ABOUT KNOWING BEKKAH...
...ABOUT WHY YOU WANTED TO HELP.
WHAT ELSE ARE YOU LYING ABOUT, ALEX?
WHAT ELSE?
NOTHING! OKAY? NOTHING.
LOOK, IT'S COMPLICATED. I DIDN'T SAY ANYTHING BECAUSE I DIDN'T KNOW HOW. YOU KNOW THAT--
DON'T TELL ME WHAT I KNOW. ALL I CAN SEE IS THAT YOU'RE AN ASSHOLE DRUG MANUFACTURER THAT NOBODY SEEMS TO LIKE AND, APPARENTLY, THE PERSON CLOSEST TO MY SISTER ON THIS GOD DAMNED ROCK.
NOT A GOOD COMBINATION FROM AN INVESTIGATOR'S STANDPOINT.
STAY THE HELL AWAY FROM ME, STAY OUT OF MY BUSINESS. ONE WARNING, ALEX. THAT'S ALL YOU GET.
AND YOU: SORRY ABOUT THE KNEE.
I LIKE HER.
SHIT.

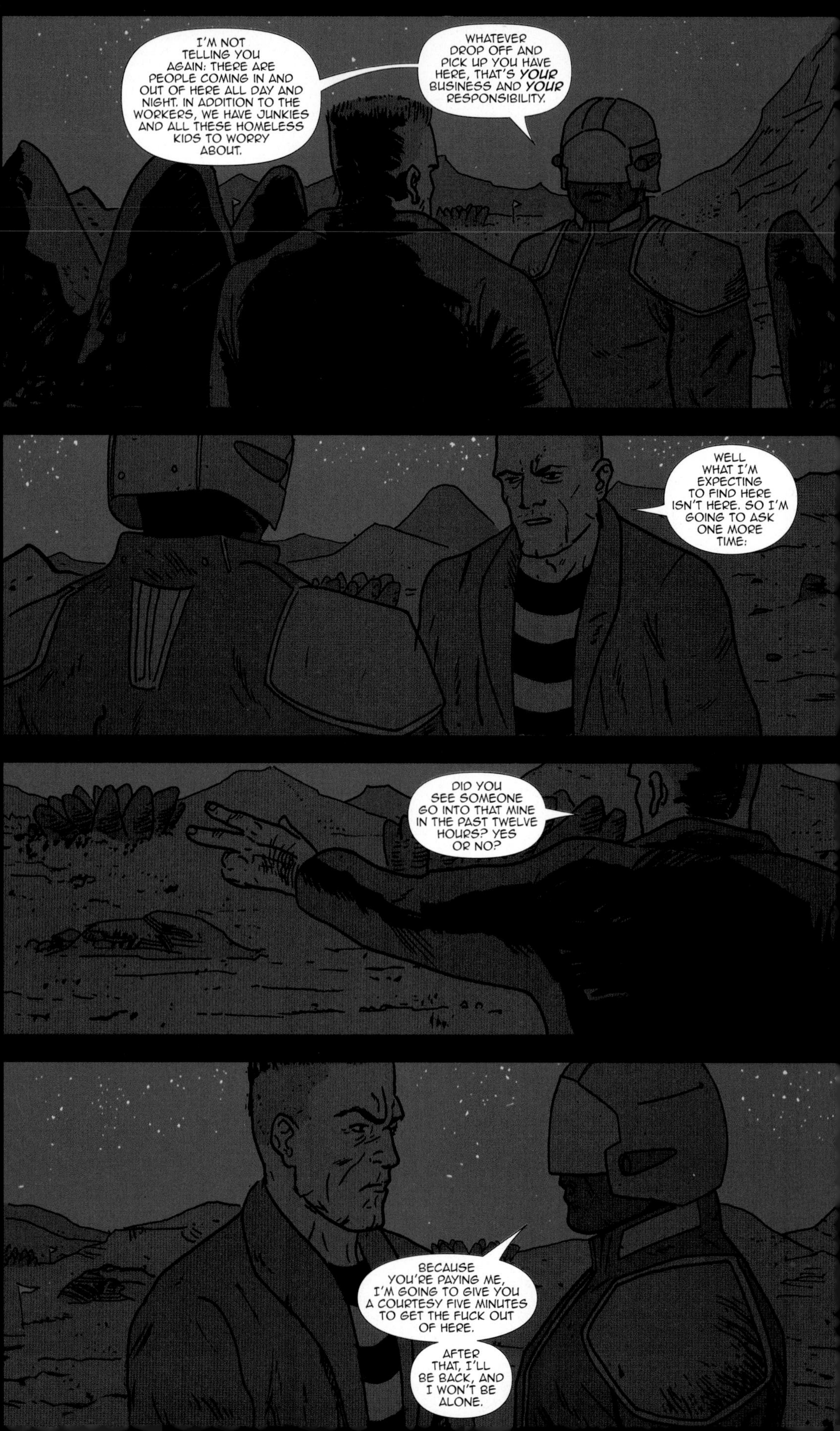
I'M NOT TELLING YOU AGAIN: THERE ARE PEOPLE COMING IN AND OUT OF HERE ALL DAY AND NIGHT. IN ADDITION TO THE WORKERS, WE HAVE JUNKIES AND ALL THESE HOMELESS KIDS TO WORRY ABOUT.
WHATEVER DROP OFF AND PICK UP YOU HAVE HERE, THAT'S *YOUR* BUSINESS AND *YOUR* RESPONSIBILITY.
WELL WHAT I'M EXPECTING TO FIND HERE ISN'T HERE. SO I'M GOING TO ASK ONE MORE TIME:
DID YOU SEE SOMEONE GO INTO THAT MINE IN THE PAST TWELVE HOURS? YES OR NO?
BECAUSE YOU'RE PAYING ME, I'M GOING TO GIVE YOU A COURTESY FIVE MINUTES TO GET THE FUCK OUT OF HERE.
AFTER THAT, I'LL BE BACK, AND I WON'T BE ALONE.

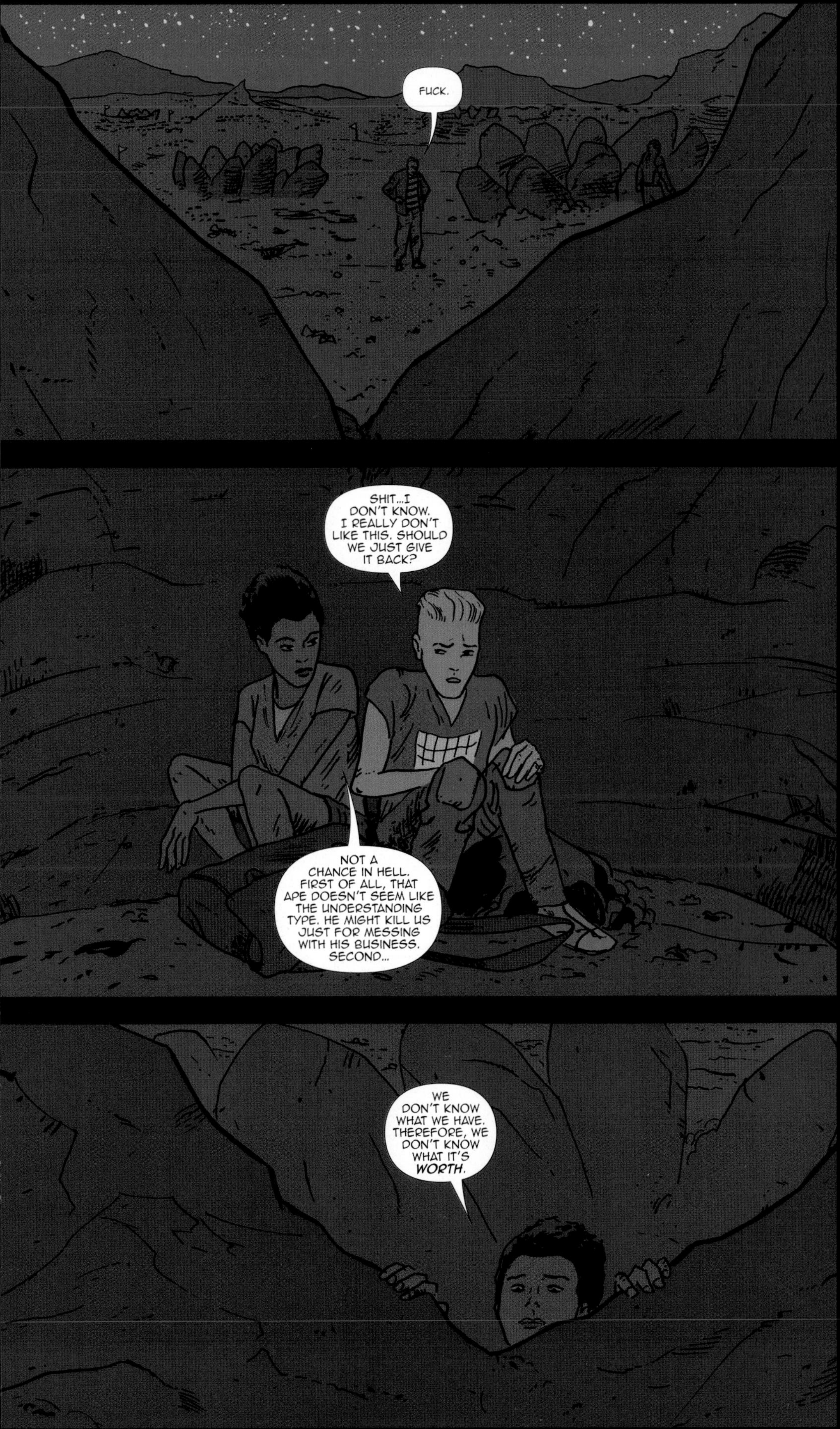
FUCK.
SHIT...I DON'T KNOW. I REALLY DON'T LIKE THIS. SHOULD WE JUST GIVE IT BACK?
NOT A CHANCE IN HELL. FIRST OF ALL, THAT APE DOESN'T SEEM LIKE THE UNDERSTANDING TYPE. HE MIGHT KILL US JUST FOR MESSING WITH HIS BUSINESS. SECOND...
WE DON'T KNOW WHAT WE HAVE. THEREFORE, WE DON'T KNOW WHAT IT'S *WORTH*.

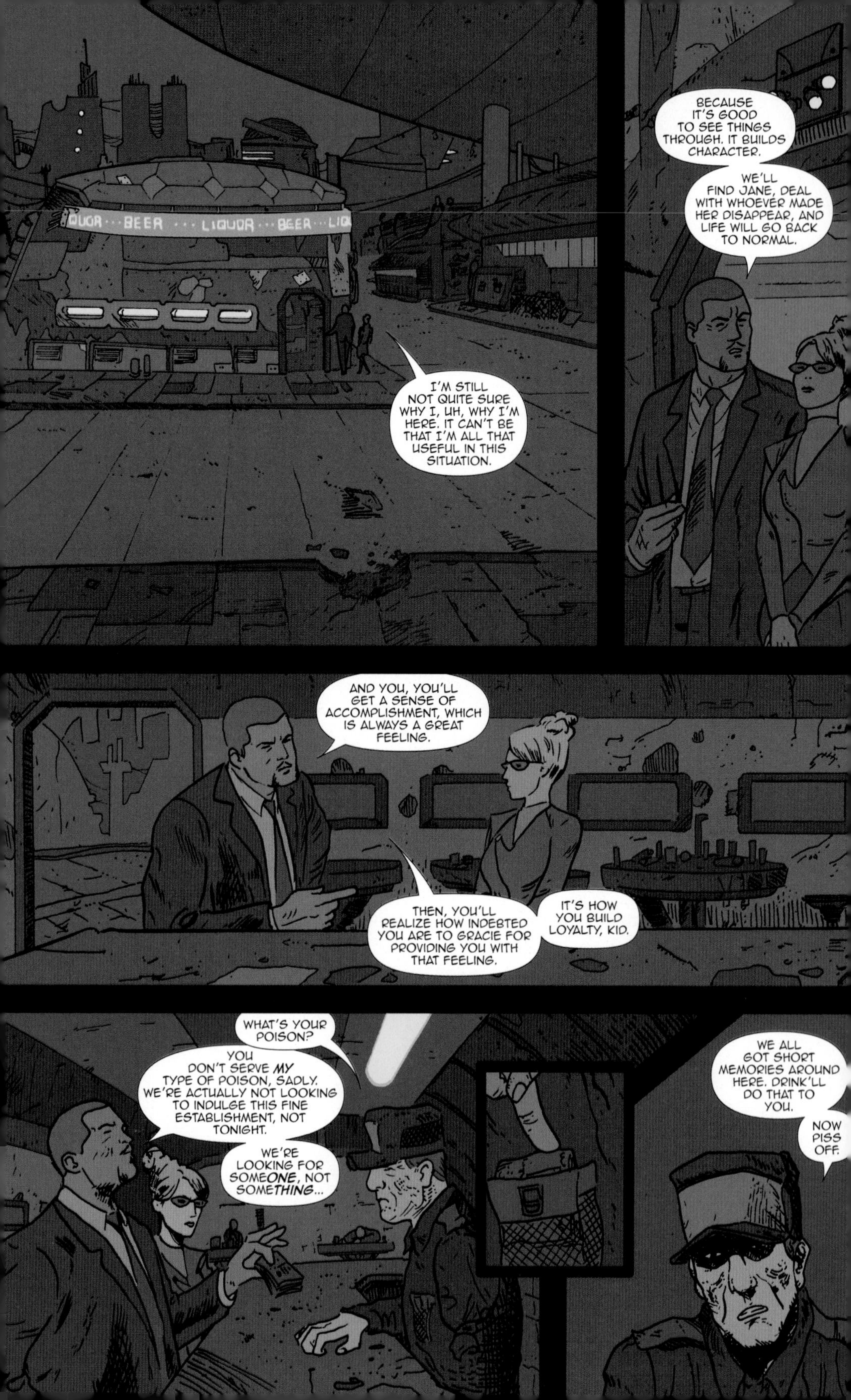
QUOR ··· BEER ··· LIQUOR ··· BEER ··· LIQ
I'M STILL NOT QUITE SURE WHY I, UH, WHY I'M HERE. IT CAN'T BE THAT I'M ALL THAT USEFUL IN THIS SITUATION.
BECAUSE IT'S GOOD TO SEE THINGS THROUGH. IT BUILDS CHARACTER.
WE'LL FIND JANE, DEAL WITH WHOEVER MADE HER DISAPPEAR, AND LIFE WILL GO BACK TO NORMAL.
AND YOU, YOU'LL GET A SENSE OF ACCOMPLISHMENT, WHICH IS ALWAYS A GREAT FEELING.
THEN, YOU'LL REALIZE HOW INDEBTED YOU ARE TO GRACIE FOR PROVIDING YOU WITH THAT FEELING.
IT'S HOW YOU BUILD LOYALTY, KID.
WHAT'S YOUR POISON?
YOU DON'T SERVE *MY* TYPE OF POISON, SADLY. WE'RE ACTUALLY NOT LOOKING TO INDULGE THIS FINE ESTABLISHMENT, NOT TONIGHT.
WE'RE LOOKING FOR SOME*ONE*, NOT SOME*THING*...
WE ALL GOT SHORT MEMORIES AROUND HERE. DRINK'LL DO THAT TO YOU.
NOW PISS OFF.

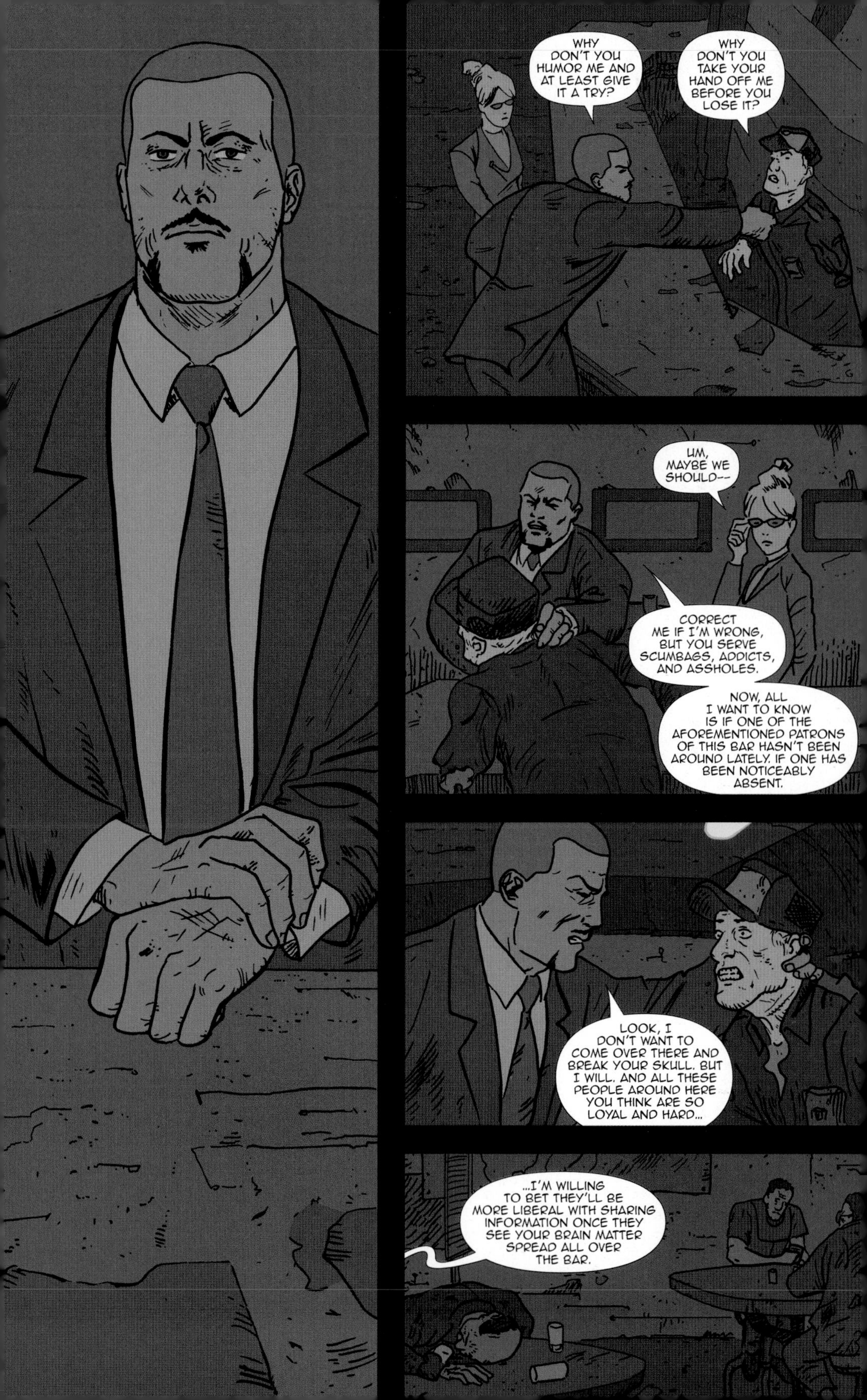
WHY DON'T YOU HUMOR ME AND AT LEAST GIVE IT A TRY?
WHY DON'T YOU TAKE YOUR HAND OFF ME BEFORE YOU LOSE IT?
UM, MAYBE WE SHOULD--
CORRECT ME IF I'M WRONG, BUT YOU SERVE SCUMBAGS, ADDICTS, AND ASSHOLES.
NOW, ALL I WANT TO KNOW IS IF ONE OF THE AFOREMENTIONED PATRONS OF THIS BAR HASN'T BEEN AROUND LATELY. IF ONE HAS BEEN NOTICEABLY ABSENT.
LOOK, I DON'T WANT TO COME OVER THERE AND BREAK YOUR SKULL. BUT I WILL. AND ALL THESE PEOPLE AROUND HERE YOU THINK ARE SO LOYAL AND HARD...
...I'M WILLING TO BET THEY'LL BE MORE LIBERAL WITH SHARING INFORMATION ONCE THEY SEE YOUR BRAIN MATTER SPREAD ALL OVER THE BAR.

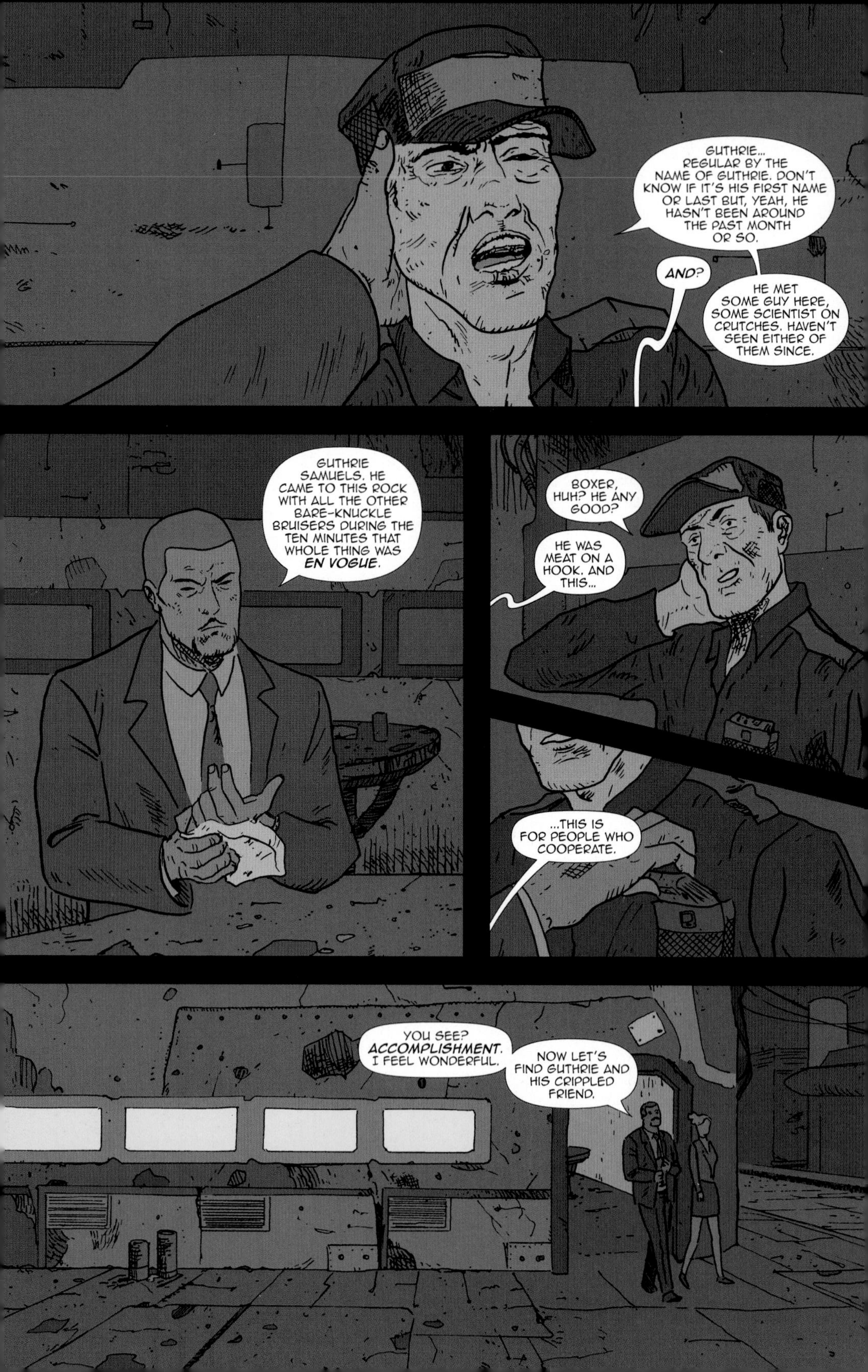
GUTHRIE... REGULAR BY THE NAME OF GUTHRIE. DON'T KNOW IF IT'S HIS FIRST NAME OR LAST BUT, YEAH, HE HASN'T BEEN AROUND THE PAST MONTH OR SO.
AND?
HE MET SOME GUY HERE, SOME SCIENTIST ON CRUTCHES. HAVEN'T SEEN EITHER OF THEM SINCE.
GUTHRIE SAMUELS. HE CAME TO THIS ROCK WITH ALL THE OTHER BARE-KNUCKLE BRUISERS DURING THE TEN MINUTES THAT WHOLE THING WAS EN VOGUE.
BOXER, HUH? HE ANY GOOD?
HE WAS MEAT ON A HOOK. AND THIS...
...THIS IS FOR PEOPLE WHO COOPERATE.
YOU SEE? ACCOMPLISHMENT. I FEEL WONDERFUL.
NOW LET'S FIND GUTHRIE AND HIS CRIPPLED FRIEND.

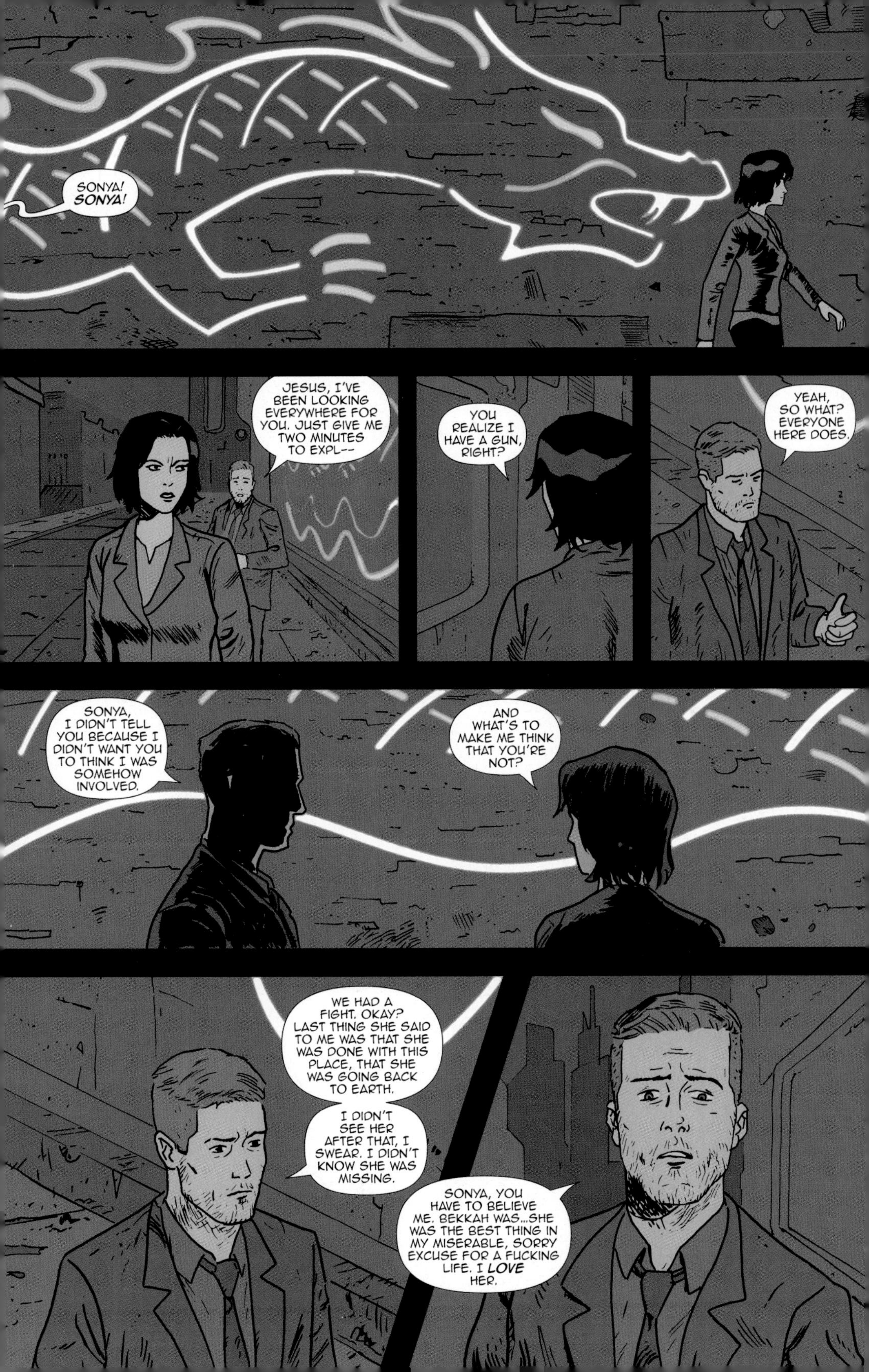
SONYA! *SONYA!*
JESUS, I'VE BEEN LOOKING EVERYWHERE FOR YOU. JUST GIVE ME TWO MINUTES TO EXPL--
YOU REALIZE I HAVE A GUN, RIGHT?
YEAH, SO WHAT? EVERYONE HERE DOES.
SONYA, I DIDN'T TELL YOU BECAUSE I DIDN'T WANT YOU TO THINK I WAS SOMEHOW INVOLVED.
AND WHAT'S TO MAKE ME THINK THAT YOU'RE NOT?
WE HAD A FIGHT. OKAY? LAST THING SHE SAID TO ME WAS THAT SHE WAS DONE WITH THIS PLACE, THAT SHE WAS GOING BACK TO EARTH.
I DIDN'T SEE HER AFTER THAT, I SWEAR. I DIDN'T KNOW SHE WAS MISSING.
SONYA, YOU HAVE TO BELIEVE ME. BEKKAH WAS...SHE WAS THE BEST THING IN MY MISERABLE, SORRY EXCUSE FOR A FUCKING LIFE. I *LOVE* HER.

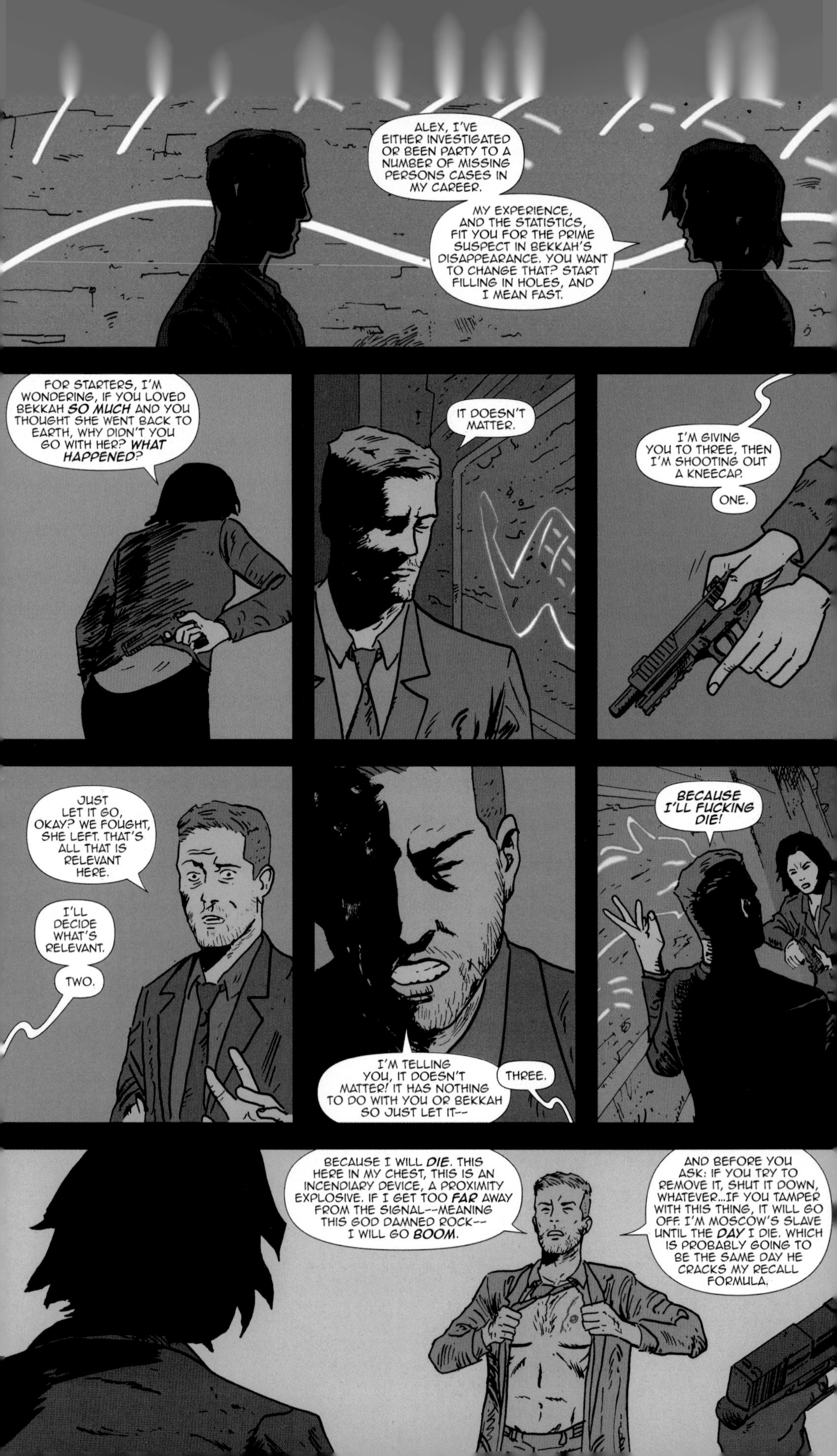
ALEX, I'VE EITHER INVESTIGATED OR BEEN PARTY TO A NUMBER OF MISSING PERSONS CASES IN MY CAREER.
MY EXPERIENCE, AND THE STATISTICS, FIT YOU FOR THE PRIME SUSPECT IN BEKKAH'S DISAPPEARANCE. YOU WANT TO CHANGE THAT? START FILLING IN HOLES, AND I MEAN FAST.
FOR STARTERS, I'M WONDERING, IF YOU LOVED BEKKAH SO MUCH AND YOU THOUGHT SHE WENT BACK TO EARTH, WHY DIDN'T YOU GO WITH HER? WHAT HAPPENED?
IT DOESN'T MATTER.
I'M GIVING YOU TO THREE, THEN I'M SHOOTING OUT A KNEECAP.
ONE.
JUST LET IT GO, OKAY? WE FOUGHT, SHE LEFT. THAT'S ALL THAT IS RELEVANT HERE.
I'LL DECIDE WHAT'S RELEVANT.
TWO.
I'M TELLING YOU, IT DOESN'T MATTER! IT HAS NOTHING TO DO WITH YOU OR BEKKAH SO JUST LET IT--
THREE.
BECAUSE I'LL FUCKING DIE!
BECAUSE I WILL DIE. THIS HERE IN MY CHEST, THIS IS AN INCENDIARY DEVICE, A PROXIMITY EXPLOSIVE. IF I GET TOO FAR AWAY FROM THE SIGNAL--MEANING THIS GOD DAMNED ROCK--I WILL GO BOOM.
AND BEFORE YOU ASK: IF YOU TRY TO REMOVE IT, SHUT IT DOWN, WHATEVER...IF YOU TAMPER WITH THIS THING, IT WILL GO OFF. I'M MOSCOW'S SLAVE UNTIL THE DAY I DIE. WHICH IS PROBABLY GOING TO BE THE SAME DAY HE CRACKS MY RECALL FORMULA.

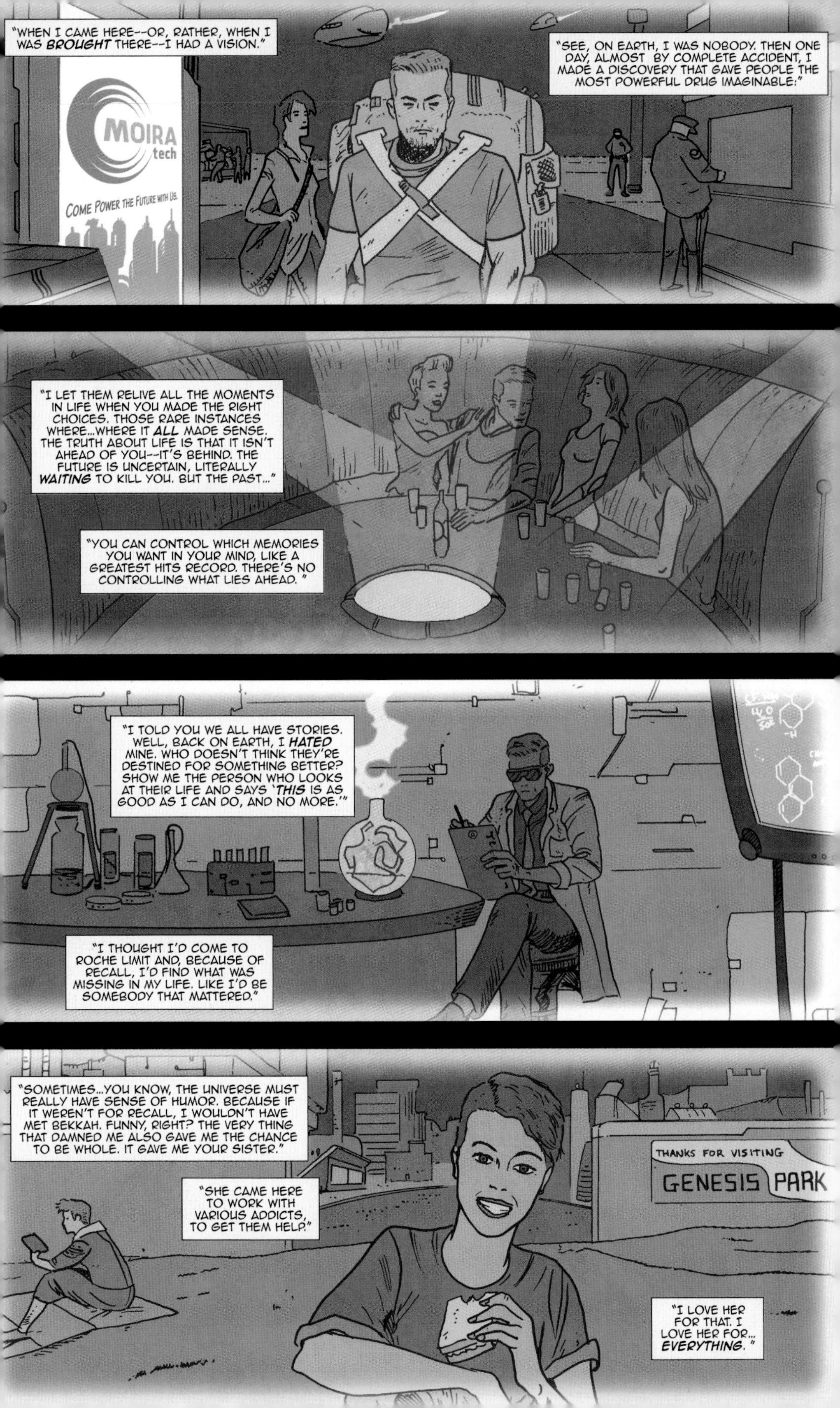

"WHEN I CAME HERE--OR, RATHER, WHEN I WAS BROUGHT THERE--I HAD A VISION."
MOIRA tech
COME POWER THE FUTURE WITH US.
"SEE, ON EARTH, I WAS NOBODY. THEN ONE DAY, ALMOST BY COMPLETE ACCIDENT, I MADE A DISCOVERY THAT GAVE PEOPLE THE MOST POWERFUL DRUG IMAGINABLE:"
"I LET THEM RELIVE ALL THE MOMENTS IN LIFE WHEN YOU MADE THE RIGHT CHOICES. THOSE RARE INSTANCES WHERE...WHERE IT ALL MADE SENSE. THE TRUTH ABOUT LIFE IS THAT IT ISN'T AHEAD OF YOU--IT'S BEHIND. THE FUTURE IS UNCERTAIN, LITERALLY WAITING TO KILL YOU. BUT THE PAST..."
"YOU CAN CONTROL WHICH MEMORIES YOU WANT IN YOUR MIND, LIKE A GREATEST HITS RECORD. THERE'S NO CONTROLLING WHAT LIES AHEAD."
"I TOLD YOU WE ALL HAVE STORIES. WELL, BACK ON EARTH, I HATED MINE. WHO DOESN'T THINK THEY'RE DESTINED FOR SOMETHING BETTER? SHOW ME THE PERSON WHO LOOKS AT THEIR LIFE AND SAYS 'THIS IS AS GOOD AS I CAN DO, AND NO MORE.'"
"I THOUGHT I'D COME TO ROCHE LIMIT AND, BECAUSE OF RECALL, I'D FIND WHAT WAS MISSING IN MY LIFE. LIKE I'D BE SOMEBODY THAT MATTERED."
"SOMETIMES...YOU KNOW, THE UNIVERSE MUST REALLY HAVE SENSE OF HUMOR. BECAUSE IF IT WEREN'T FOR RECALL, I WOULDN'T HAVE MET BEKKAH. FUNNY, RIGHT? THE VERY THING THAT DAMNED ME ALSO GAVE ME THE CHANCE TO BE WHOLE. IT GAVE ME YOUR SISTER."
THANKS FOR VISITING
GENESIS PARK
"SHE CAME HERE TO WORK WITH VARIOUS ADDICTS, TO GET THEM HELP."
"I LOVE HER FOR THAT. I LOVE HER FOR... EVERYTHING."

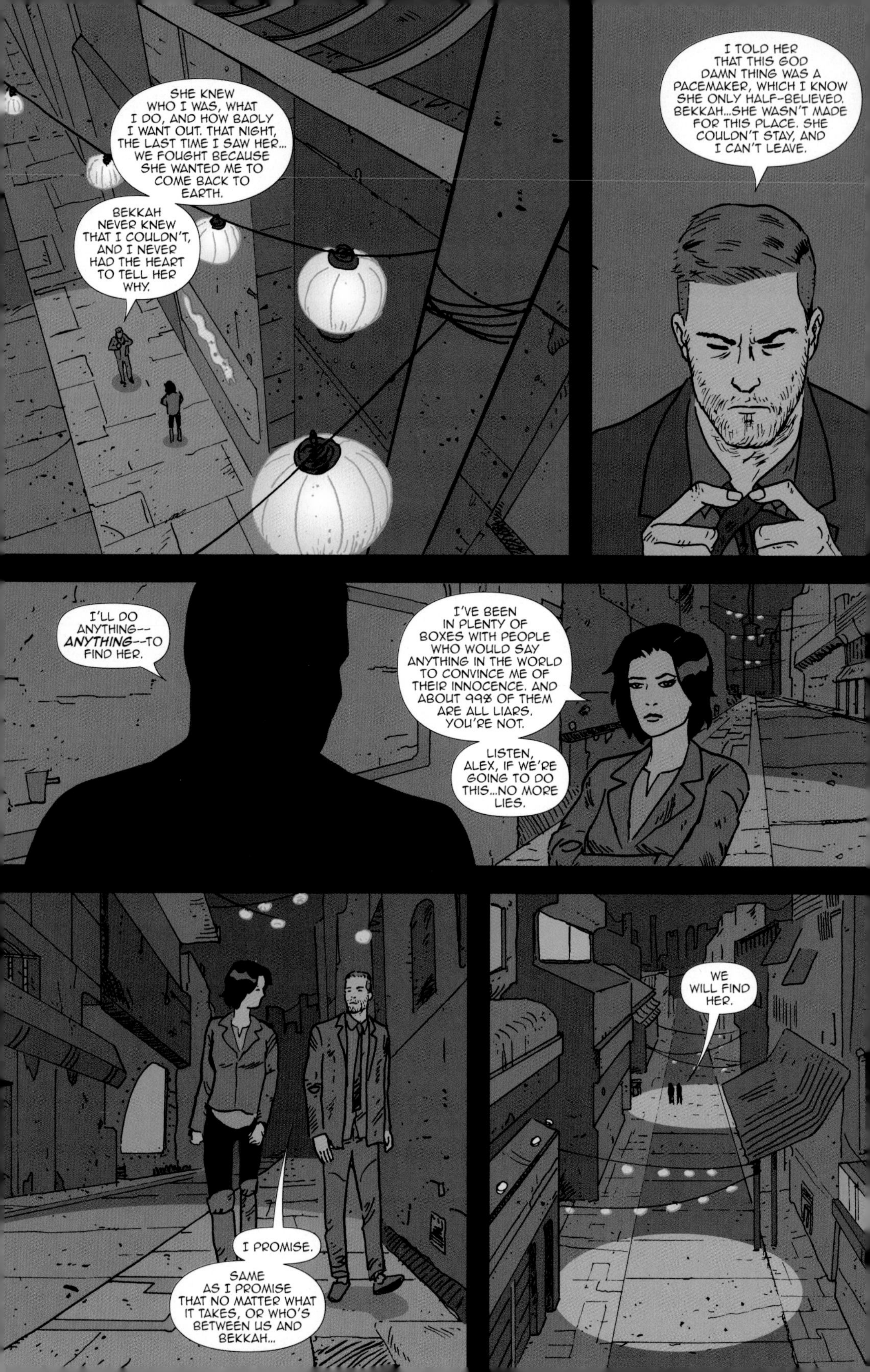
SHE KNEW WHO I WAS, WHAT I DO, AND HOW BADLY I WANT OUT. THAT NIGHT, THE LAST TIME I SAW HER... WE FOUGHT BECAUSE SHE WANTED ME TO COME BACK TO EARTH.
BEKKAH NEVER KNEW THAT I COULDN'T, AND I NEVER HAD THE HEART TO TELL HER WHY.
I TOLD HER THAT THIS GOD DAMN THING WAS A PACEMAKER, WHICH I KNOW SHE ONLY HALF-BELIEVED. BEKKAH...SHE WASN'T MADE FOR THIS PLACE. SHE COULDN'T STAY, AND I CAN'T LEAVE.
I'LL DO ANYTHING-- *ANYTHING*--TO FIND HER.
I'VE BEEN IN PLENTY OF BOXES WITH PEOPLE WHO WOULD SAY ANYTHING IN THE WORLD TO CONVINCE ME OF THEIR INNOCENCE. AND ABOUT 99% OF THEM ARE ALL LIARS. YOU'RE NOT.
LISTEN, ALEX, IF WE'RE GOING TO DO THIS...NO MORE LIES.
I PROMISE.
SAME AS I PROMISE THAT NO MATTER WHAT IT TAKES, OR WHO'S BETWEEN US AND BEKKAH...
WE WILL FIND HER.

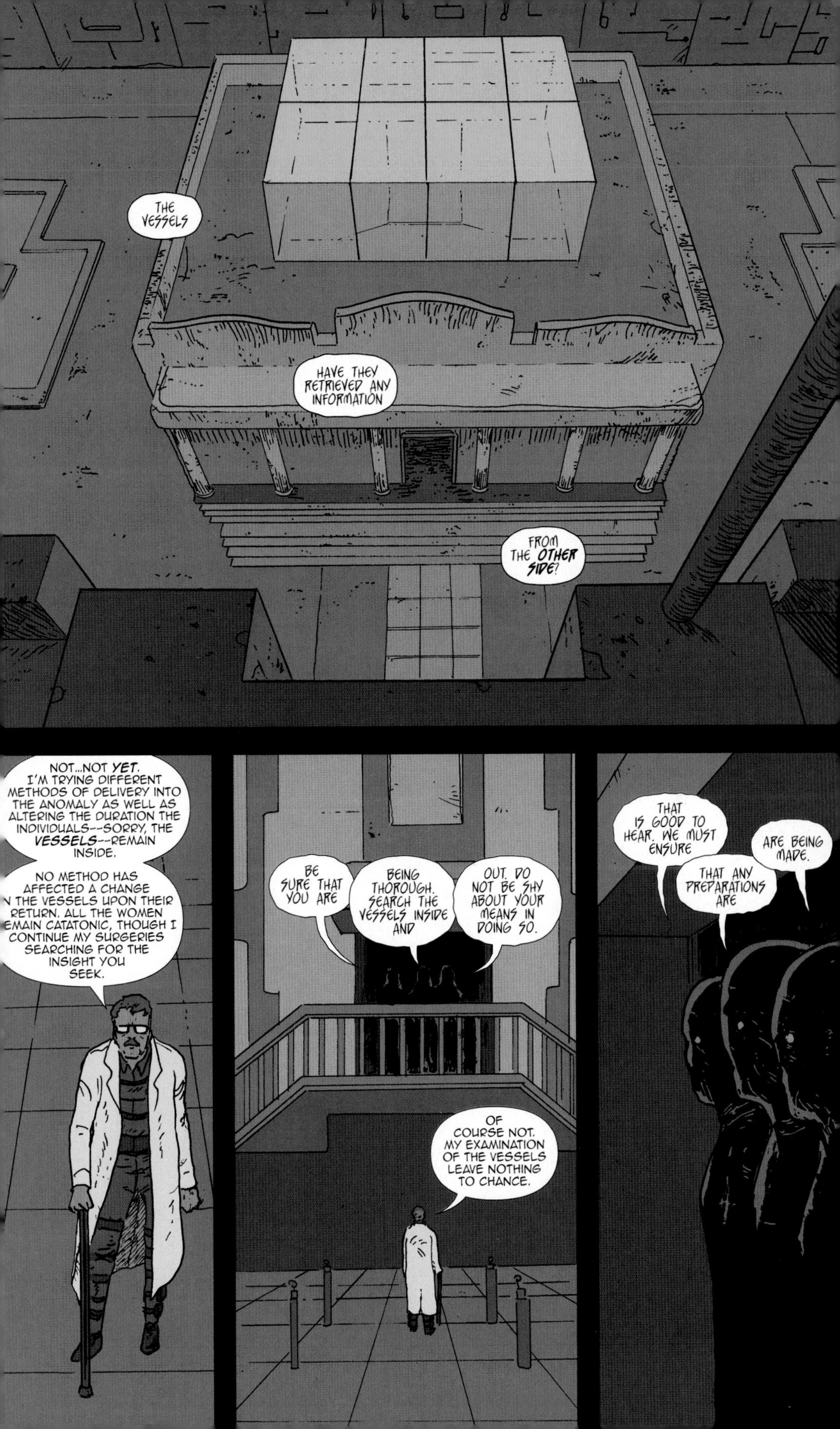

THE VESSELS
HAVE THEY RETRIEVED ANY INFORMATION
FROM THE **OTHER SIDE**?
NOT...NOT **YET**. I'M TRYING DIFFERENT METHODS OF DELIVERY INTO THE ANOMALY AS WELL AS ALTERING THE DURATION THE INDIVIDUALS--SORRY, THE **VESSELS**--REMAIN INSIDE.
NO METHOD HAS AFFECTED A CHANGE N THE VESSELS UPON THEIR RETURN. ALL THE WOMEN EMAIN CATATONIC, THOUGH I CONTINUE MY SURGERIES SEARCHING FOR THE INSIGHT YOU SEEK.
BE SURE THAT YOU ARE
BEING THOROUGH. SEARCH THE VESSELS INSIDE AND
OUT. DO NOT BE SHY ABOUT YOUR MEANS IN DOING SO.
OF COURSE NOT. MY EXAMINATION OF THE VESSELS LEAVE NOTHING TO CHANCE.
THAT IS GOOD TO HEAR. WE MUST ENSURE
THAT ANY PREPARATIONS ARE
ARE BEING MADE.

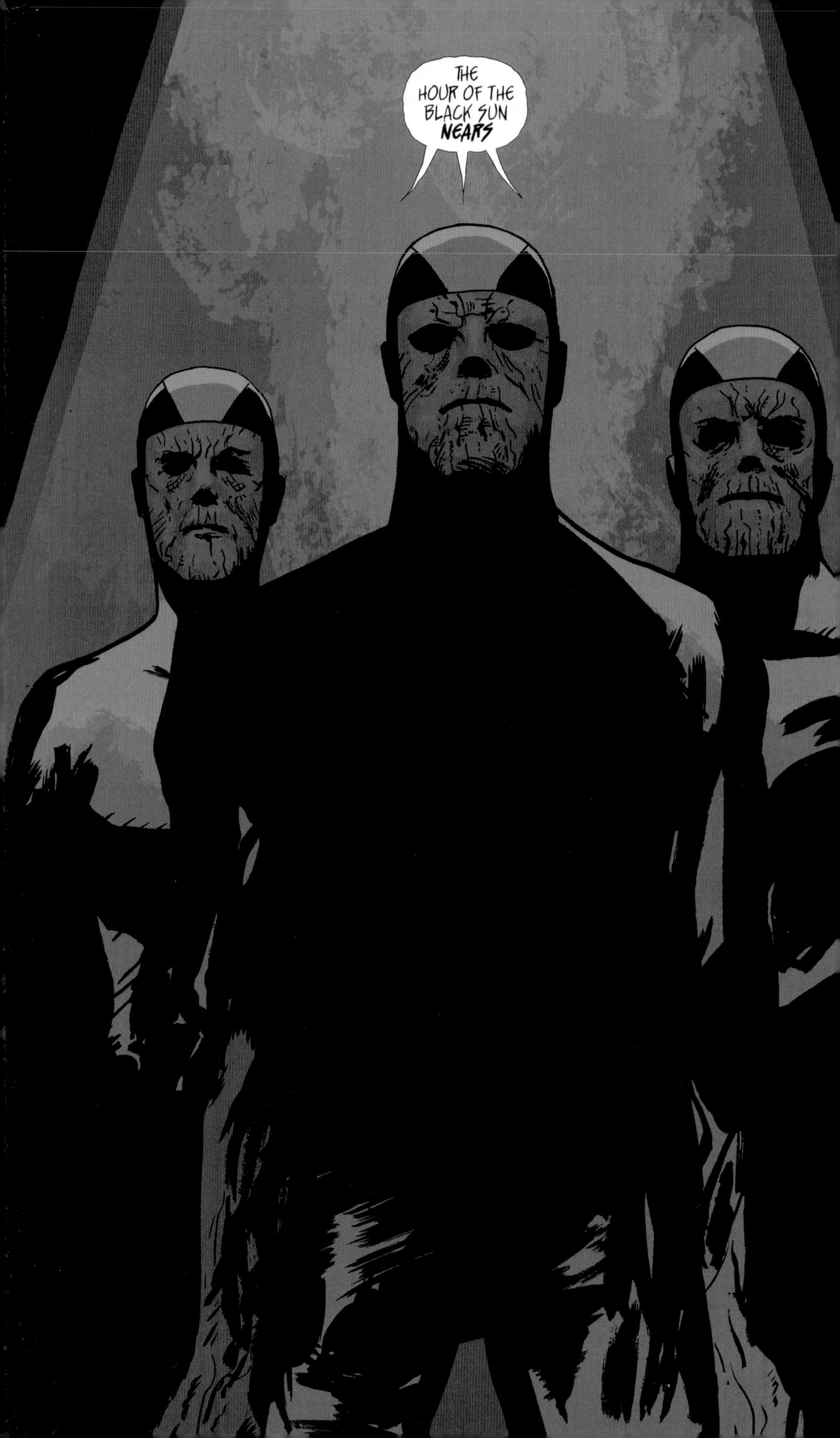
THE HOUR OF THE BLACK SUN NEARS

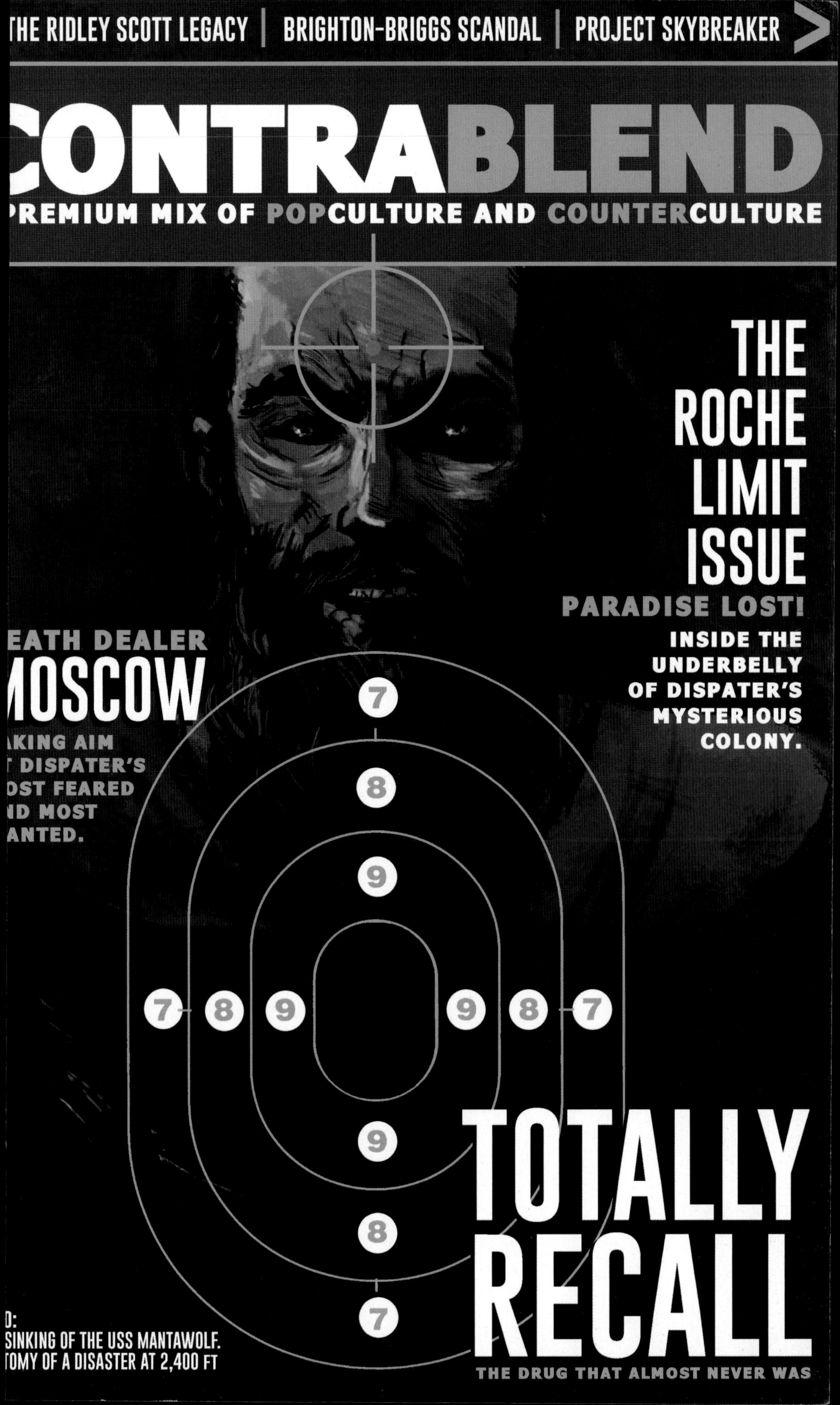

THE RIDLEY SCOTT LEGACY | BRIGHTON-BRIGGS SCANDAL | PROJECT SKYBREAKER
CONTRABLEND
PREMIUM MIX OF POPCULTURE AND COUNTERCULTURE
THE ROCHE LIMIT ISSUE
PARADISE LOST!
INSIDE THE UNDERBELLY OF DISPATER'S MYSTERIOUS COLONY.
EATH DEALER
MOSCOW
AKING AIM
DISPATER'S
OST FEARED
D MOST
ANTED.
7
8
9
7 8 9 9 8 7
9
8
7
TOTALLY RECALL
THE DRUG THAT ALMOST NEVER WAS
SINKING OF THE USS MANTAWOLF.
TOMY OF A DISASTER AT 2,400 FT

TOTALLY RECALL

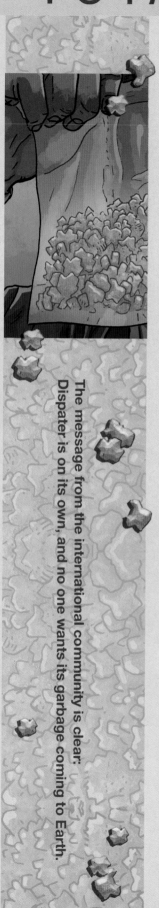

The message from the international community is clear: Dispater is on its own, and no one wants its garbage coming to Earth.

IT'S THE HOTTEST DRUG across the world, though hardly anyone get it—at least on Earth. Recall is the drug that almost never was, a maybe shouldn't be. It was discovered—or engineered, no one certain—by chemist Alex Ford in his private lab in Madison, Wiscons Working with minerals transported back from Dispater's Roche Li Colony, Ford is said to be the one and only person who knows how manufacture the drug. Some say Recall takes you on journey to anot place, unknown, unfamiliar; most say it takes you back to a spec point in your life, that you live your memory. For all the mystery, thing is certain: Recall is the vanity drug of the wealthy elite, and i getting increasingly difficult—and dangerous—to obtain.

Transport to and from Dispater has become a dicey, pricey expediti As crime rates soar and the moneyed enclaves that were the foundat of the colony are abandoned or overrun, travel to and from Dispater become, as most know, less and less appealing. It's risky, expensi and no Earthly borders are enthusiastic about welcoming back any the denizens that have decayed the once glamorous space colony fr the inside out. Because of that, regulations are strict, border contro tight, and the punishment for those convicted of smuggl anything—let alone an illegal drug—from Dispater can be up to twe years in prison.

DRUG OF CHOICE//ROCHE LIMIT

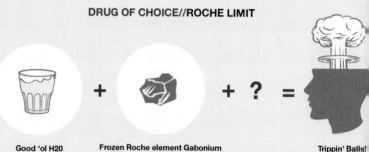

Good 'ol H20
from Earth

Frozen Roche element Gabonium
(1/4 size standard ice cube.)

Trippin' Balls!

A recipe for Recall. SOURCE//a bathroom stall in a Brooklyn ba

The message from the international community is clear: Dispater is its own, and no one wants its garbage coming to Earth. So why r trying to get to Dispater and back—a dubious ambition by itself—w an illegal drug in tow? The answer is obvious—money.

The going rate in the United States for a batch of Recall ranges fr $10,000 all the way up to $25,000. And that doesn't include the tra expenses for this particularly bold drug mule. The mystery, though, why. There are many who think Recall is a myth, an urban leger maybe even the wild imagination of naive rich kids who are all too e to rip off. The science, or at least the mystery behind the science, he to underscore the idea that Recall is a fiction at worst, placebo at be

"I have no idea what it is. The molecular properties alone...have y ever heard of the principle that the more you look at something, the le you know about it? I've never truly experienced that until I studi Recall."

These are the words of Lawrence Dimuri, PhD, and life scien researcher at MIT.

THE DRUG THAT ALMOST NEVER WAS.

BY AMANDA LYNN

's baffling to some of the greatest minds of the science community, though, is somehow understood ›rd, described by nearly all of his colleagues as "unfocused." This is where one of the greatest leaps r—if the science of Recall is an enigma to Dimuri, how has it become, allegedly, Ford's domain? ng into his history, you see the makings of an average life. Middle of his class at a middle of the pack ›rsity; unenthusiastic work evaluations; few published papers—enough just to get by.

Alex Ford mystery will remain just that, it would seem. Word from Dispater says he's the property of :ow, an underworld figure who is nearly as mythical as Recall itself. Most agree that Ford is alive on ater, but he and his formula are prisoners there, and there's no parole for that kind of sentence.

ALL FANTASIZE about the past. Through rose-tinted glasses, we envision a life less ordinary through rtunities missed, chances not taken, decisions made bad. We zigged when we should have zagged. ory is a powerful drug, an opiate that gives us hope and warmth, taking us back to the best parts or all too brief existence. The promise of Recall is too good to pass up: the opportunity to inhabit these ories, to, seemingly, relive them, flesh and bone. The sad truth is memory, as we know it, is limited. n never replicate the electricity of a first kiss, the sensation of a lost lover's embrace, or the way your born feels in your arms. But Recall, it's said, can give you back these experiences—for a moment, ever brief, whether real or not, users say you are back.

real, man, I swear," I was told by a source who, for ous reasons, chose to remain anonymous. We spoke ength about the sensation of Recall, yet he always ged the specifics. Until, at last, he opened up, fully, "Every time, I'm back with my fiancée; it's a nal day, just us at the beach...together. She died two s later, car crash. But for those few hours the drug s, we're together again, and I don't even know what's g to happen—the memory is pure, it's actual. I'd nd my entire life's fortune living that day if I could."

ilar stories exist in abundance, as well as the asional hallucinogenic tale that many attribute to the bad trip or the result of someone being scammed. for those who do experience the real deal, the lts, and their stories, are powerful, moving, and even r words seem too real to be a lie.

'D SPEND MY ENTIRE LIFE'S FORTUNE LIVING THAT DAY IF I COULD."

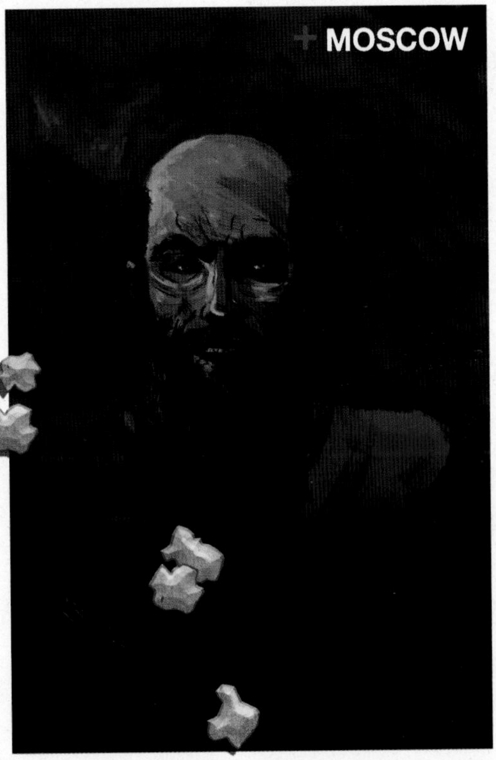
+ MOSCOW

A sketch composite of Moscow. SOURCE//as described by the few who, allegedly, have seen him.

RTAIN THEORIES OF RELATIVITY say that time exists the same way as space—all around us, happening the time. It's our mind that makes time linear; we couldn't handle the sensation of time otherwise. t's what deja vu is, it's said—we feel like we've experienced something before because we have. Or we depending on how deep into the physics of time you want to go.

s Recall simply unlock our minds, freeing them from the constraints of linear existence? One thing that users agree on is that while they are reliving these memories, they are more or less voyeurs. They cannot r what's already happened, they can't change the past to impact the present. What's done is done. Yet t doesn't seem to diminish Recall's power, and that speaks to the burden of existence.

ybe we don't want the responsibility of the future's promise; maybe it's better to let the beauty of the t absorb and free us. If that's our true heart's desire, than there is nothing more powerful than what call offers.

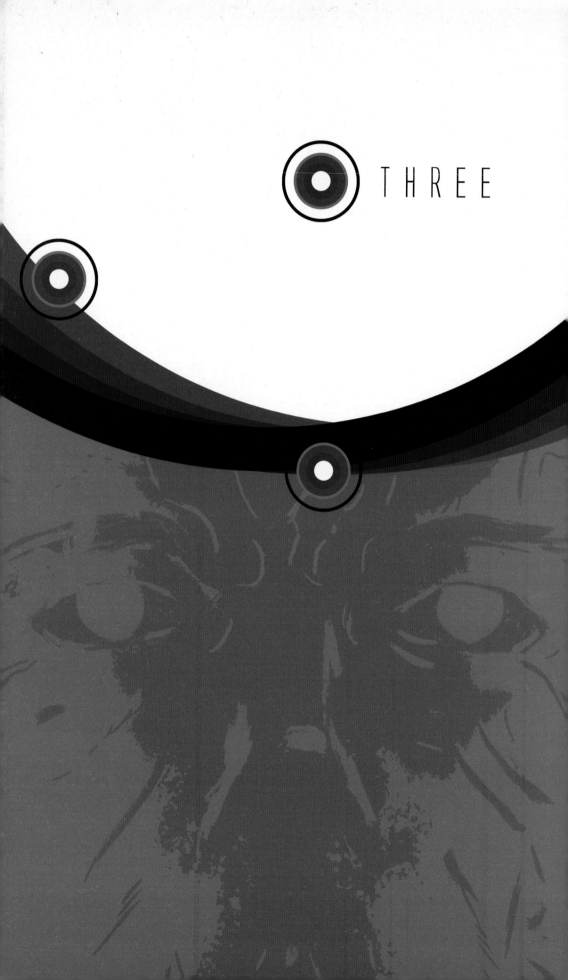

THREE

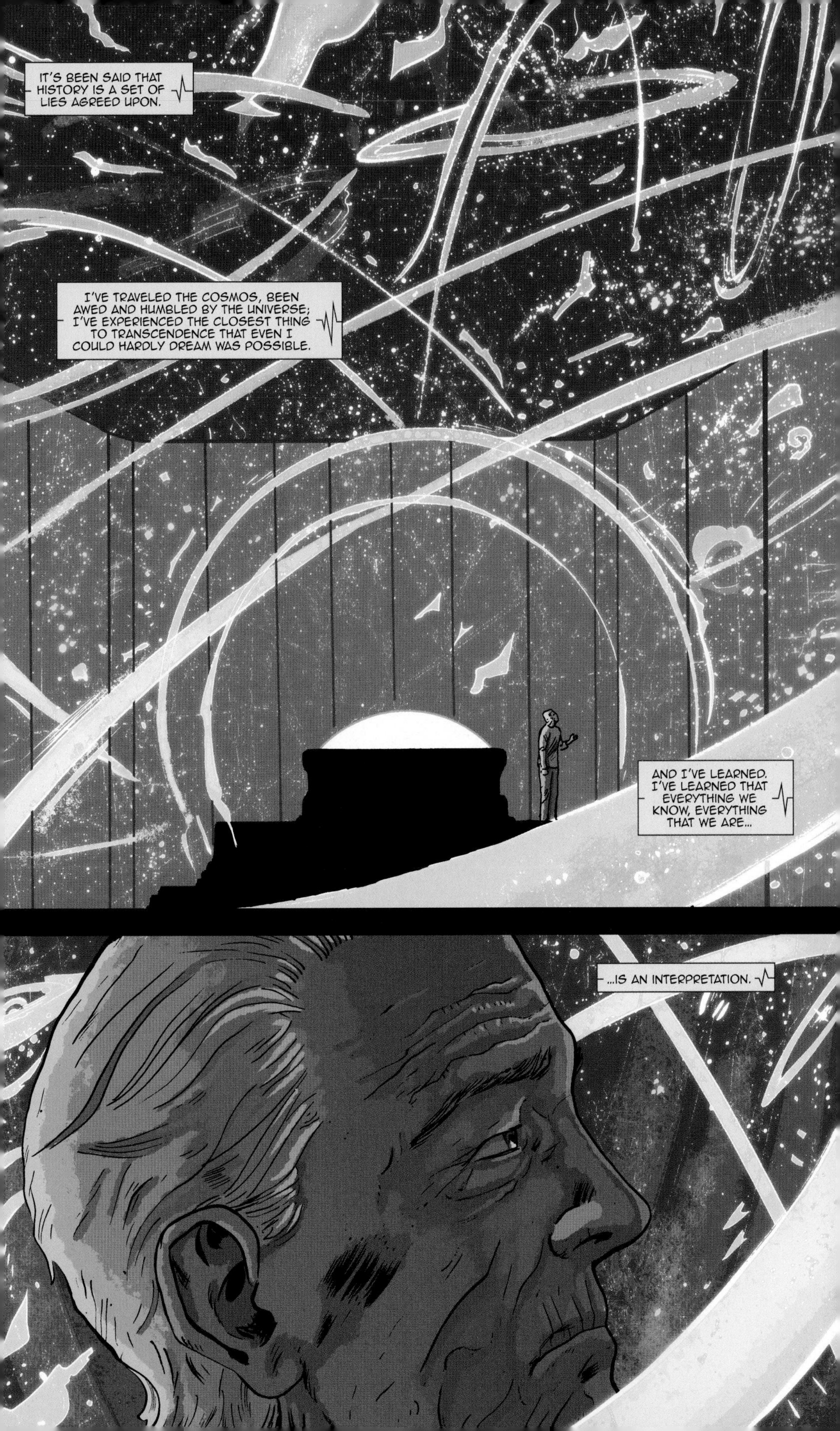
IT'S BEEN SAID THAT HISTORY IS A SET OF LIES AGREED UPON.
I'VE TRAVELED THE COSMOS, BEEN AWED AND HUMBLED BY THE UNIVERSE; I'VE EXPERIENCED THE CLOSEST THING TO TRANSCENDENCE THAT EVEN I COULD HARDLY DREAM WAS POSSIBLE.
AND I'VE LEARNED. I'VE LEARNED THAT EVERYTHING WE KNOW, EVERYTHING THAT WE ARE...
...IS AN INTERPRETATION.

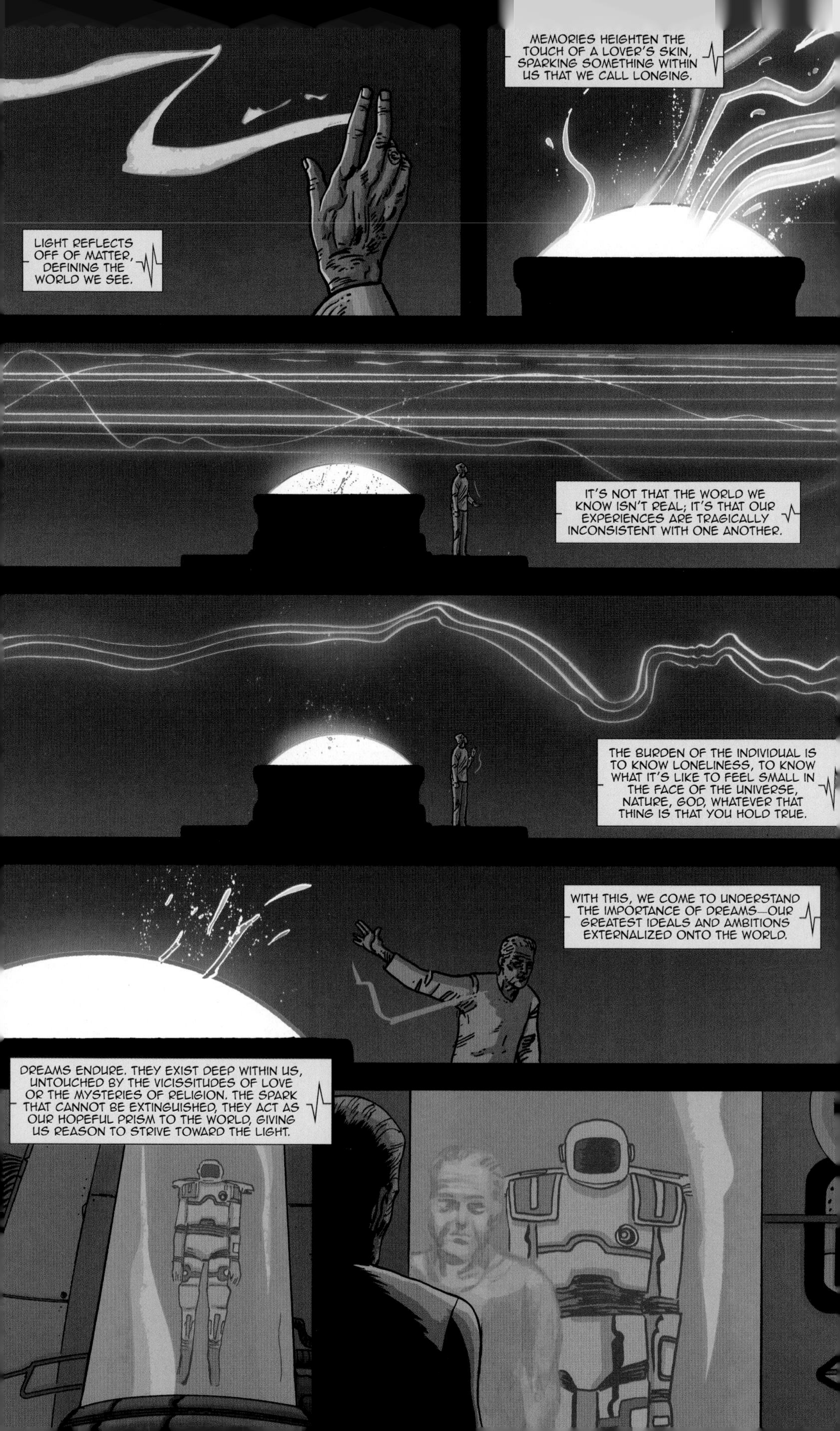
LIGHT REFLECTS OFF OF MATTER, DEFINING THE WORLD WE SEE.
MEMORIES HEIGHTEN THE TOUCH OF A LOVER'S SKIN, SPARKING SOMETHING WITHIN US THAT WE CALL LONGING.
IT'S NOT THAT THE WORLD WE KNOW ISN'T REAL; IT'S THAT OUR EXPERIENCES ARE TRAGICALLY INCONSISTENT WITH ONE ANOTHER.
THE BURDEN OF THE INDIVIDUAL IS TO KNOW LONELINESS, TO KNOW WHAT IT'S LIKE TO FEEL SMALL IN THE FACE OF THE UNIVERSE, NATURE, GOD, WHATEVER THAT THING IS THAT YOU HOLD TRUE.
WITH THIS, WE COME TO UNDERSTAND THE IMPORTANCE OF DREAMS—OUR GREATEST IDEALS AND AMBITIONS EXTERNALIZED ONTO THE WORLD.
DREAMS ENDURE. THEY EXIST DEEP WITHIN US, UNTOUCHED BY THE VICISSITUDES OF LOVE OR THE MYSTERIES OF RELIGION. THE SPARK THAT CANNOT BE EXTINGUISHED, THEY ACT AS OUR HOPEFUL PRISM TO THE WORLD, GIVING US REASON TO STRIVE TOWARD THE LIGHT.

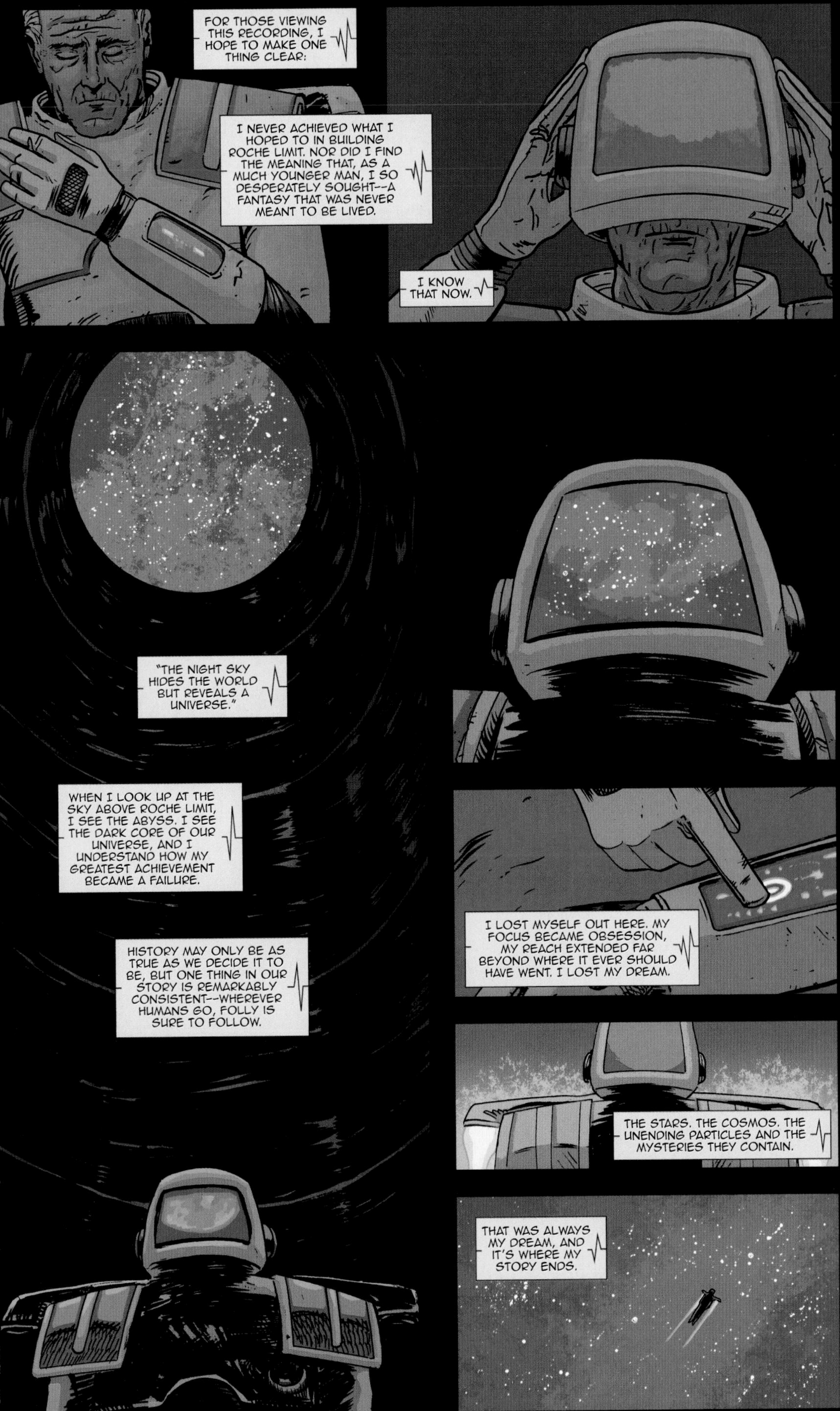
FOR THOSE VIEWING THIS RECORDING, I HOPE TO MAKE ONE THING CLEAR:
I NEVER ACHIEVED WHAT I HOPED TO IN BUILDING ROCHE LIMIT. NOR DID I FIND THE MEANING THAT, AS A MUCH YOUNGER MAN, I SO DESPERATELY SOUGHT--A FANTASY THAT WAS NEVER MEANT TO BE LIVED.
I KNOW THAT NOW.
"THE NIGHT SKY HIDES THE WORLD BUT REVEALS A UNIVERSE."
WHEN I LOOK UP AT THE SKY ABOVE ROCHE LIMIT, I SEE THE ABYSS. I SEE THE DARK CORE OF OUR UNIVERSE, AND I UNDERSTAND HOW MY GREATEST ACHIEVEMENT BECAME A FAILURE.
HISTORY MAY ONLY BE AS TRUE AS WE DECIDE IT TO BE, BUT ONE THING IN OUR STORY IS REMARKABLY CONSISTENT--WHEREVER HUMANS GO, FOLLY IS SURE TO FOLLOW.
I LOST MYSELF OUT HERE. MY FOCUS BECAME OBSESSION, MY REACH EXTENDED FAR BEYOND WHERE IT EVER SHOULD HAVE WENT. I LOST MY DREAM.
THE STARS. THE COSMOS. THE UNENDING PARTICLES AND THE MYSTERIES THEY CONTAIN.
THAT WAS ALWAYS MY DREAM, AND IT'S WHERE MY STORY ENDS.

ROCHE LIMIT IN FOCU

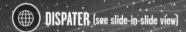

DISPATER (see slide-in-slide view)

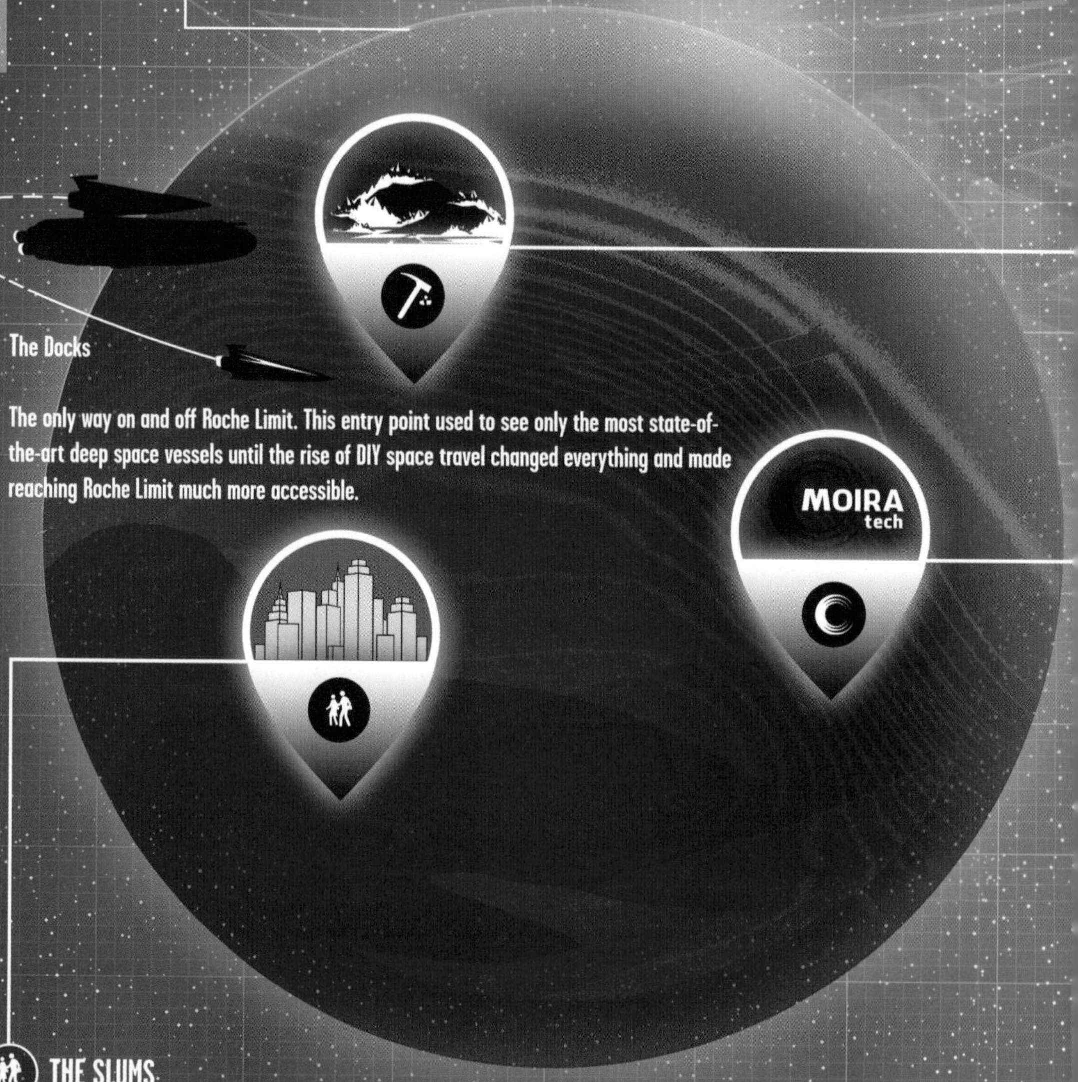
MOIRA
tech

The Docks

The only way on and off Roche Limit. This entry point used to see only the most state-of-the-art deep space vessels until the rise of DIY space travel changed everything and made reaching Roche Limit much more accessible.

THE SLUMS

Constructed in the tradition of Chicago's Pullman neighborhood, this area of Roche Limit was designed to temporarily house who were part of the Moiratech compound project. As construction dragged beyond its targeted completion date requiring m more laborers—and travel to Roche Limit became more accessible—the population of The Slums grew exponentially. The infrastructure is built mainly of found materials, particularly scrap from the Moiratech construction.

THE MINES

The mines were once the central focus of Moiratech's investment in Roche Limit. Speculation abounded that a mineral existed within the planet's core that could provide limitless, clean energy. This wishful thinking has since been debunked, though small mining outfits are still operational, hopeful of a discovery that could change the course of mankind. So far, the only notable find has been Gaborium, the mineral used to make the popular colony drug known as "Recall."

MOIRATECH COMPOUND

Once the nucleus of Roche Limit, this was the walled compound housing the colony's elite, particularly the three Moiratech founders—Shay Thompson, Phillip Murdock, and Leo Maxwell, the "explorernauts" as they've been dubbed. As crime grew amongst the worker population and more and more of the wealthy elite returned to Earth, the Compound slowly began to lose its luster. When the explorernauts went missing—presumed murdered at the hands of their own construction team—the Compound became an abandoned, yet still sealed, ghost town.

« PREVIOUS SLIDE

DISPATER

-Like Earth, most of the topography is made of silicates and metals.

-An abundance of water is located beneath the surface. Mining for it revealed a mineral native only to Dispater. That mineral is used to make the popular drug "Recall."

Its surface area is approximately the size of India.

NEXT SLIDE »

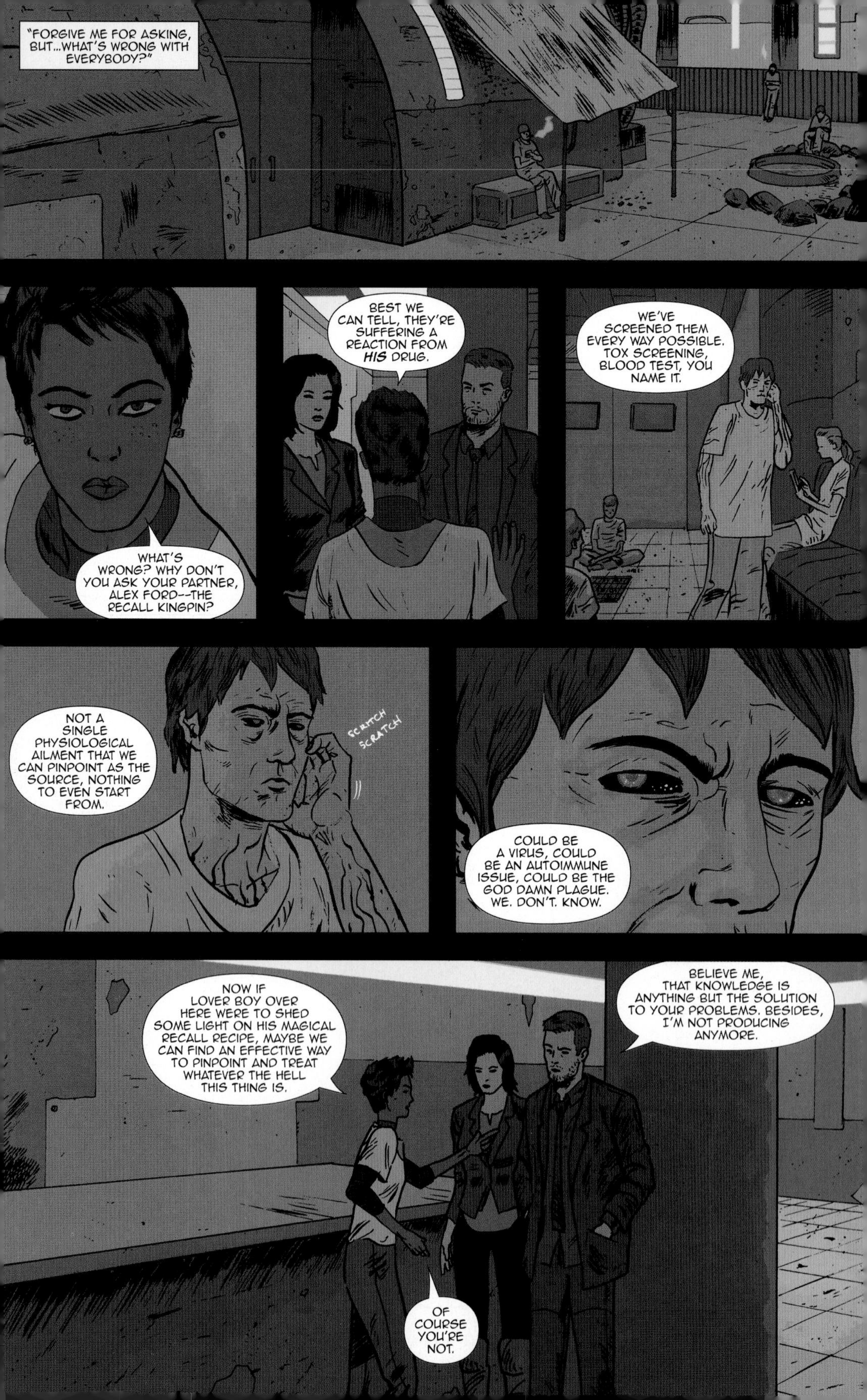
"FORGIVE ME FOR ASKING, BUT...WHAT'S WRONG WITH EVERYBODY?"
WHAT'S WRONG? WHY DON'T YOU ASK YOUR PARTNER, ALEX FORD--THE RECALL KINGPIN?
BEST WE CAN TELL, THEY'RE SUFFERING A REACTION FROM HIS DRUG.
WE'VE SCREENED THEM EVERY WAY POSSIBLE. TOX SCREENING, BLOOD TEST, YOU NAME IT.
NOT A SINGLE PHYSIOLOGICAL AILMENT THAT WE CAN PINPOINT AS THE SOURCE, NOTHING TO EVEN START FROM.
SCRATCH SCRATCH
COULD BE A VIRUS, COULD BE AN AUTOIMMUNE ISSUE, COULD BE THE GOD DAMN PLAGUE. WE. DON'T. KNOW.
NOW IF LOVER BOY OVER HERE WERE TO SHED SOME LIGHT ON HIS MAGICAL RECALL RECIPE, MAYBE WE CAN FIND AN EFFECTIVE WAY TO PINPOINT AND TREAT WHATEVER THE HELL THIS THING IS.
BELIEVE ME, THAT KNOWLEDGE IS ANYTHING BUT THE SOLUTION TO YOUR PROBLEMS. BESIDES, I'M NOT PRODUCING ANYMORE.
OF COURSE YOU'RE NOT.

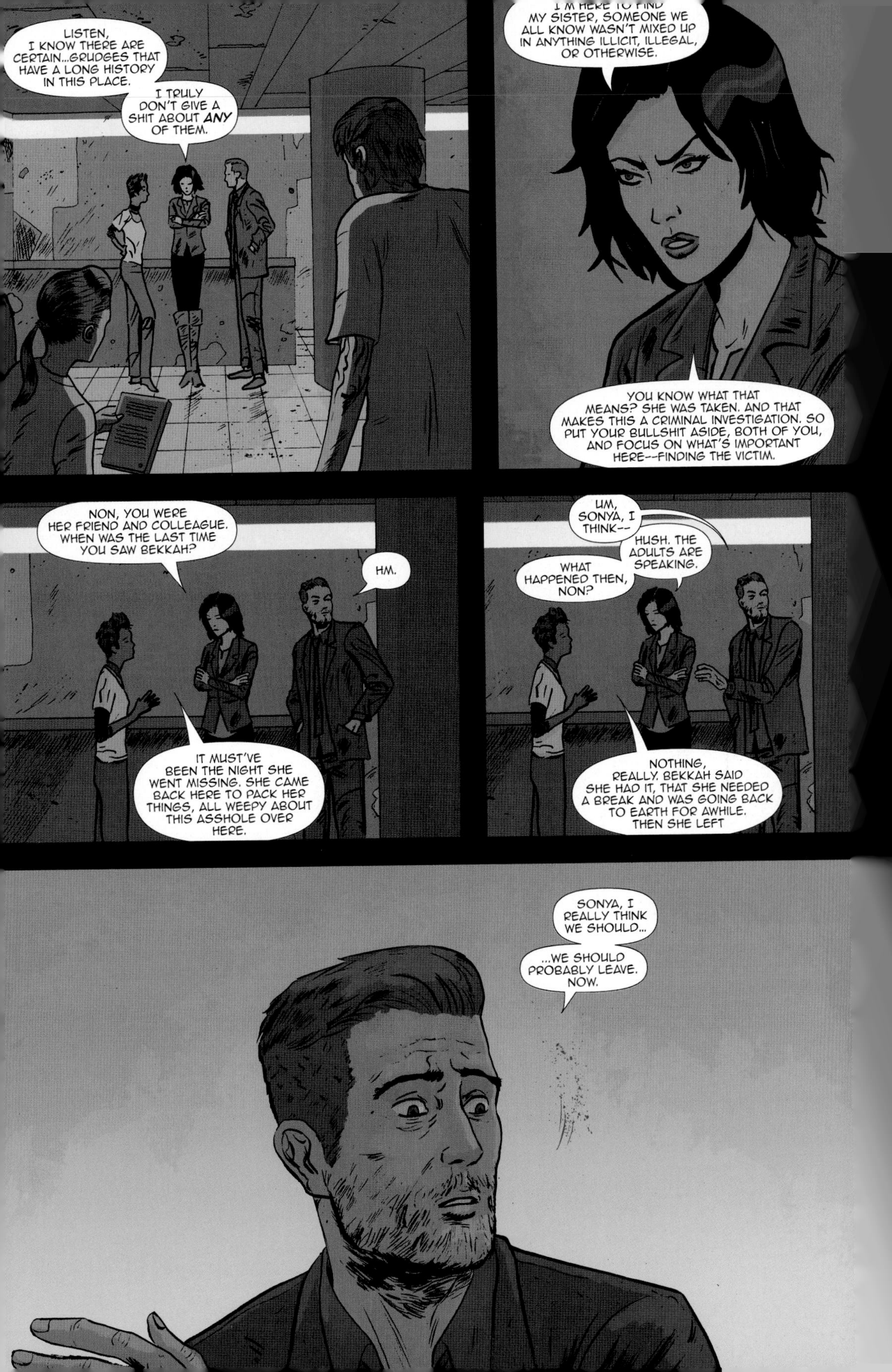

LISTEN, I KNOW THERE ARE CERTAIN...GRUDGES THAT HAVE A LONG HISTORY IN THIS PLACE.
I TRULY DON'T GIVE A SHIT ABOUT *ANY* OF THEM.
I'M HERE TO FIND MY SISTER, SOMEONE WE ALL KNOW WASN'T MIXED UP IN ANYTHING ILLICIT, ILLEGAL, OR OTHERWISE.
YOU KNOW WHAT THAT MEANS? SHE WAS TAKEN. AND THAT MAKES THIS A CRIMINAL INVESTIGATION. SO PUT YOUR BULLSHIT ASIDE, BOTH OF YOU, AND FOCUS ON WHAT'S IMPORTANT HERE--FINDING THE VICTIM.
NON, YOU WERE HER FRIEND AND COLLEAGUE. WHEN WAS THE LAST TIME YOU SAW BEKKAH?
HM.
IT MUST'VE BEEN THE NIGHT SHE WENT MISSING. SHE CAME BACK HERE TO PACK HER THINGS, ALL WEEPY ABOUT THIS ASSHOLE OVER HERE.
UM, SONYA, I THINK--
HUSH. THE ADULTS ARE SPEAKING.
WHAT HAPPENED THEN, NON?
NOTHING, REALLY. BEKKAH SAID SHE HAD IT, THAT SHE NEEDED A BREAK AND WAS GOING BACK TO EARTH FOR AWHILE. THEN SHE LEFT
SONYA, I REALLY THINK WE SHOULD...
...WE SHOULD PROBABLY LEAVE. NOW.

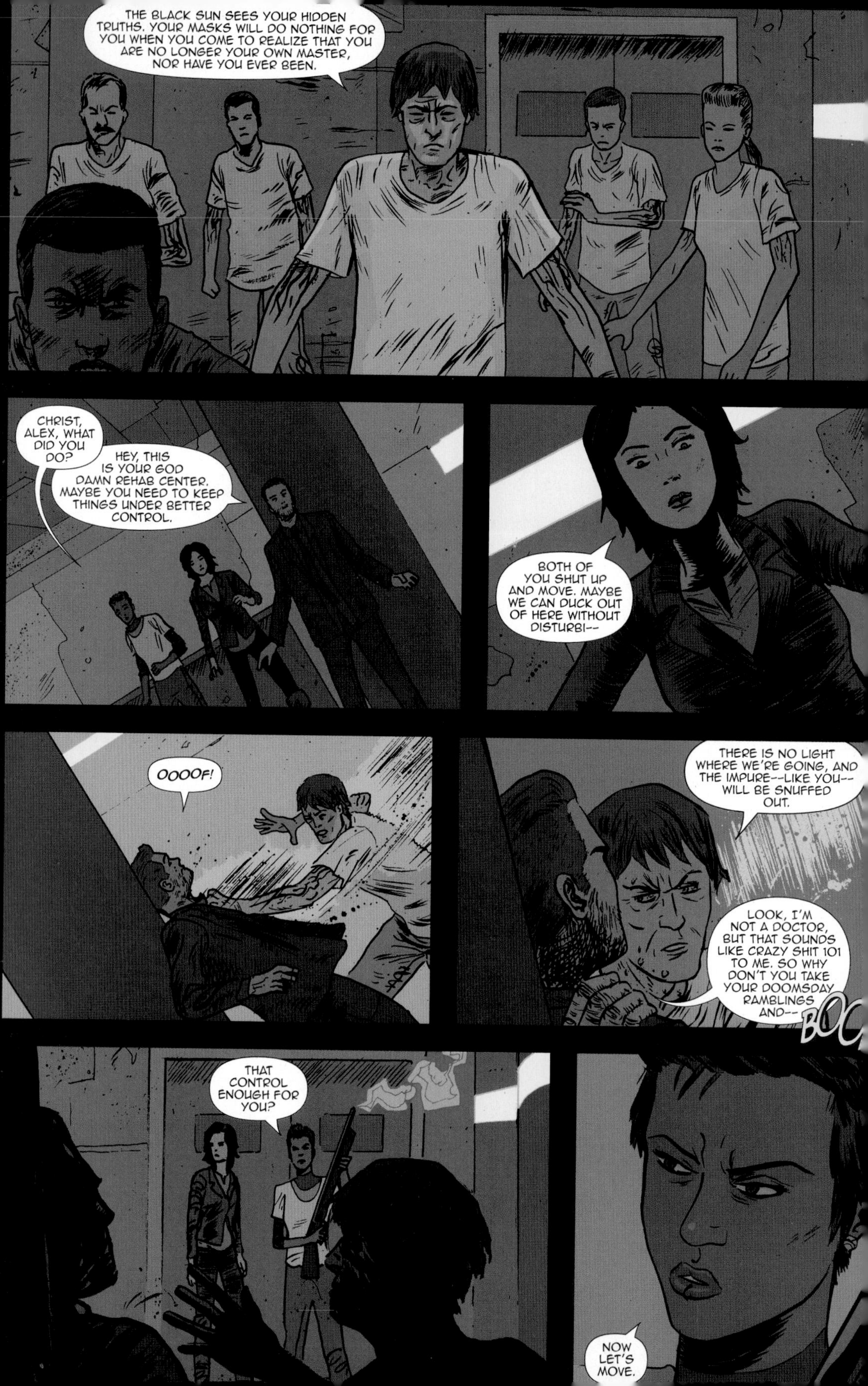
THE BLACK SUN SEES YOUR HIDDEN TRUTHS. YOUR MASKS WILL DO NOTHING FOR YOU WHEN YOU COME TO REALIZE THAT YOU ARE NO LONGER YOUR OWN MASTER, NOR HAVE YOU EVER BEEN.
CHRIST, ALEX, WHAT DID YOU DO?
HEY, THIS IS YOUR GOD DAMN REHAB CENTER. MAYBE YOU NEED TO KEEP THINGS UNDER BETTER CONTROL.
BOTH OF YOU SHUT UP AND MOVE. MAYBE WE CAN DUCK OUT OF HERE WITHOUT DISTURBI--
OOOOF!
THERE IS NO LIGHT WHERE WE'RE GOING, AND THE IMPURE--LIKE YOU--WILL BE SNUFFED OUT.
LOOK, I'M NOT A DOCTOR, BUT THAT SOUNDS LIKE CRAZY SHIT 101 TO ME. SO WHY DON'T YOU TAKE YOUR DOOMSDAY RAMBLINGS AND--
BOO
THAT CONTROL ENOUGH FOR YOU?
NOW LET'S MOVE.

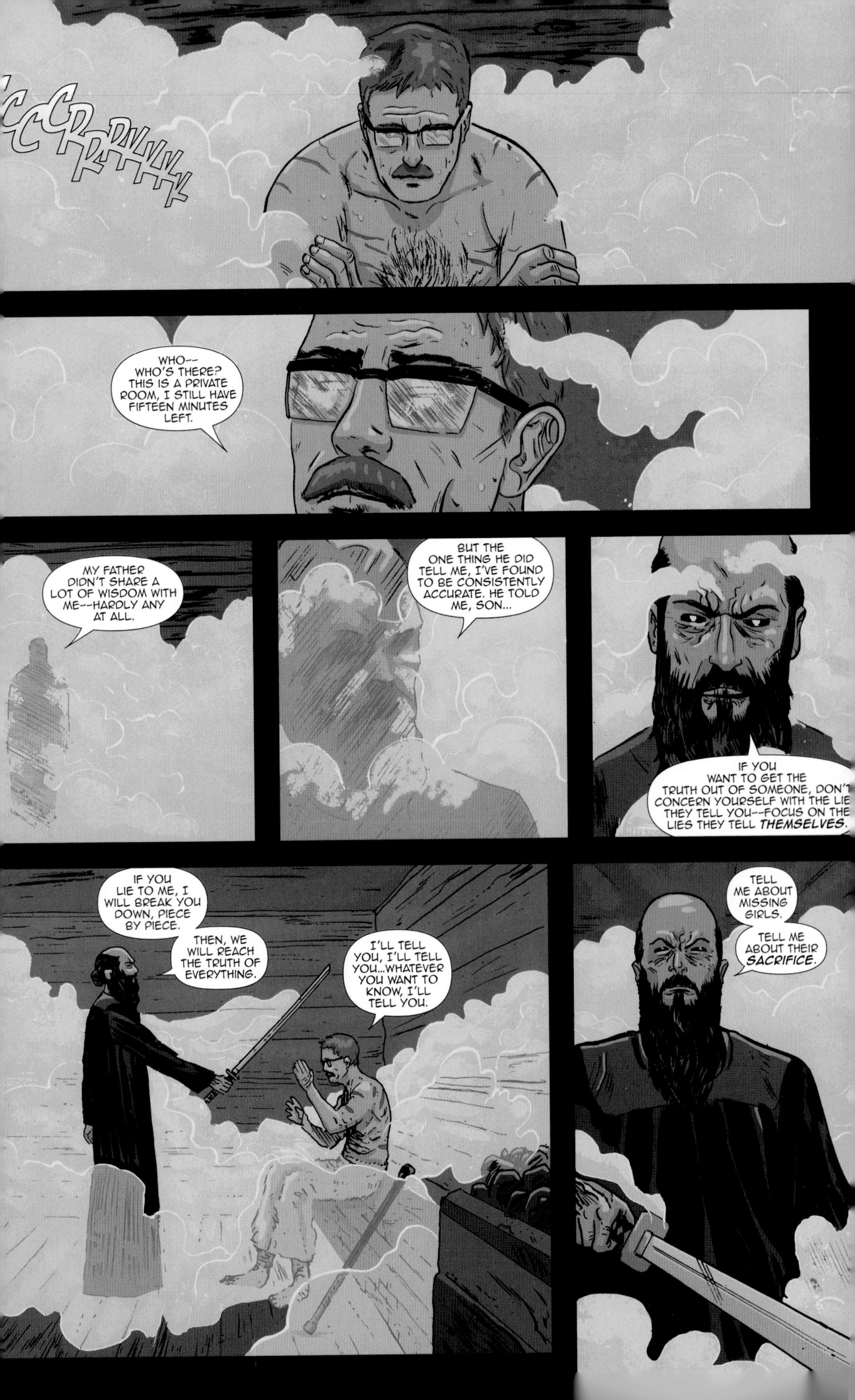
CCCRRRVLVLVLK
WHO-- WHO'S THERE? THIS IS A PRIVATE ROOM, I STILL HAVE FIFTEEN MINUTES LEFT.
MY FATHER DIDN'T SHARE A LOT OF WISDOM WITH ME--HARDLY ANY AT ALL.
BUT THE ONE THING HE DID TELL ME, I'VE FOUND TO BE CONSISTENTLY ACCURATE. HE TOLD ME, SON...
IF YOU WANT TO GET THE TRUTH OUT OF SOMEONE, DON'T CONCERN YOURSELF WITH THE LIES THEY TELL YOU--FOCUS ON THE LIES THEY TELL *THEMSELVES*.
IF YOU LIE TO ME, I WILL BREAK YOU DOWN, PIECE BY PIECE.
THEN, WE WILL REACH THE TRUTH OF EVERYTHING.
I'LL TELL YOU, I'LL TELL YOU...WHATEVER YOU WANT TO KNOW, I'LL TELL YOU.
TELL ME ABOUT MISSING GIRLS.
TELL ME ABOUT THEIR *SACRIFICE*.

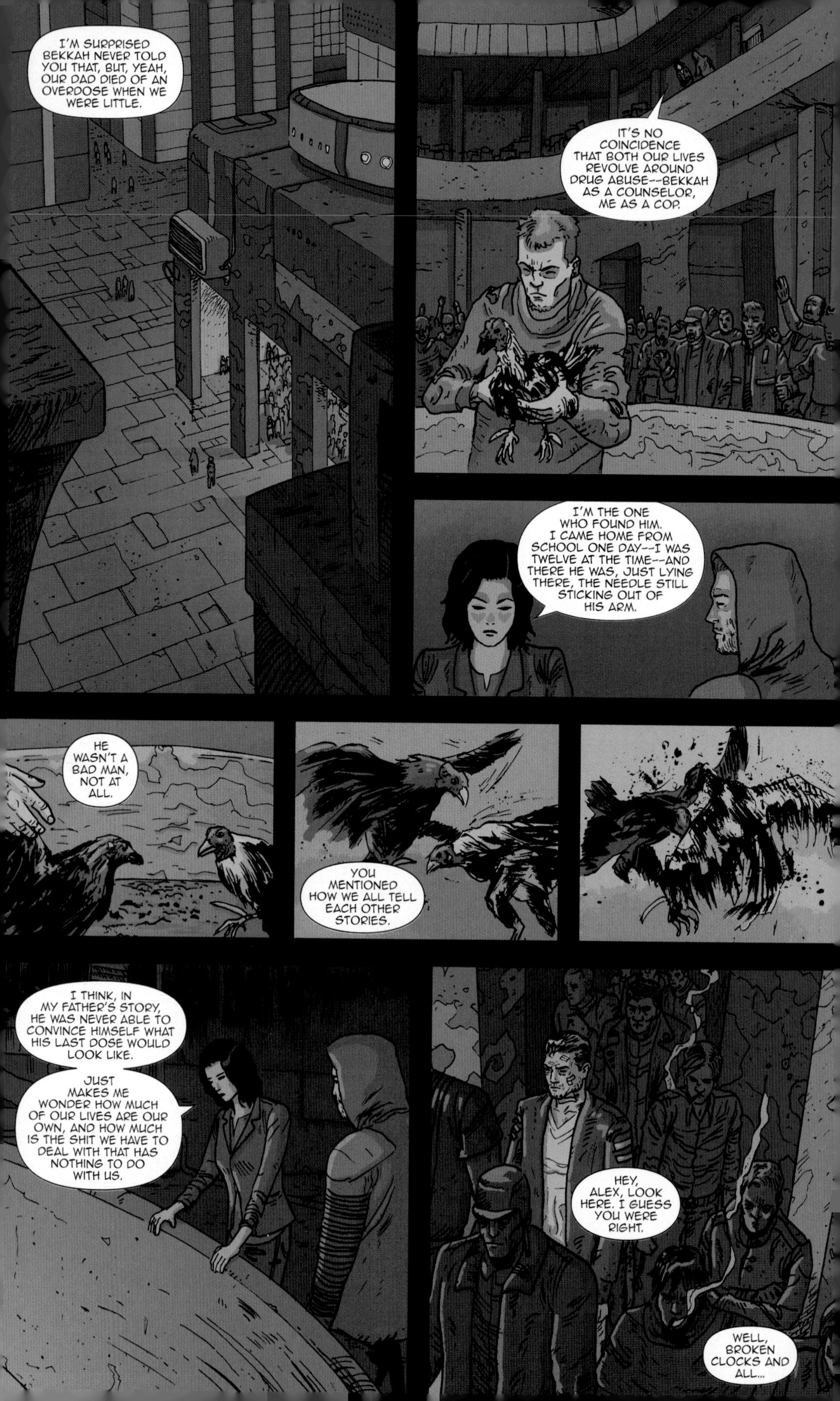
I'M SURPRISED BEKKAH NEVER TOLD YOU THAT, BUT, YEAH, OUR DAD DIED OF AN OVERDOSE WHEN WE WERE LITTLE.
IT'S NO COINCIDENCE THAT BOTH OUR LIVES REVOLVE AROUND DRUG ABUSE--BEKKAH AS A COUNSELOR, ME AS A COP.
I'M THE ONE WHO FOUND HIM. I CAME HOME FROM SCHOOL ONE DAY--I WAS TWELVE AT THE TIME--AND THERE HE WAS, JUST LYING THERE, THE NEEDLE STILL STICKING OUT OF HIS ARM.
HE WASN'T A BAD MAN, NOT AT ALL.
YOU MENTIONED HOW WE ALL TELL EACH OTHER STORIES.
I THINK, IN MY FATHER'S STORY, HE WAS NEVER ABLE TO CONVINCE HIMSELF WHAT HIS LAST DOSE WOULD LOOK LIKE.
JUST MAKES ME WONDER HOW MUCH OF OUR LIVES ARE OUR OWN, AND HOW MUCH IS THE SHIT WE HAVE TO DEAL WITH THAT HAS NOTHING TO DO WITH US.
HEY, ALEX, LOOK HERE. I GUESS YOU WERE RIGHT.
WELL, BROKEN CLOCKS AND ALL...

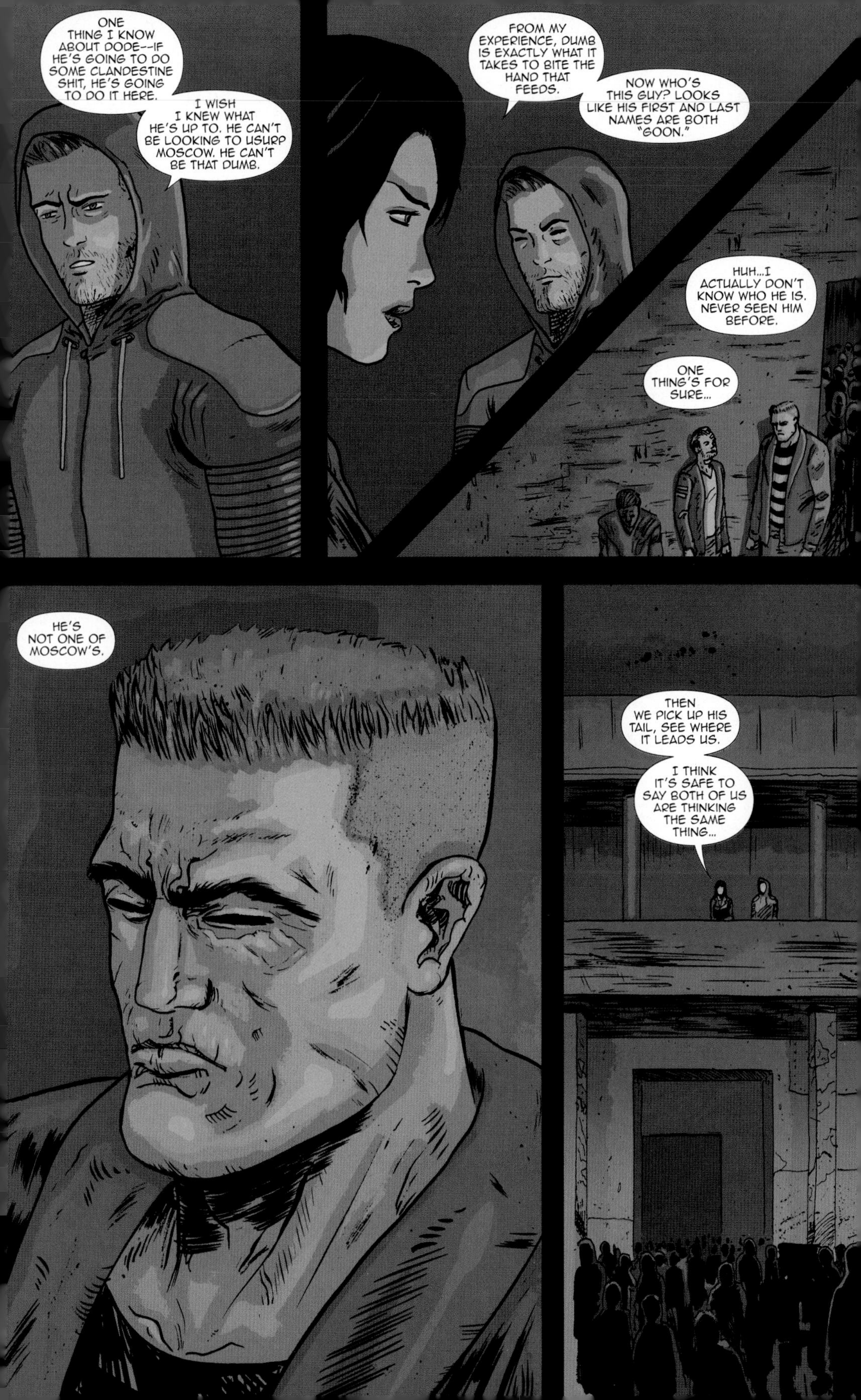
ONE THING I KNOW ABOUT DODE--IF HE'S GOING TO DO SOME CLANDESTINE SHIT, HE'S GOING TO DO IT HERE.
I WISH I KNEW WHAT HE'S UP TO. HE CAN'T BE LOOKING TO USURP MOSCOW. HE CAN'T BE THAT DUMB.
FROM MY EXPERIENCE, DUMB IS EXACTLY WHAT IT TAKES TO BITE THE HAND THAT FEEDS.
NOW WHO'S THIS GUY? LOOKS LIKE HIS FIRST AND LAST NAMES ARE BOTH "GOON."
HUH...I ACTUALLY DON'T KNOW WHO HE IS. NEVER SEEN HIM BEFORE.
ONE THING'S FOR SURE...
HE'S NOT ONE OF MOSCOW'S.
THEN WE PICK UP HIS TAIL, SEE WHERE IT LEADS US.
I THINK IT'S SAFE TO SAY BOTH OF US ARE THINKING THE SAME THING...

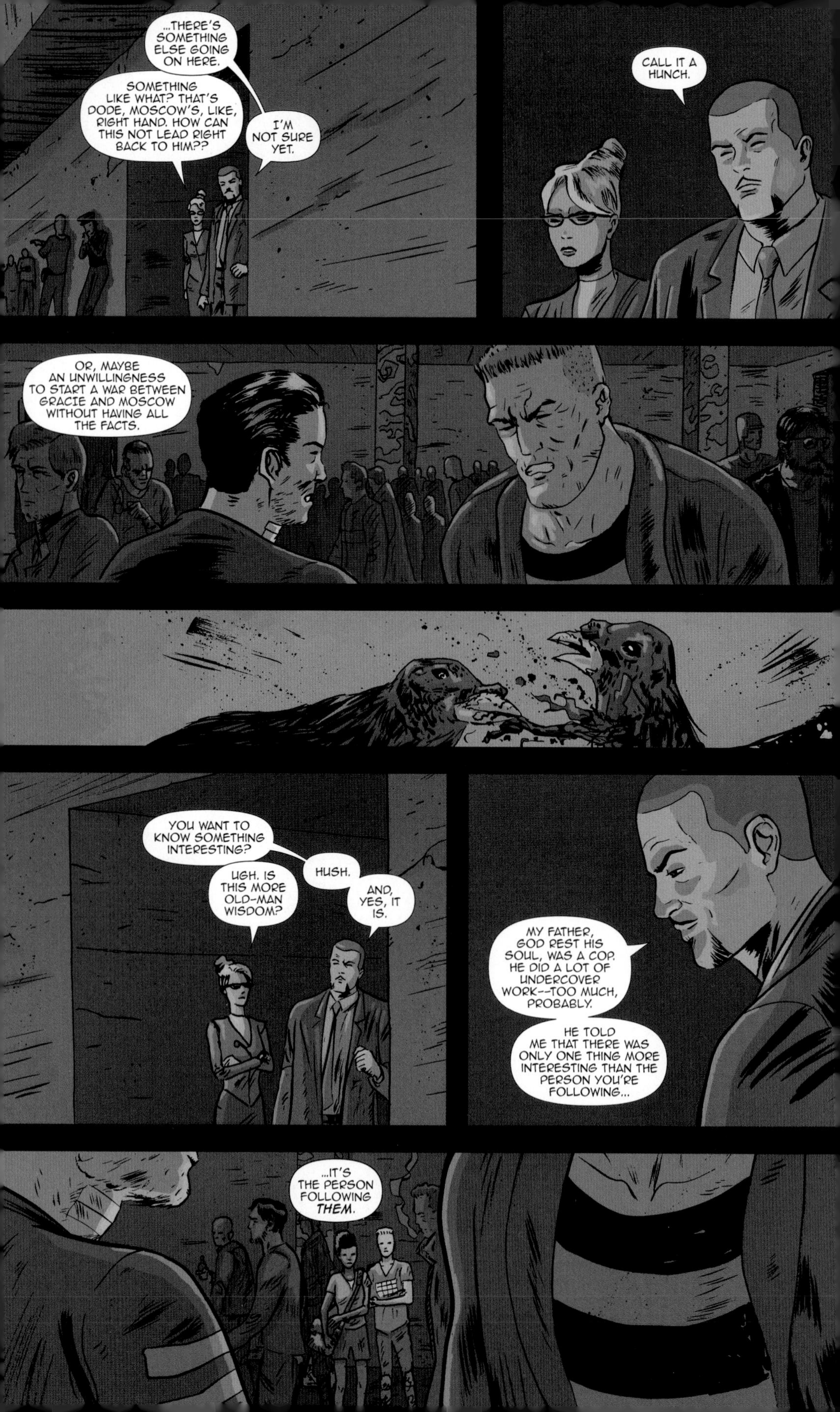
...THERE'S SOMETHING ELSE GOING ON HERE.
SOMETHING LIKE WHAT? THAT'S DODE, MOSCOW'S, LIKE, RIGHT HAND. HOW CAN THIS NOT LEAD RIGHT BACK TO HIM??
I'M NOT SURE YET.
CALL IT A HUNCH.
OR, MAYBE AN UNWILLINGNESS TO START A WAR BETWEEN GRACIE AND MOSCOW WITHOUT HAVING ALL THE FACTS.
YOU WANT TO KNOW SOMETHING INTERESTING?
UGH. IS THIS MORE OLD-MAN WISDOM?
HUSH.
AND, YES, IT IS.
MY FATHER, GOD REST HIS SOUL, WAS A COP. HE DID A LOT OF UNDERCOVER WORK--TOO MUCH, PROBABLY.
HE TOLD ME THAT THERE WAS ONLY ONE THING MORE INTERESTING THAN THE PERSON YOU'RE FOLLOWING...
...IT'S THE PERSON FOLLOWING *THEM*.

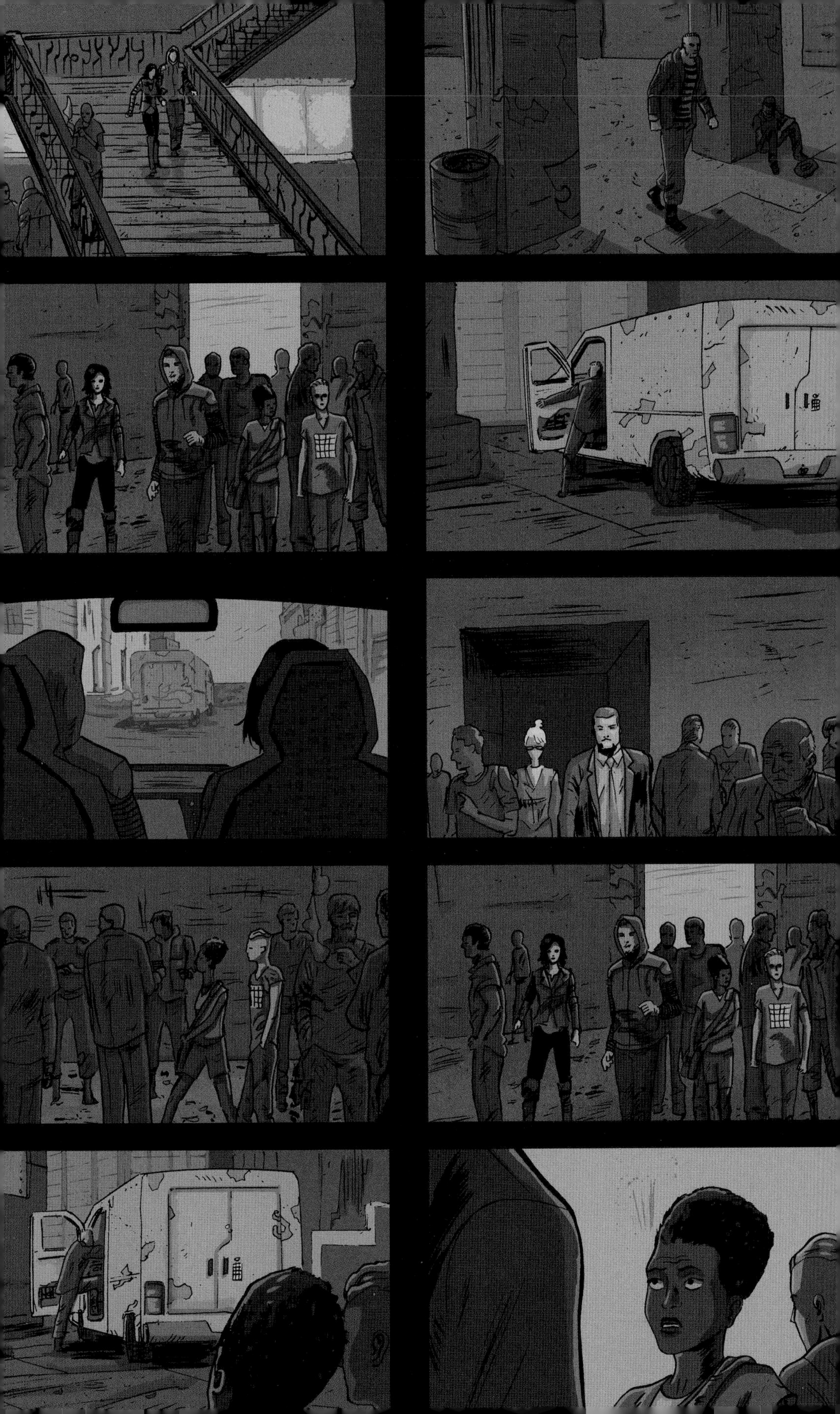

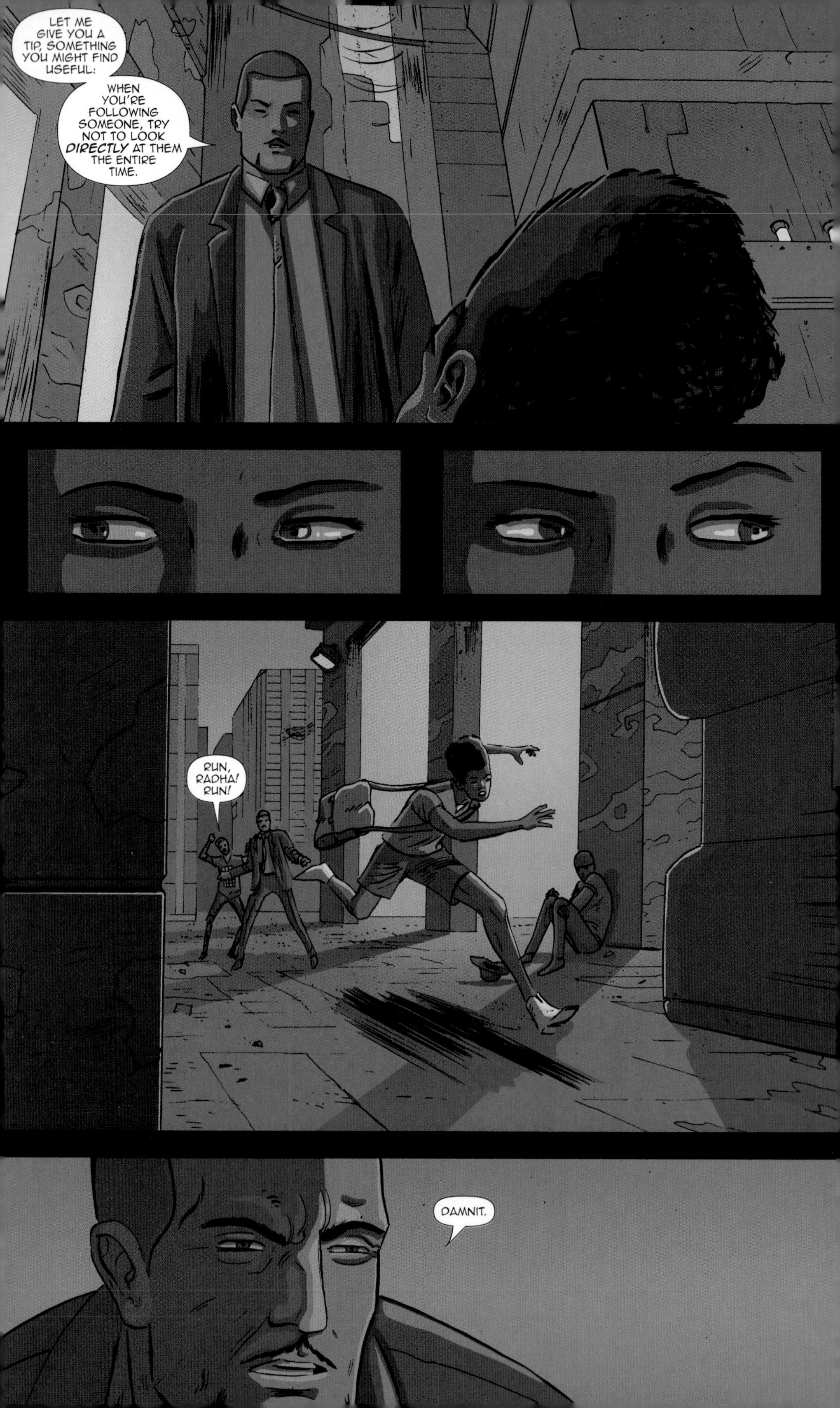
LET ME GIVE YOU A TIP, SOMETHING YOU MIGHT FIND USEFUL:
WHEN YOU'RE FOLLOWING SOMEONE, TRY NOT TO LOOK *DIRECTLY* AT THEM THE ENTIRE TIME.
RUN, RADHA! RUN!
DAMNIT.

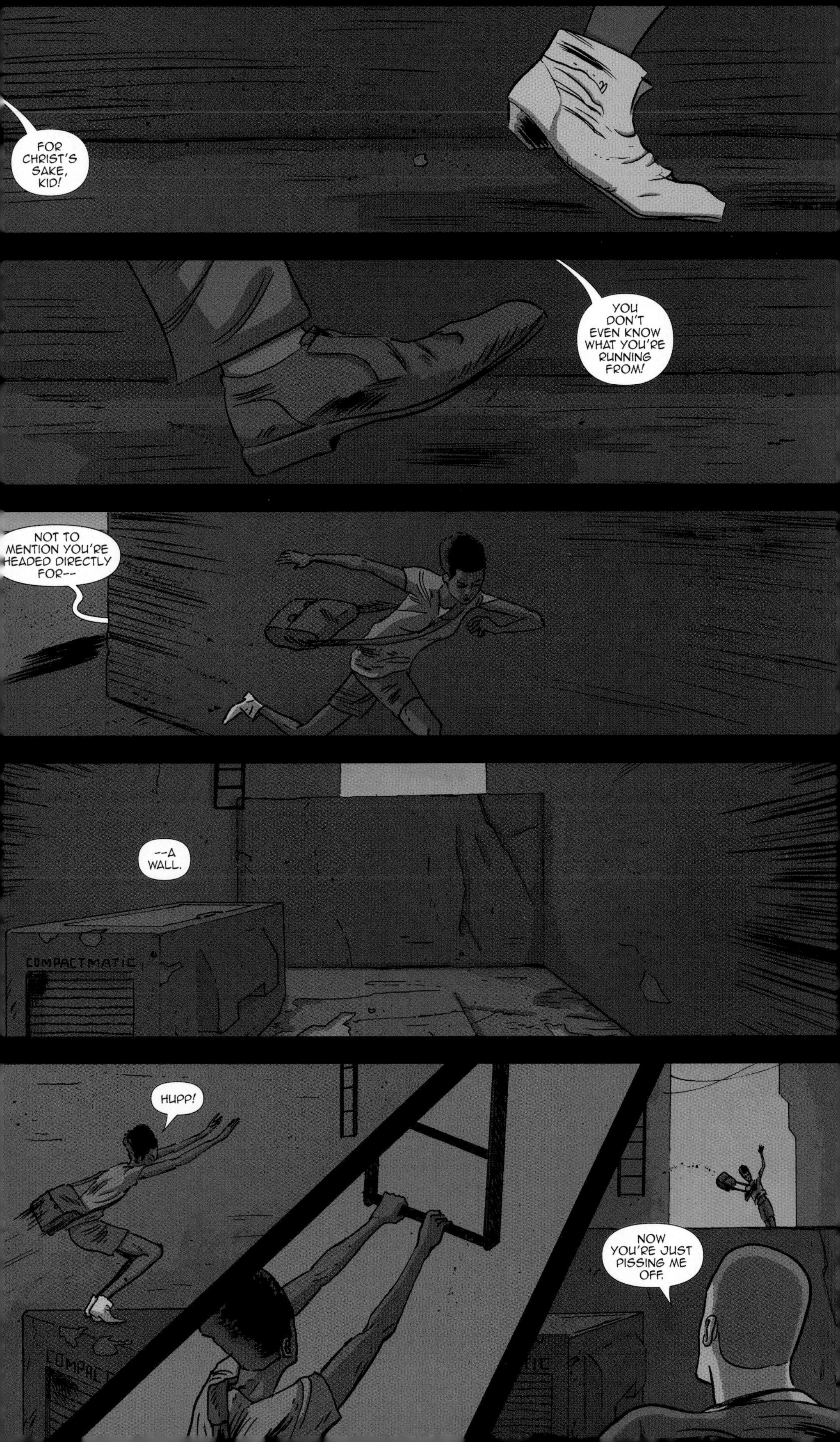
FOR CHRIST'S SAKE, KID!
YOU DON'T EVEN KNOW WHAT YOU'RE RUNNING FROM!
NOT TO MENTION YOU'RE HEADED DIRECTLY FOR--
--A WALL.
COMPACTMATIC
HUPP!
NOW YOU'RE JUST PISSING ME OFF.

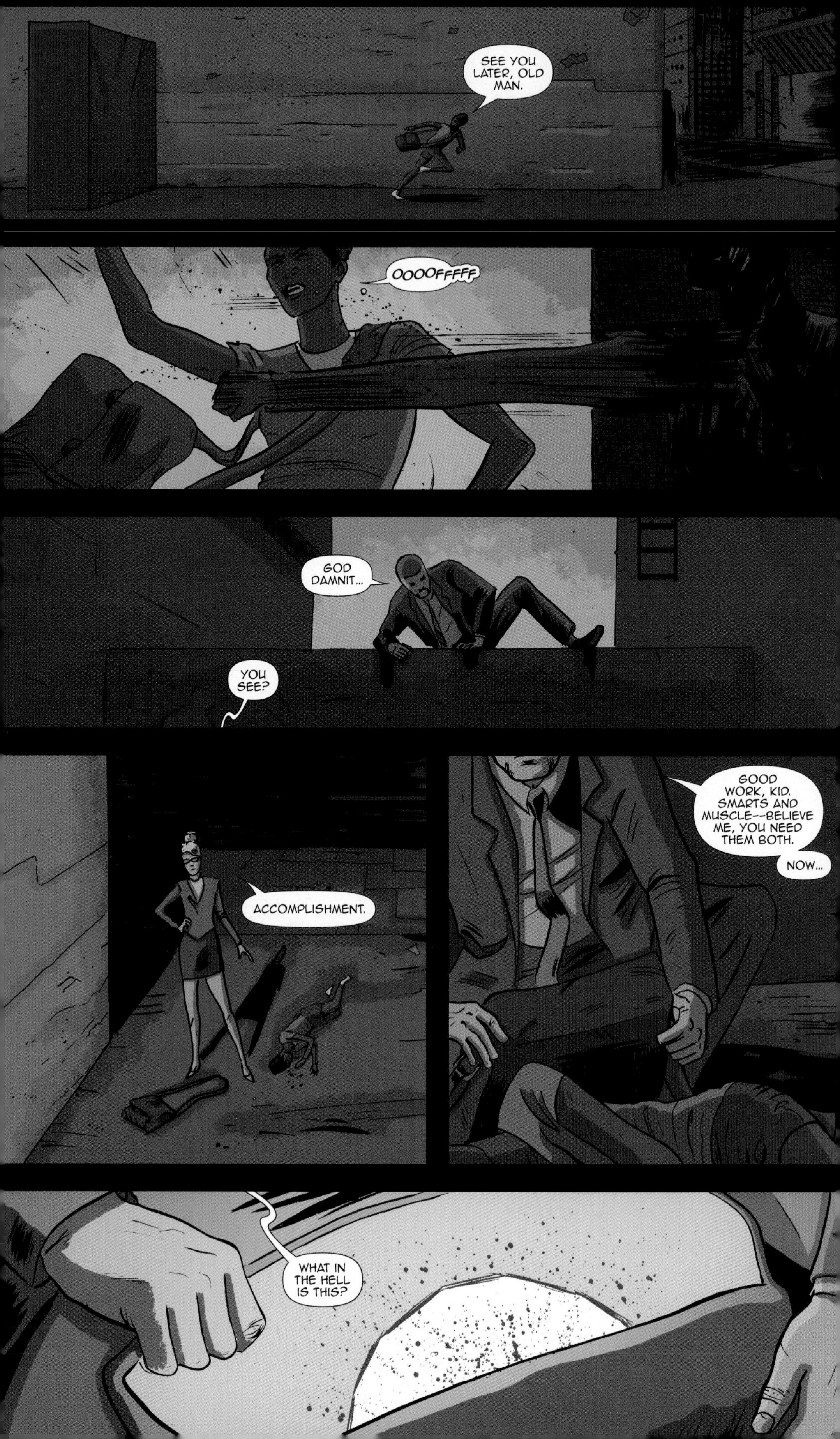
SEE YOU LATER, OLD MAN.
OOOOFFFFF
GOD DAMNIT...
YOU SEE?
ACCOMPLISHMENT.
GOOD WORK, KID. SMARTS AND MUSCLE--BELIEVE ME, YOU NEED THEM BOTH.
NOW...
WHAT IN THE HELL IS THIS?

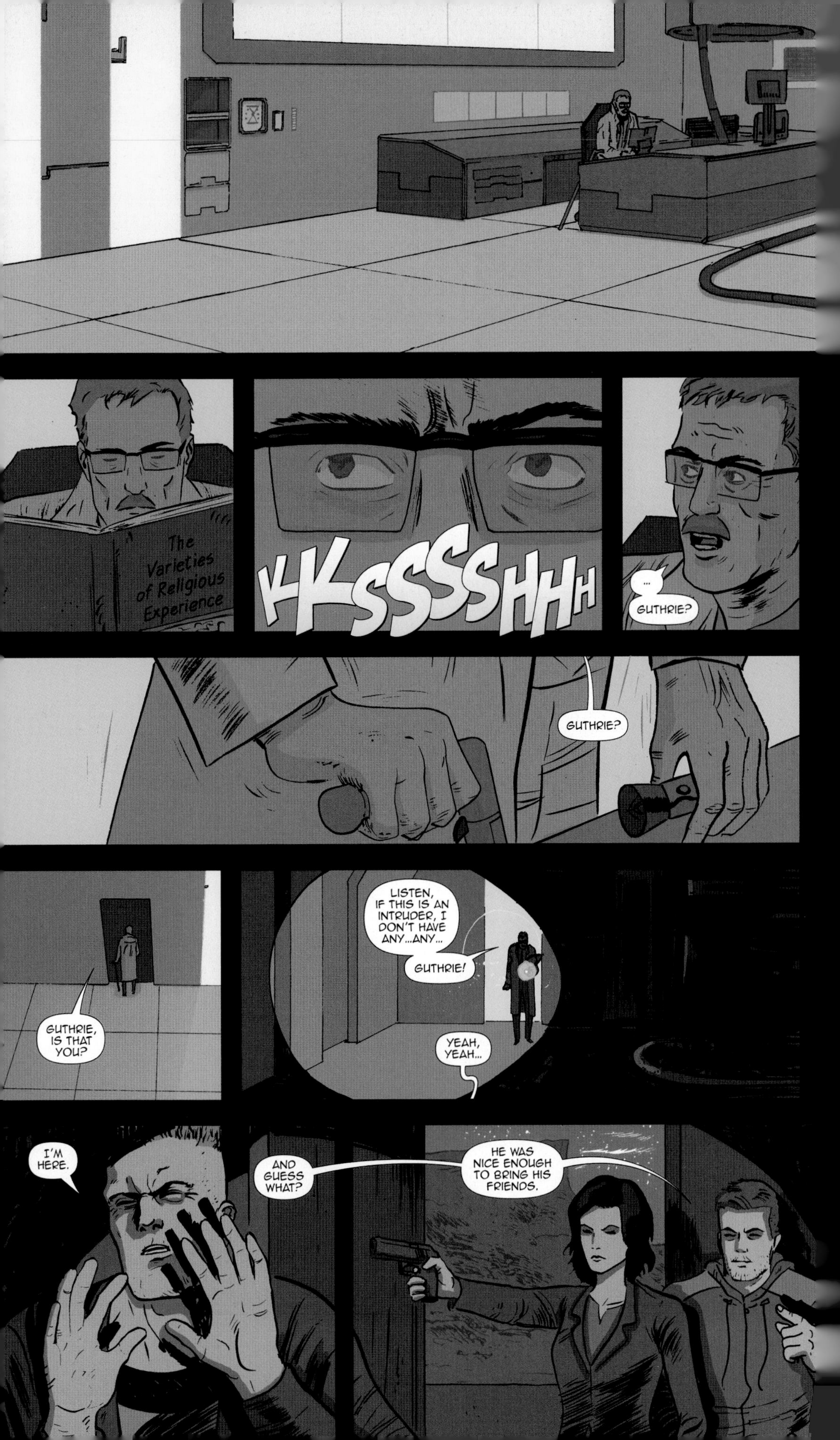
The Varieties of Religious Experience
KKSSSSSHHH
...
GUTHRIE?
GUTHRIE?
GUTHRIE, IS THAT YOU?
LISTEN, IF THIS IS AN INTRUDER, I DON'T HAVE ANY...ANY...
GUTHRIE!
YEAH, YEAH...
I'M HERE.
AND GUESS WHAT?
HE WAS NICE ENOUGH TO BRING HIS FRIENDS.

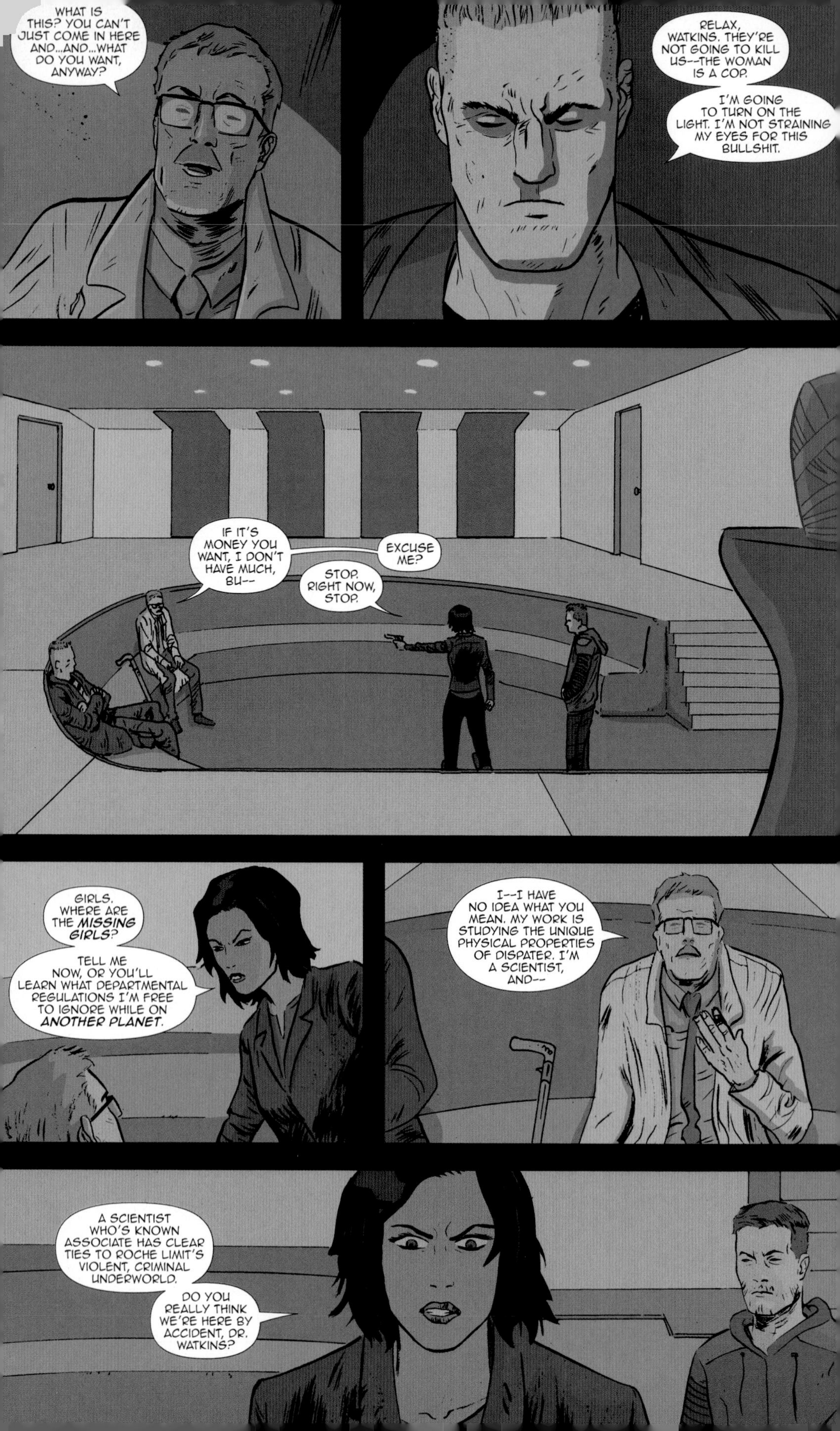
WHAT IS THIS? YOU CAN'T JUST COME IN HERE AND...AND...WHAT DO YOU WANT, ANYWAY?
RELAX, WATKINS. THEY'RE NOT GOING TO KILL US--THE WOMAN IS A COP.
I'M GOING TO TURN ON THE LIGHT. I'M NOT STRAINING MY EYES FOR THIS BULLSHIT.
IF IT'S MONEY YOU WANT, I DON'T HAVE MUCH, BU--
EXCUSE ME?
STOP. RIGHT NOW, STOP.
GIRLS. WHERE ARE THE MISSING GIRLS?
TELL ME NOW, OR YOU'LL LEARN WHAT DEPARTMENTAL REGULATIONS I'M FREE TO IGNORE WHILE ON ANOTHER PLANET.
I--I HAVE NO IDEA WHAT YOU MEAN. MY WORK IS STUDYING THE UNIQUE PHYSICAL PROPERTIES OF DISPATER. I'M A SCIENTIST, AND--
A SCIENTIST WHO'S KNOWN ASSOCIATE HAS CLEAR TIES TO ROCHE LIMIT'S VIOLENT, CRIMINAL UNDERWORLD.
DO YOU REALLY THINK WE'RE HERE BY ACCIDENT, DR. WATKINS?

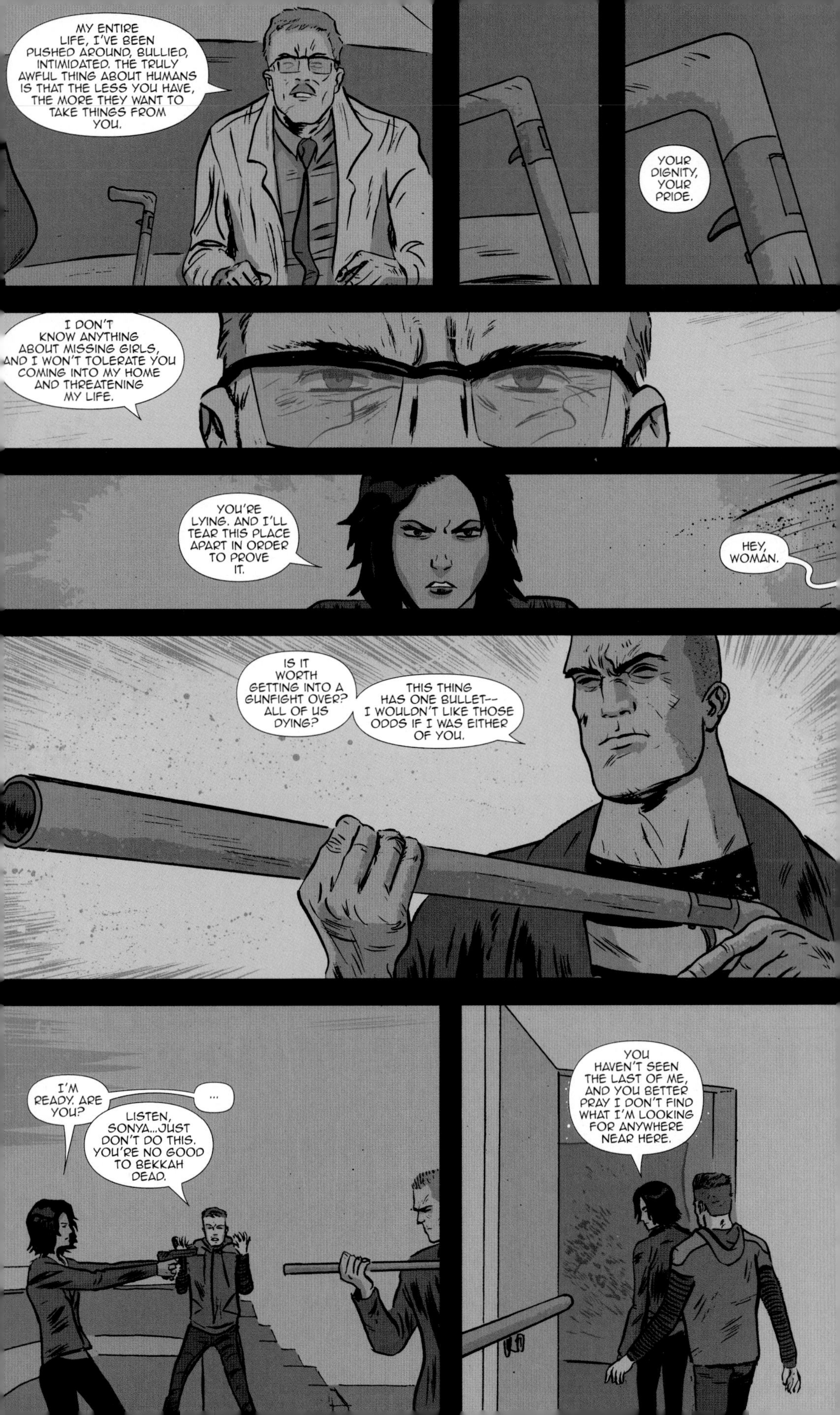
MY ENTIRE LIFE, I'VE BEEN PUSHED AROUND, BULLIED, INTIMIDATED. THE TRULY AWFUL THING ABOUT HUMANS IS THAT THE LESS YOU HAVE, THE MORE THEY WANT TO TAKE THINGS FROM YOU.
YOUR DIGNITY, YOUR PRIDE.
I DON'T KNOW ANYTHING ABOUT MISSING GIRLS, AND I WON'T TOLERATE YOU COMING INTO MY HOME AND THREATENING MY LIFE.
YOU'RE LYING. AND I'LL TEAR THIS PLACE APART IN ORDER TO PROVE IT.
HEY, WOMAN.
IS IT WORTH GETTING INTO A GUNFIGHT OVER? ALL OF US DYING?
THIS THING HAS ONE BULLET-- I WOULDN'T LIKE THOSE ODDS IF I WAS EITHER OF YOU.
I'M READY. ARE YOU?
...
LISTEN, SONYA...JUST DON'T DO THIS. YOU'RE NO GOOD TO BEKKAH DEAD.
YOU HAVEN'T SEEN THE LAST OF ME, AND YOU BETTER PRAY I DON'T FIND WHAT I'M LOOKING FOR ANYWHERE NEAR HERE.

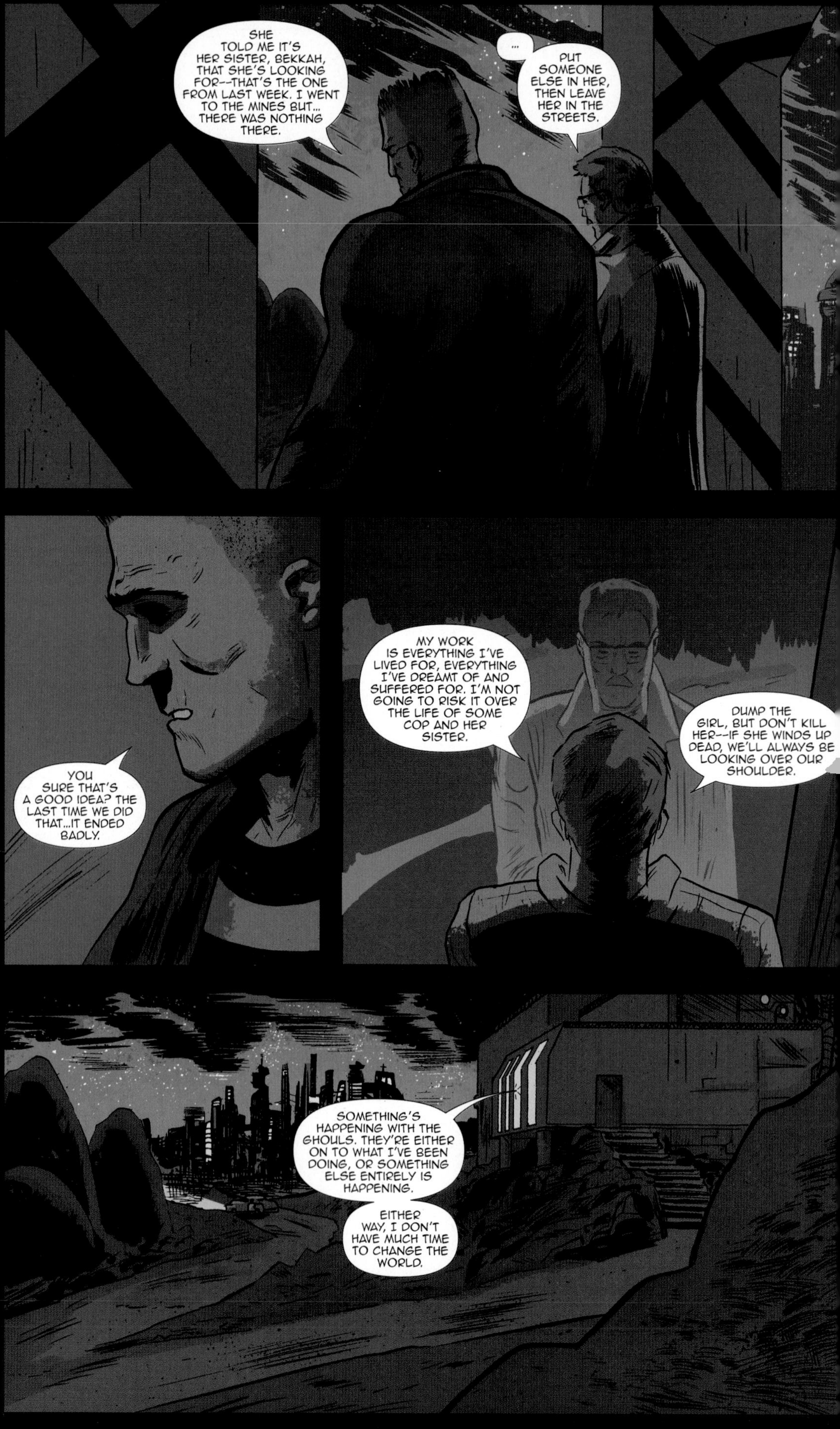
SHE TOLD ME IT'S HER SISTER, BEKKAH, THAT SHE'S LOOKING FOR--THAT'S THE ONE FROM LAST WEEK. I WENT TO THE MINES BUT... THERE WAS NOTHING THERE.
...
PUT SOMEONE ELSE IN HER, THEN LEAVE HER IN THE STREETS.
YOU SURE THAT'S A GOOD IDEA? THE LAST TIME WE DID THAT...IT ENDED BADLY.
MY WORK IS EVERYTHING I'VE LIVED FOR, EVERYTHING I'VE DREAMT OF AND SUFFERED FOR. I'M NOT GOING TO RISK IT OVER THE LIFE OF SOME COP AND HER SISTER.
DUMP THE GIRL, BUT DON'T KILL HER--IF SHE WINDS UP DEAD, WE'LL ALWAYS BE LOOKING OVER OUR SHOULDER.
SOMETHING'S HAPPENING WITH THE GHOULS. THEY'RE EITHER ON TO WHAT I'VE BEEN DOING, OR SOMETHING ELSE ENTIRELY IS HAPPENING.
EITHER WAY, I DON'T HAVE MUCH TIME TO CHANGE THE WORLD.

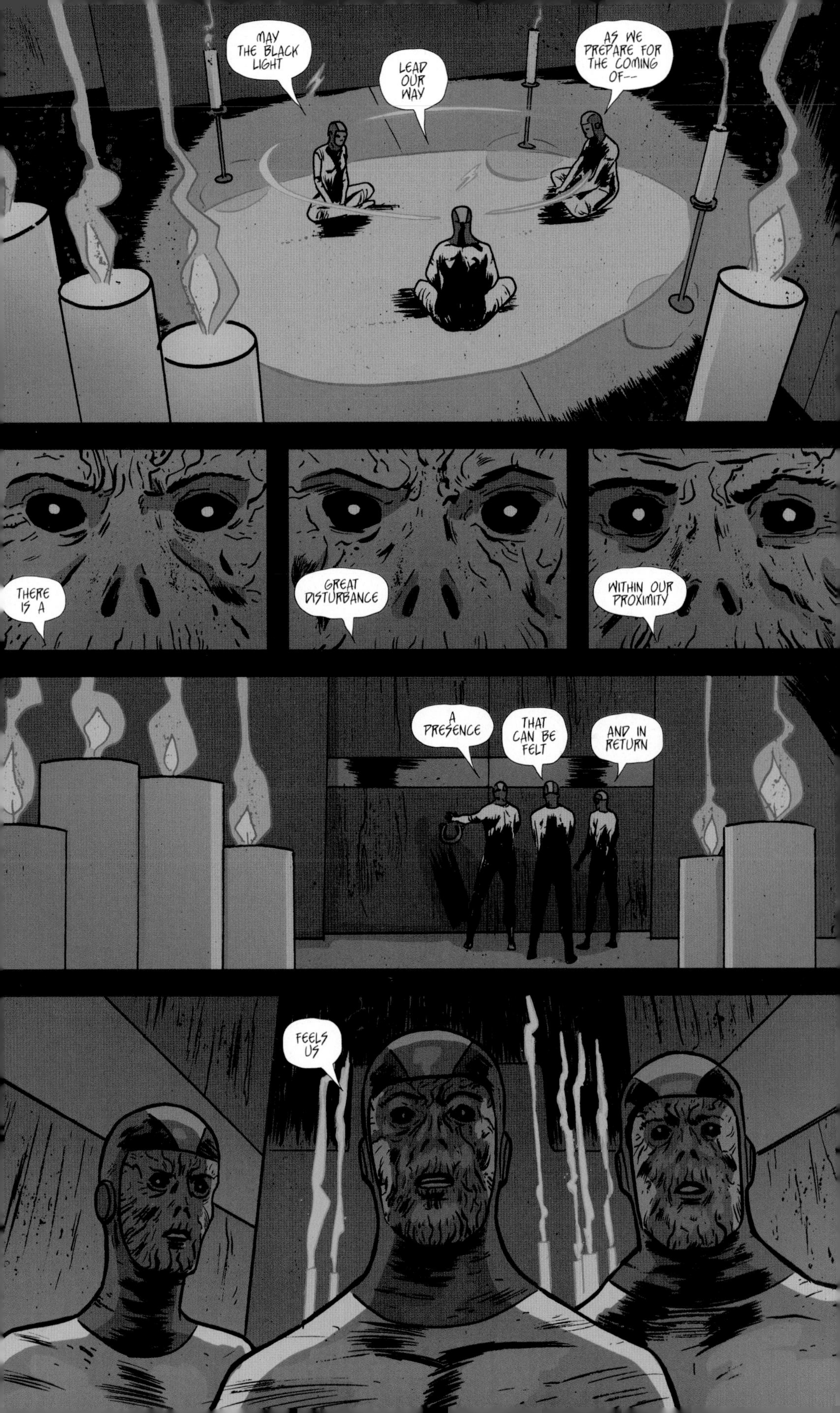
MAY THE BLACK LIGHT
LEAD OUR WAY
AS WE PREPARE FOR THE COMING OF--
THERE IS A
GREAT DISTURBANCE
WITHIN OUR PROXIMITY
A PRESENCE
THAT CAN BE FELT
AND IN RETURN
FEELS US

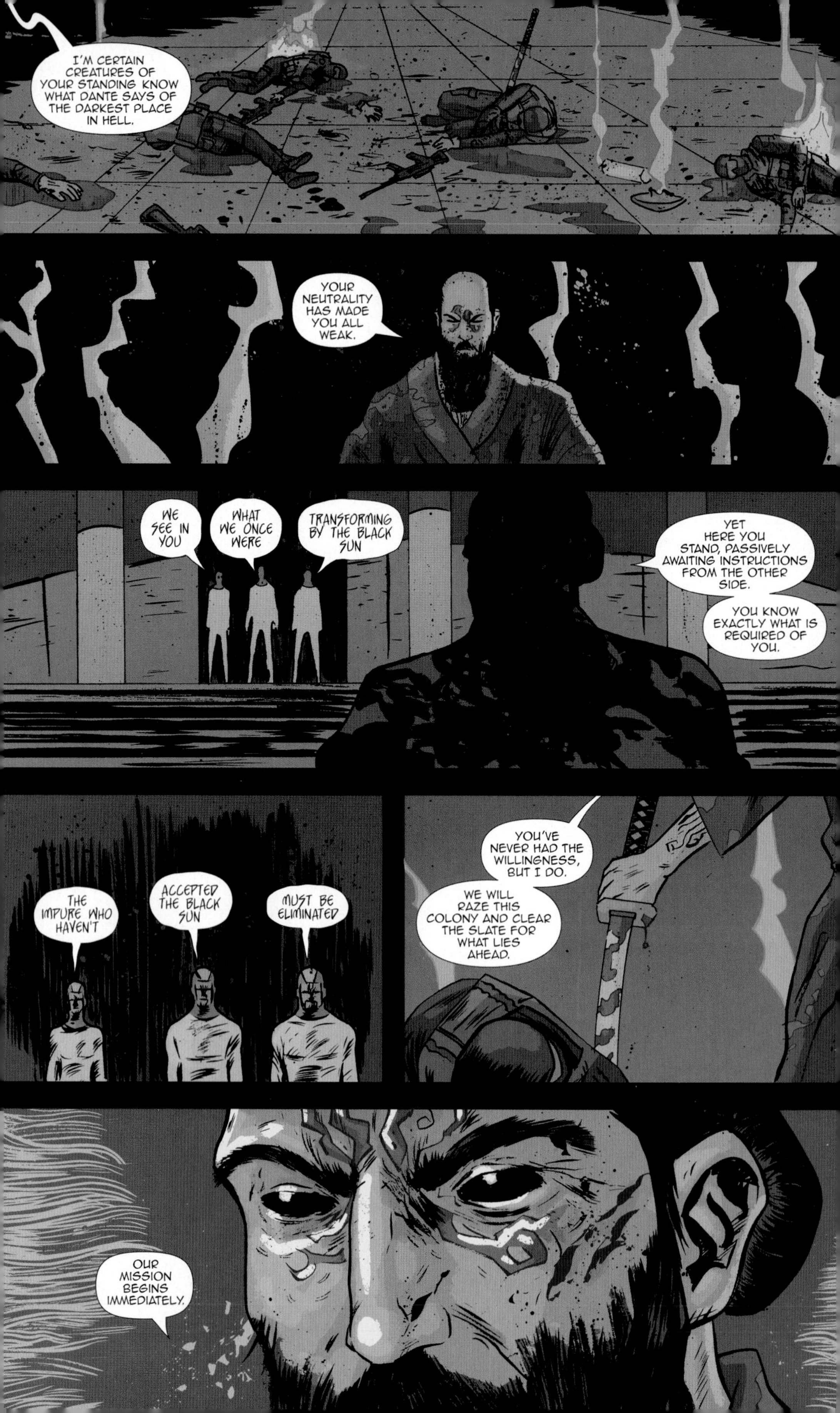
I'M CERTAIN CREATURES OF YOUR STANDING KNOW WHAT DANTE SAYS OF THE DARKEST PLACE IN HELL.
YOUR NEUTRALITY HAS MADE YOU ALL WEAK.
WE SEE IN YOU
WHAT WE ONCE WERE
TRANSFORMING BY THE BLACK SUN
YET HERE YOU STAND, PASSIVELY AWAITING INSTRUCTIONS FROM THE OTHER SIDE.
YOU KNOW EXACTLY WHAT IS REQUIRED OF YOU.
THE IMPURE WHO HAVEN'T
ACCEPTED THE BLACK SUN
MUST BE ELIMINATED
YOU'VE NEVER HAD THE WILLINGNESS, BUT I DO.
WE WILL RAZE THIS COLONY AND CLEAR THE SLATE FOR WHAT LIES AHEAD.
OUR MISSION BEGINS IMMEDIATELY.

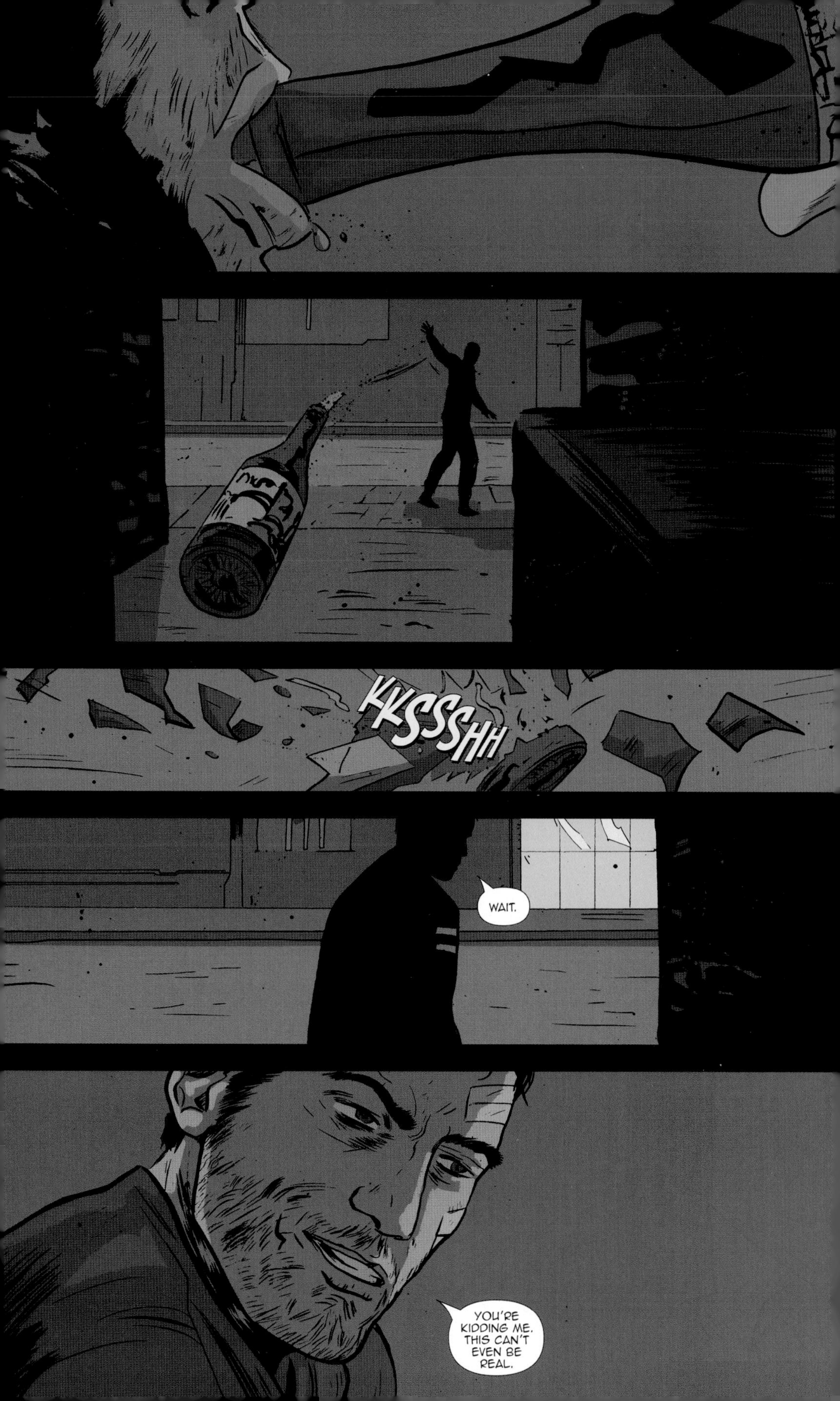
KKSSSHH
WAIT.
YOU'RE KIDDING ME. THIS CAN'T EVEN BE REAL.

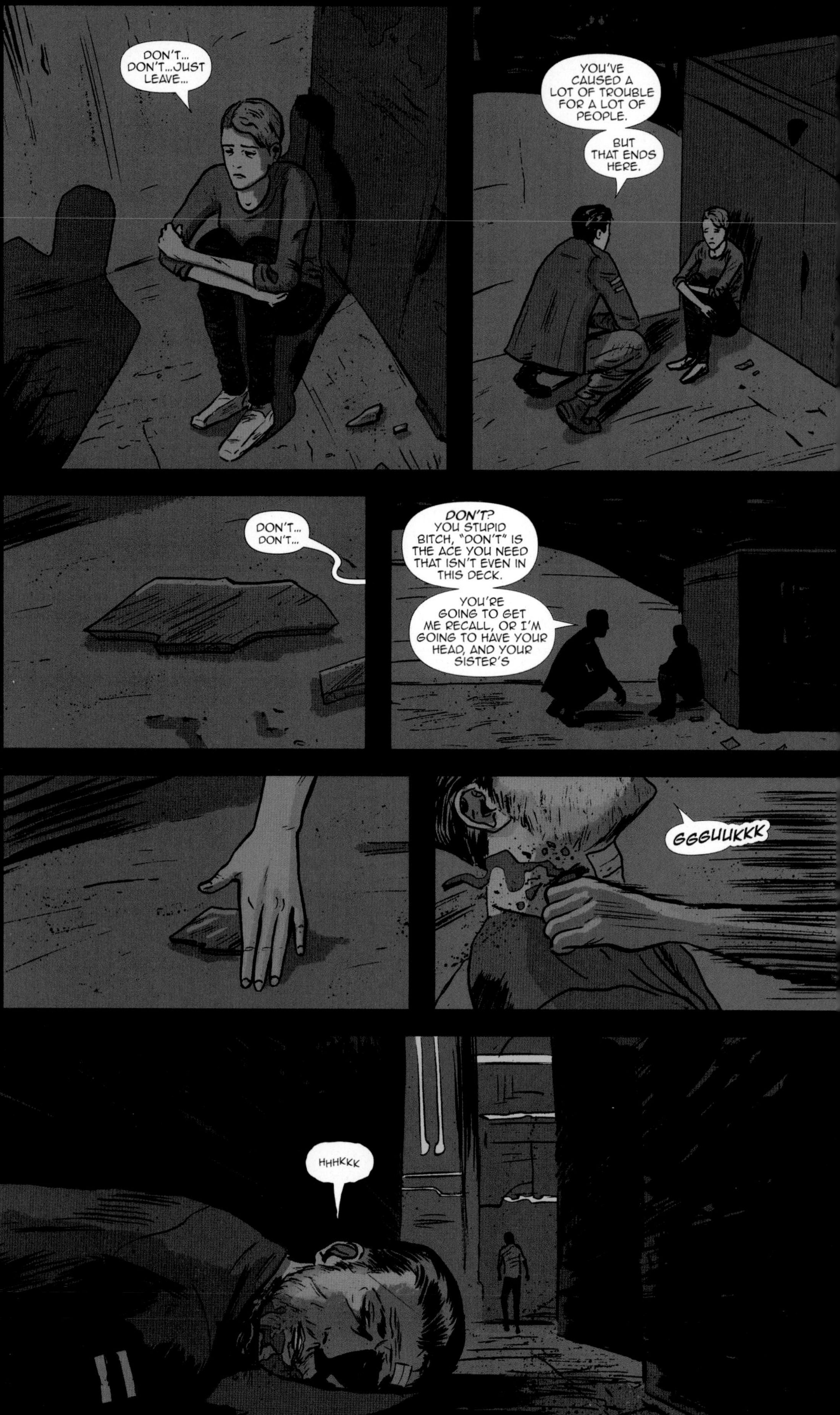
DON'T... DON'T...JUST LEAVE...
YOU'VE CAUSED A LOT OF TROUBLE FOR A LOT OF PEOPLE.
BUT THAT ENDS HERE.
DON'T... DON'T...
DON'T? YOU STUPID BITCH, "DON'T" IS THE ACE YOU NEED THAT ISN'T EVEN IN THIS DECK.
YOU'RE GOING TO GET ME RECALL, OR I'M GOING TO HAVE YOUR HEAD, AND YOUR SISTER'S
GGGUUKKK
HHHKKK

CASE FOR FINANCIAL SUPPORT
FROM DR. ABRAHAM J. WATKINS
TO THE WALLERS FOUNDATION

PRESS

DOCUMENT REPRODUCTION SERVICES

Mr. Davis R. Emery
President
Wallers Foundation
4815 Menard Avenue
Chicago, Illinois 60618

Dear Mr. Emery:

First, I apologize for the antiquated instrument used for producing this message. My employers on Roche Limit don't allow modern technology to be used within the MoiraTech compound. Not anymore.

I write to make my case for support of my research and preliminary findings that, without a doubt in my mind, has the potential to change the world.

My entire career, I've always compartmentalized the scientific and the spiritual into two very distinct camps. While they both center on the search for meaning to humanity's greatest mysteries, they never seem to ask the same questions. In my highly classified work on the Roche Limit Colony, I never sought after this kind of existential pursuit. My work was...different, guided by the goals of my employers. Yet, as you surely know, life oftentimes gives us answers to questions we haven't asked, and the discovery I've made is nothing short of breathtaking.

We all share the same fundamental questions about life—who we are, where we came from, where we are going. Science will point to evolution, fossil data, and the like; religion will cite scripture and the always nebulous sensation of faith. Through pure happenstance, my work has come to intersect the two.

We, as people, want to feel that our lives have meaning, that we're unique creations with an agency all our own. We strive to be remarkably independent in so many ways. Yet what is it that makes us so hungry to understand and maintain our individualism? What makes us stake our claim as our own person, not to be subjugated as part of the masses?

The answer is simple: the human soul. It exists, and I've found it.

CASE FOR FINANCIAL SUPPORT

FROM DR. ABRAHAM J. WATKINS
TO THE WALLERS FOUNDATION

I know it seems preposterous, but it s true and it s real. We no longer need to fear the emptiness in our lives, we no longer need to struggle with who we are. It s all right there, deep within us. We just need to understand it.

Because of the delicate nature of my current research and the character of the people I work for, I'm afraid I can't divulge how I've made this discovery or what I've learned so far. I don't trust that information getting released, and I fear what might happen, especially if my employers were to uncover my work. They'd use it for their own twisted gains.

All I ask of you is safe passage off of this planet. Give me that and a lab, and I will provide you with what might be the greatest discovery in humanity s history. I'll produce a soul and place it right in front of you, if that's what it takes. But I do need to get off of Dispater and away from this colony as soon as possible. It's not safe here, and I fear what's in store for Roche Limit's future.

I've included a number where I can be reached—leave a message there, and I'll be sure to receive it within a week. We can proceed from there.

I look forward to changing the world together.

Sincerely,

Dr. Abraham Watkins

CASE FOR FINANCIAL SUPPORT

FROM DR. ABRAHAM J. WATKINS
TO THE WALLERS FOUNDATION

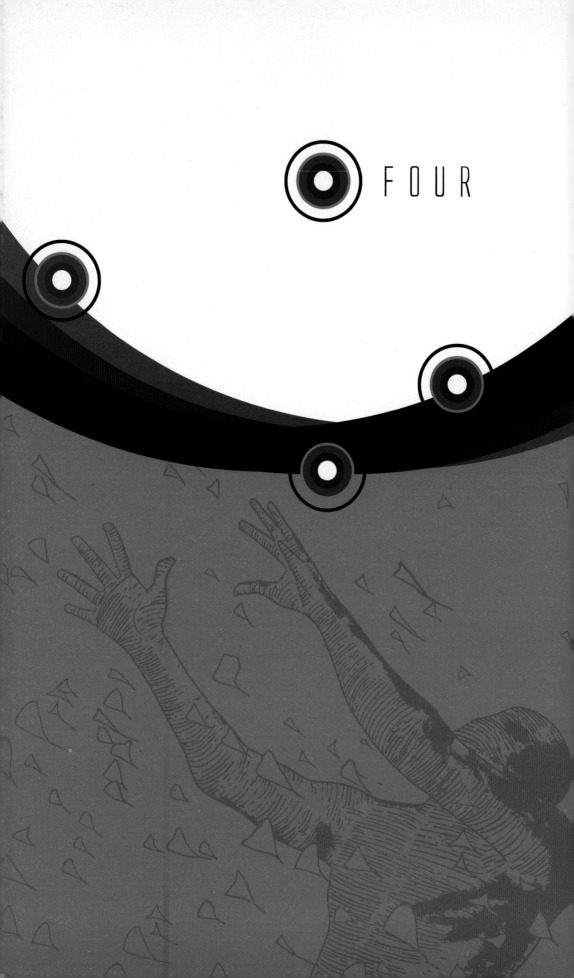

FOUR

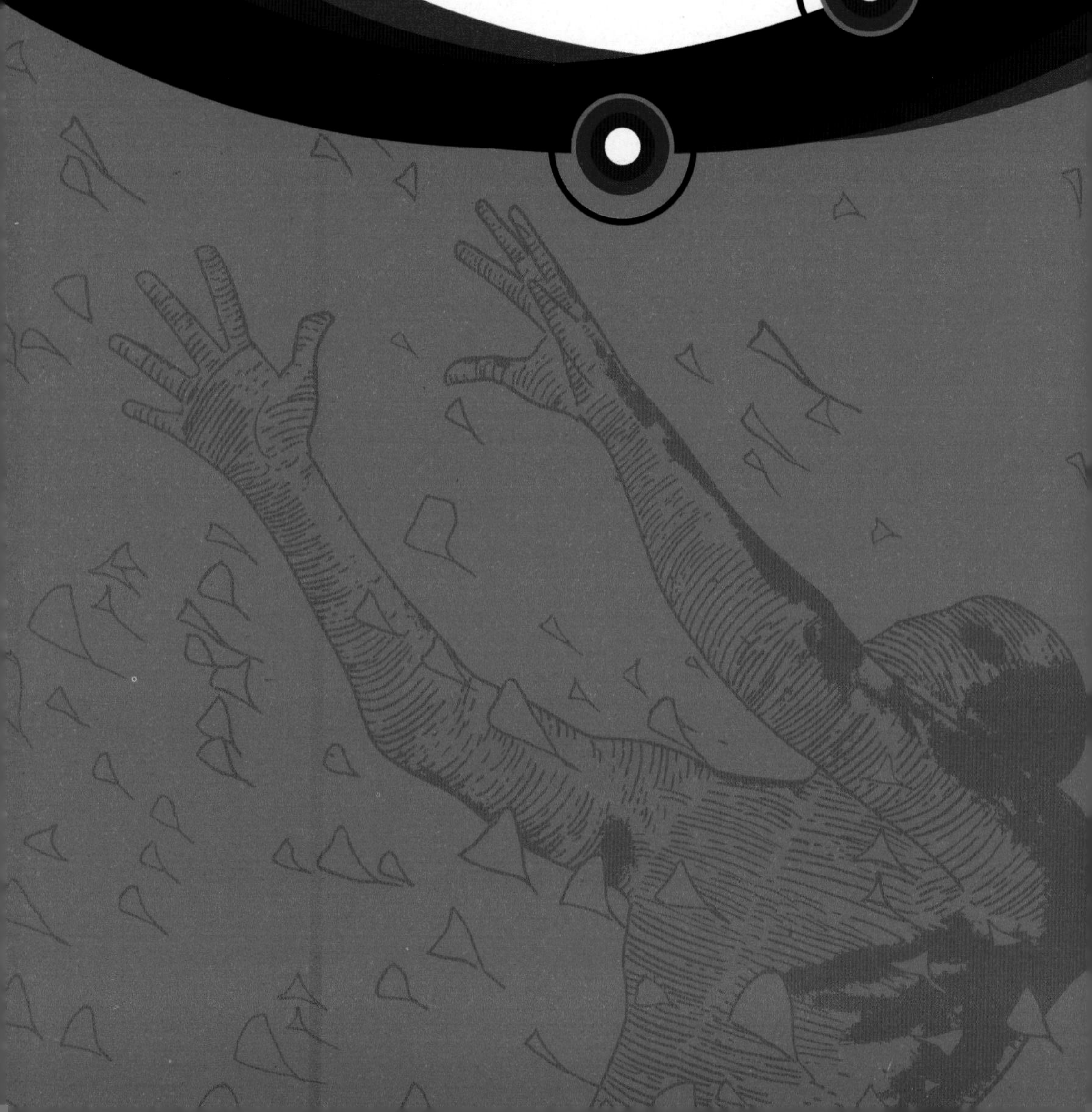

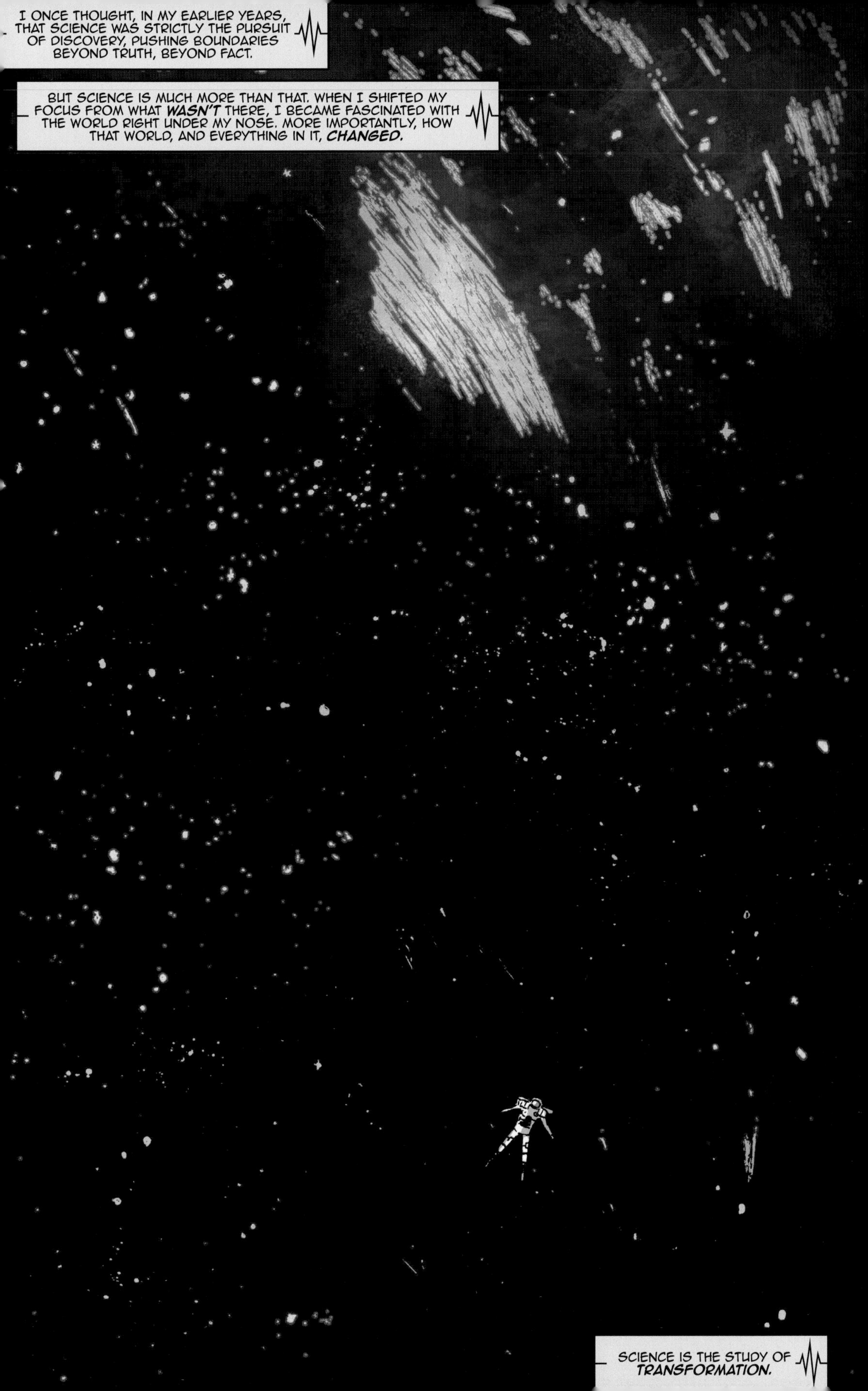
I ONCE THOUGHT, IN MY EARLIER YEARS, THAT SCIENCE WAS STRICTLY THE PURSUIT OF DISCOVERY, PUSHING BOUNDARIES BEYOND TRUTH, BEYOND FACT.
BUT SCIENCE IS MUCH MORE THAN THAT. WHEN I SHIFTED MY FOCUS FROM WHAT **WASN'T** THERE, I BECAME FASCINATED WITH THE WORLD RIGHT UNDER MY NOSE. MORE IMPORTANTLY, HOW THAT WORLD, AND EVERYTHING IN IT, ***CHANGED.***
SCIENCE IS THE STUDY OF ***TRANSFORMATION.***

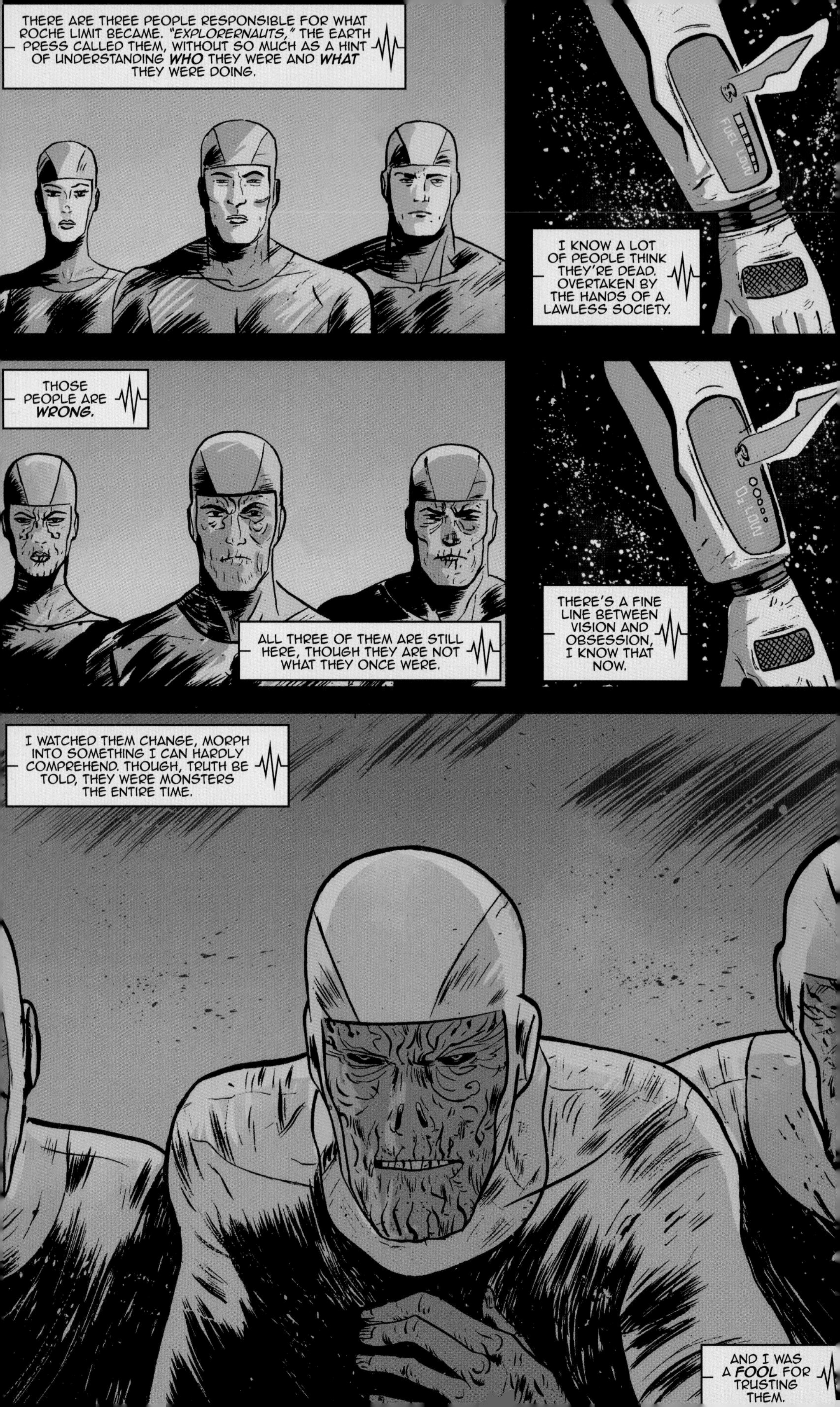
THERE ARE THREE PEOPLE RESPONSIBLE FOR WHAT ROCHE LIMIT BECAME. "*EXPLORERNAUTS*," THE EARTH PRESS CALLED THEM, WITHOUT SO MUCH AS A HINT OF UNDERSTANDING ***WHO*** THEY WERE AND ***WHAT*** THEY WERE DOING.
FUEL LOW
I KNOW A LOT OF PEOPLE THINK THEY'RE DEAD. OVERTAKEN BY THE HANDS OF A LAWLESS SOCIETY.
THOSE PEOPLE ARE ***WRONG.***
ALL THREE OF THEM ARE STILL HERE, THOUGH THEY ARE NOT WHAT THEY ONCE WERE.
O_2 LOW
THERE'S A FINE LINE BETWEEN VISION AND OBSESSION, I KNOW THAT NOW.
I WATCHED THEM CHANGE, MORPH INTO SOMETHING I CAN HARDLY COMPREHEND. THOUGH, TRUTH BE TOLD, THEY WERE MONSTERS THE ENTIRE TIME.
AND I WAS A ***FOOL*** FOR TRUSTING THEM.

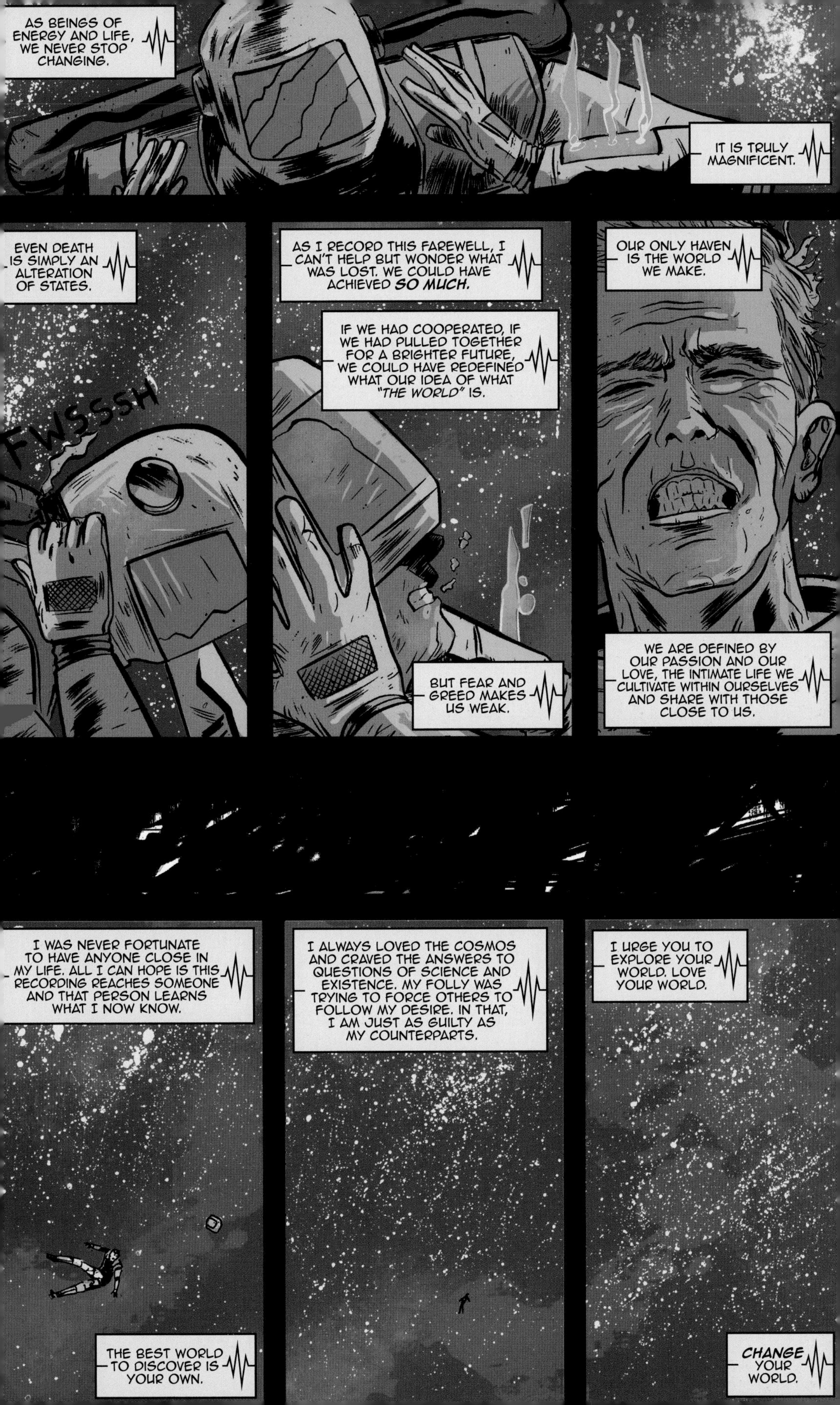
AS BEINGS OF ENERGY AND LIFE, WE NEVER STOP CHANGING.
IT IS TRULY MAGNIFICENT.
EVEN DEATH IS SIMPLY AN ALTERATION OF STATES.
FWSSSH
AS I RECORD THIS FAREWELL, I CAN'T HELP BUT WONDER WHAT WAS LOST. WE COULD HAVE ACHIEVED SO MUCH.
IF WE HAD COOPERATED, IF WE HAD PULLED TOGETHER FOR A BRIGHTER FUTURE, WE COULD HAVE REDEFINED WHAT OUR IDEA OF WHAT "THE WORLD" IS.
BUT FEAR AND GREED MAKES US WEAK.
OUR ONLY HAVEN IS THE WORLD WE MAKE.
WE ARE DEFINED BY OUR PASSION AND OUR LOVE, THE INTIMATE LIFE WE CULTIVATE WITHIN OURSELVES AND SHARE WITH THOSE CLOSE TO US.
I WAS NEVER FORTUNATE TO HAVE ANYONE CLOSE IN MY LIFE. ALL I CAN HOPE IS THIS RECORDING REACHES SOMEONE AND THAT PERSON LEARNS WHAT I NOW KNOW.
THE BEST WORLD TO DISCOVER IS YOUR OWN.
I ALWAYS LOVED THE COSMOS AND CRAVED THE ANSWERS TO QUESTIONS OF SCIENCE AND EXISTENCE. MY FOLLY WAS TRYING TO FORCE OTHERS TO FOLLOW MY DESIRE. IN THAT, I AM JUST AS GUILTY AS MY COUNTERPARTS.
I URGE YOU TO EXPLORE YOUR WORLD. LOVE YOUR WORLD.
CHANGE YOUR WORLD.

ANOMALY

-More questions than answers exist when it comes to the anomaly that hovers over Dispater. For years, physicists believed it was a black hole, or at least an event that behaved like a black hole. But the space exploration team, Genysis 2, dispelled that theory after studying the anomaly from just beyond its event horizon.

GENYSIS 2

-Regarding Genysis 2, speculation abounds that what was made public from their four years of orbital research is a fraction of what they actually learned. Of the four crew members, two returned to Earth suffering from psychological trauma akin to bipolar disorder and schizophrenia, one committed suicide on the journey home, and one, Visnhy Laurel, returned unfazed. In fact, Laurel went on to lead a productive life as CEO of Moiratech.

-Of the findings that the Genysis 2 did produce, two have captured the imaginations of the international community—and conspiracy theorists—and have led to much speculation. The first finding, made by Jake Wexman (who tragically took is own life two months before returning to Earth), was the theory that the anomaly is a wormhole—that it acts as a portal to another galaxy far beyond our current knowledge of space. Wexman's claim, though, is highly theoretical, based mainly on speculative assumptions of time and gravity. The other finding is a simple recording a Genysis orb captured while collecting visual data. Most disregard the audio clip as space clatter, though many argue over the repetition of sound, as if it was a message being conveyed.

PREVIOUS SLIDE

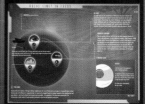

‹‹ ››

NEXT SLIDE

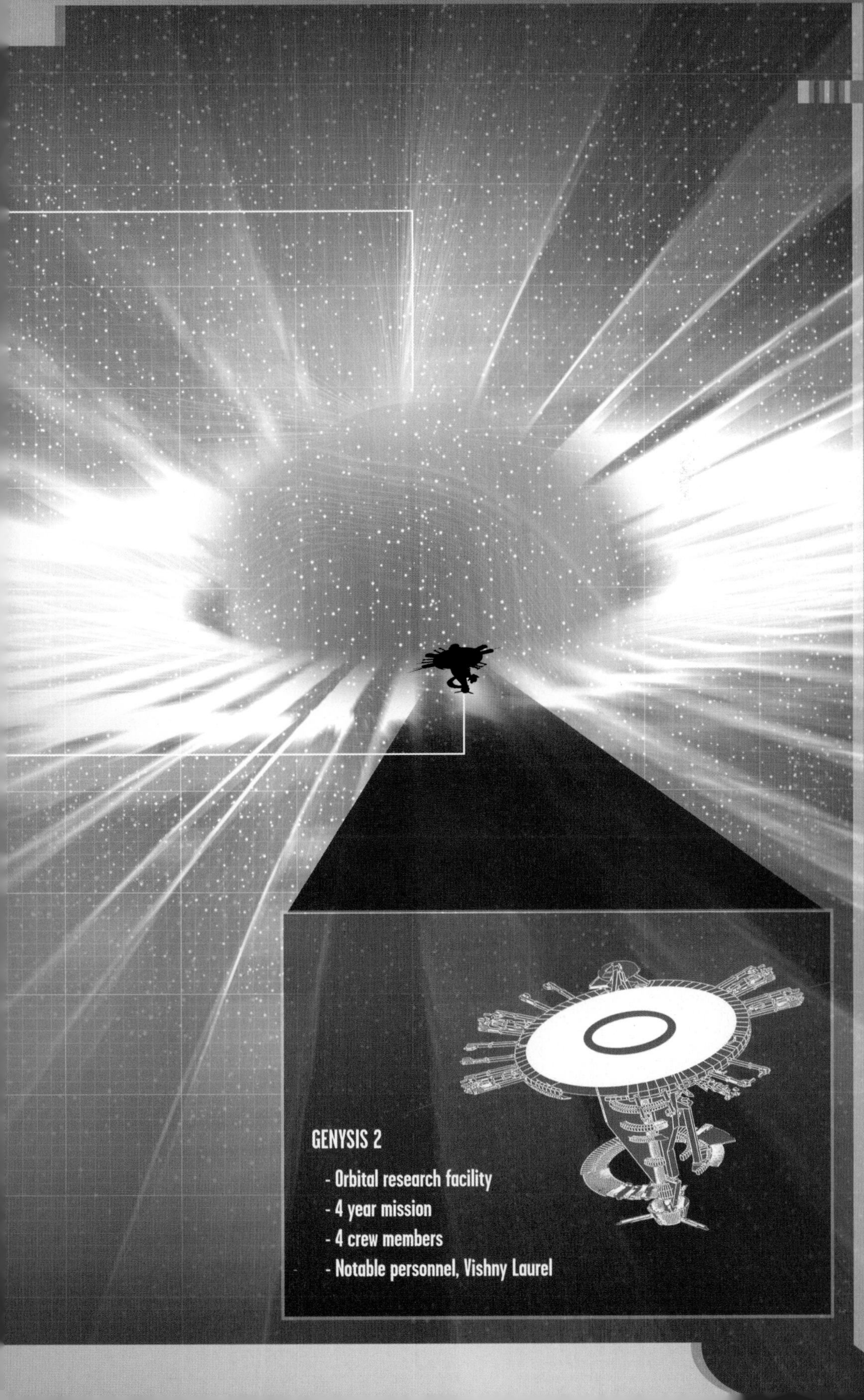
GENYSIS 2
- Orbital research facility
- 4 year mission
- 4 crew members
- Notable personnel, Vishny Laurel

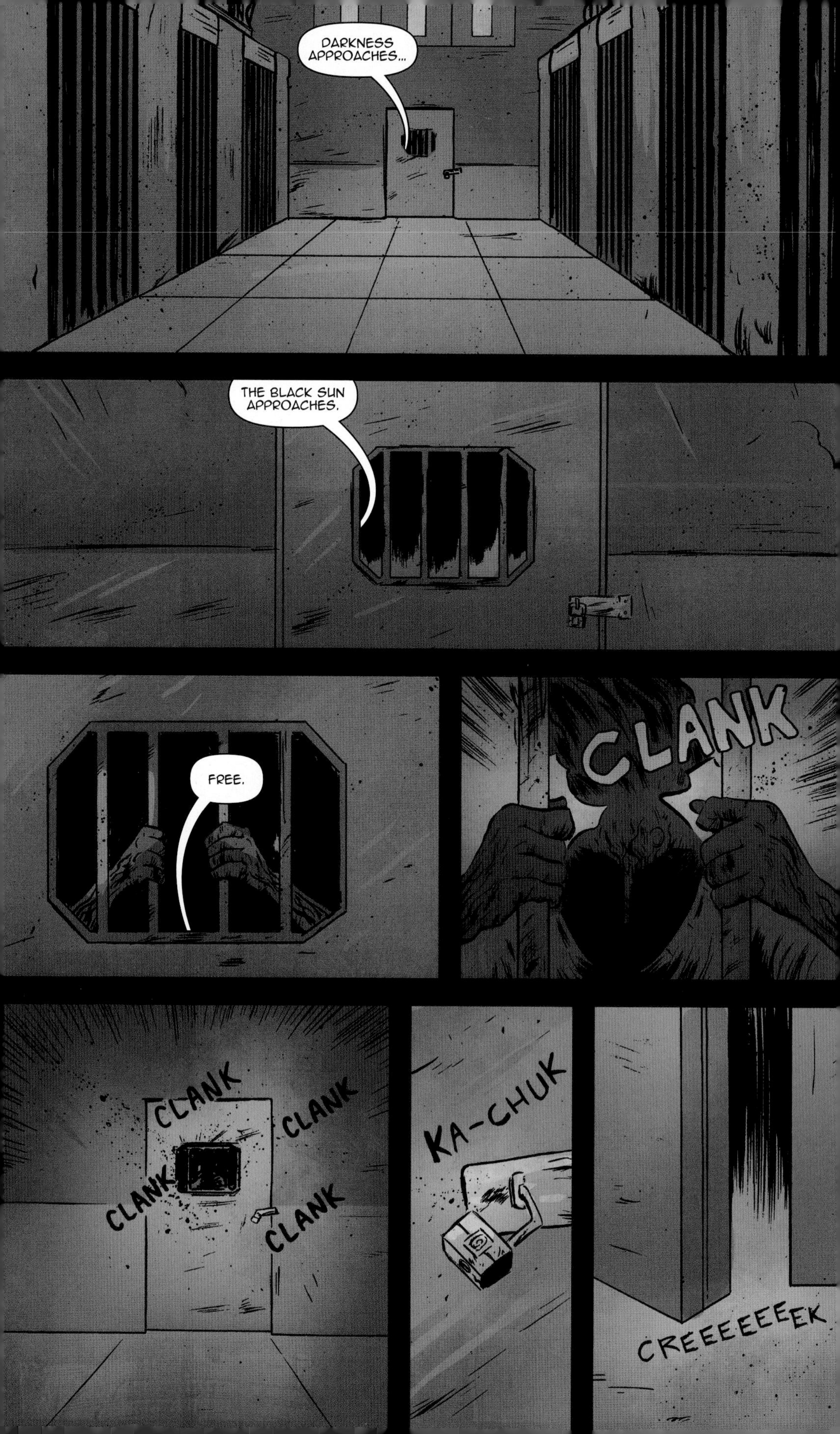

DARKNESS APPROACHES...
THE BLACK SUN APPROACHES.
FREE.
CLANK
CLANK
CLANK
CLANK
CLANK
KA-CHUK
CREEEEEEEEK

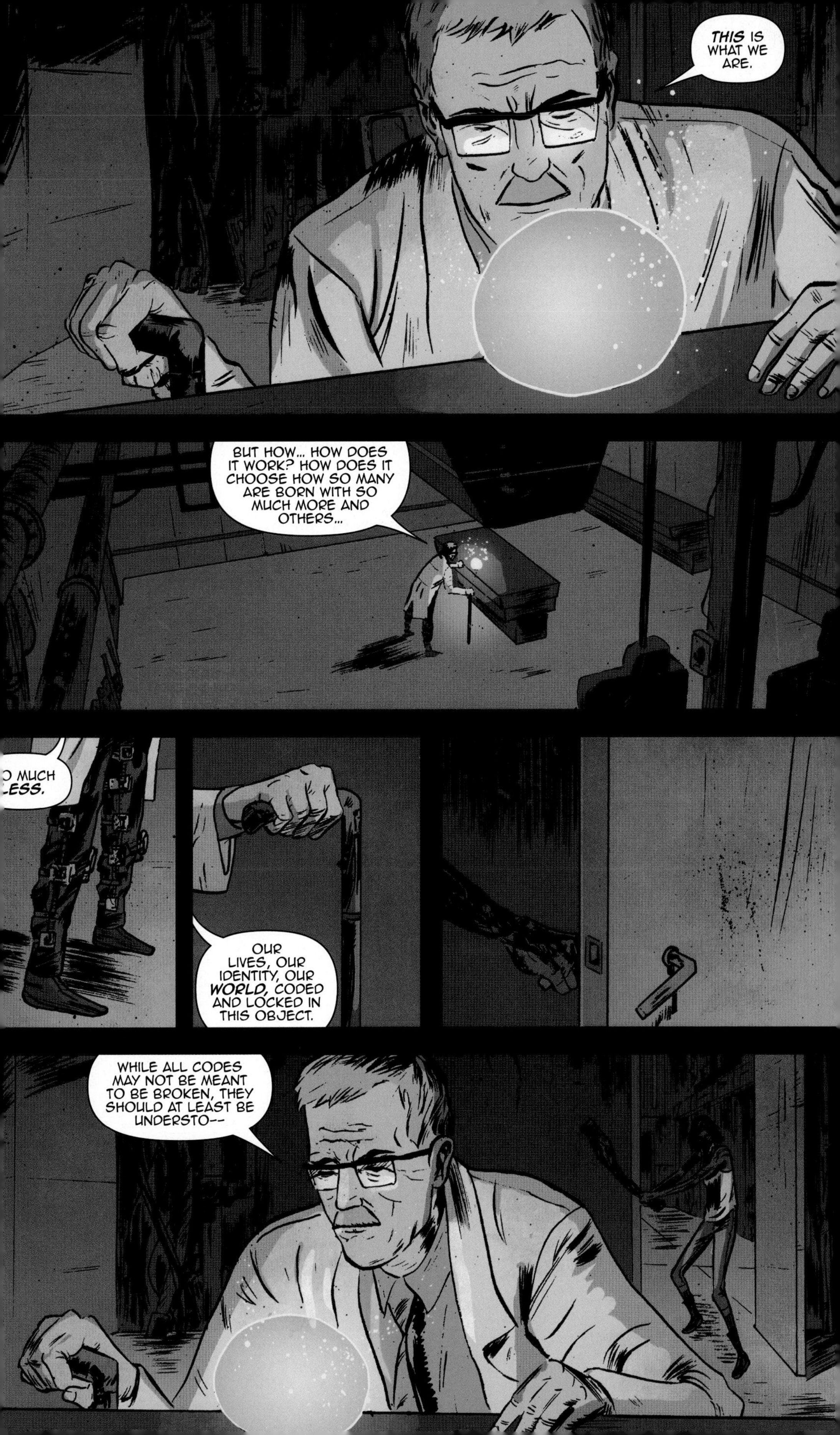
THIS IS WHAT WE ARE.
BUT HOW... HOW DOES IT WORK? HOW DOES IT CHOOSE HOW SO MANY ARE BORN WITH SO MUCH MORE AND OTHERS...
O MUCH LESS.
OUR LIVES, OUR IDENTITY, OUR WORLD, CODED AND LOCKED IN THIS OBJECT.
WHILE ALL CODES MAY NOT BE MEANT TO BE BROKEN, THEY SHOULD AT LEAST BE UNDERSTO--

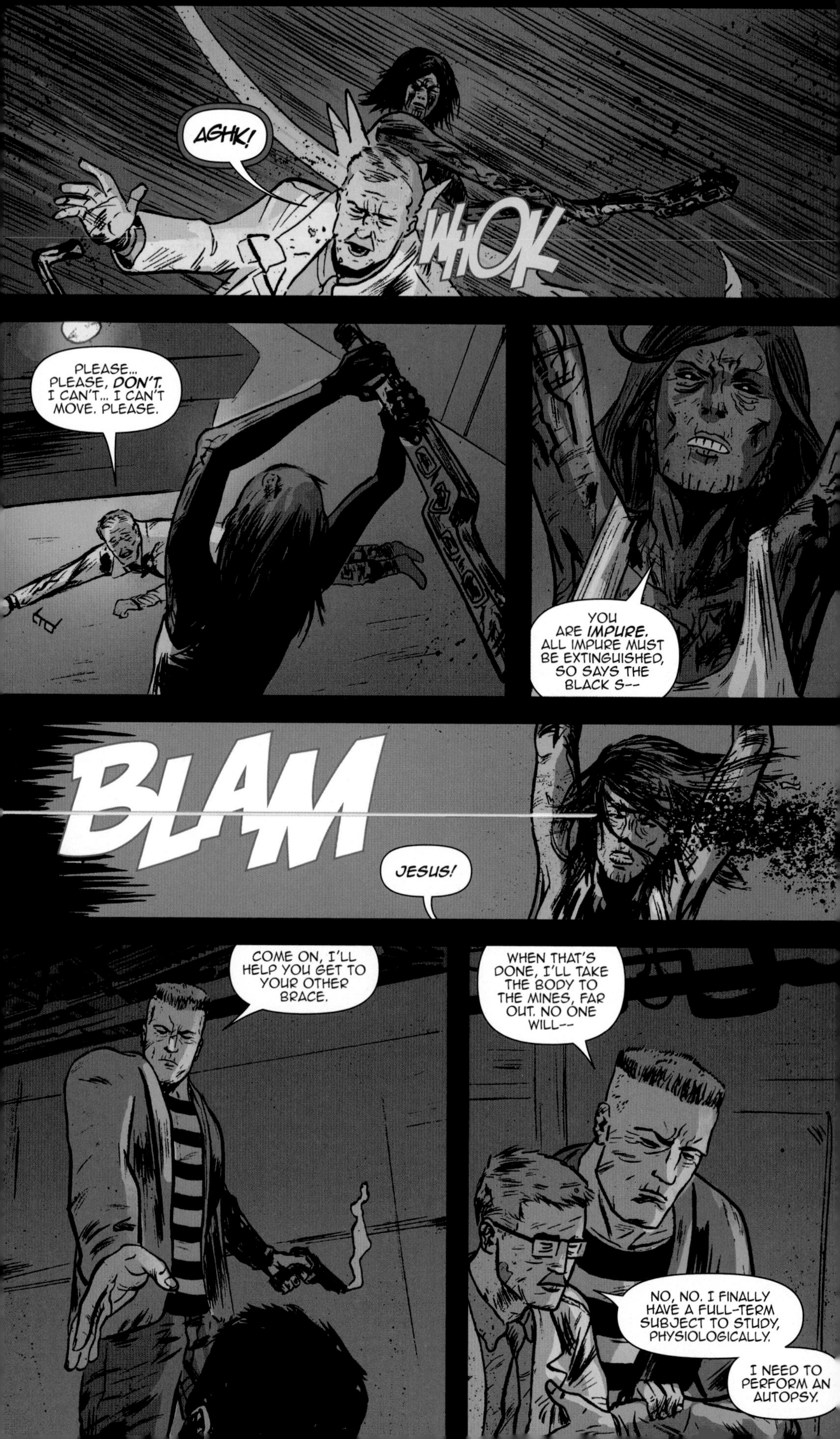
AGHK!
WHOK
PLEASE... PLEASE, *DON'T.* I CAN'T... I CAN'T MOVE. PLEASE.
YOU ARE *IMPURE.* ALL IMPURE MUST BE EXTINGUISHED, SO SAYS THE BLACK S--
BLAM
JESUS!
COME ON, I'LL HELP YOU GET TO YOUR OTHER BRACE.
WHEN THAT'S DONE, I'LL TAKE THE BODY TO THE MINES, FAR OUT. NO ONE WILL--
NO, NO. I FINALLY HAVE A FULL-TERM SUBJECT TO STUDY, PHYSIOLOGICALLY.
I NEED TO PERFORM AN AUTOPSY.

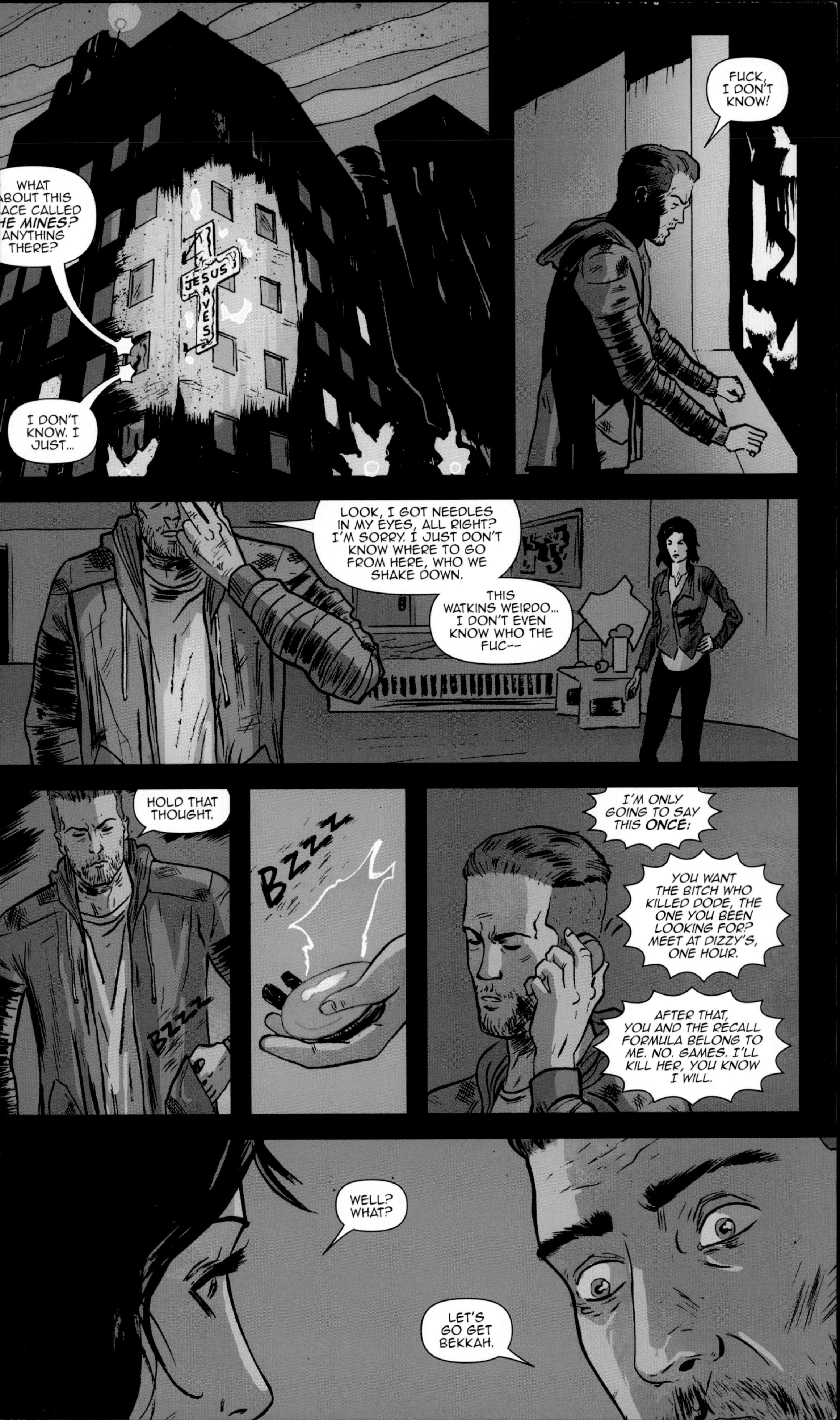
WHAT ABOUT THIS ACE CALLED HE MINES? ANYTHING THERE?
I DON'T KNOW. I JUST...
FUCK, I DON'T KNOW!
LOOK, I GOT NEEDLES IN MY EYES, ALL RIGHT? I'M SORRY. I JUST DON'T KNOW WHERE TO GO FROM HERE, WHO WE SHAKE DOWN.
THIS WATKINS WEIRDO... I DON'T EVEN KNOW WHO THE FUC--
HOLD THAT THOUGHT.
BZZZ
BZZZ
I'M ONLY GOING TO SAY THIS ONCE:
YOU WANT THE BITCH WHO KILLED DODE, THE ONE YOU BEEN LOOKING FOR? MEET AT DIZZY'S, ONE HOUR.
AFTER THAT, YOU AND THE RECALL FORMULA BELONG TO ME. NO. GAMES. I'LL KILL HER, YOU KNOW I WILL.
WELL? WHAT?
LET'S GO GET BEKKAH.

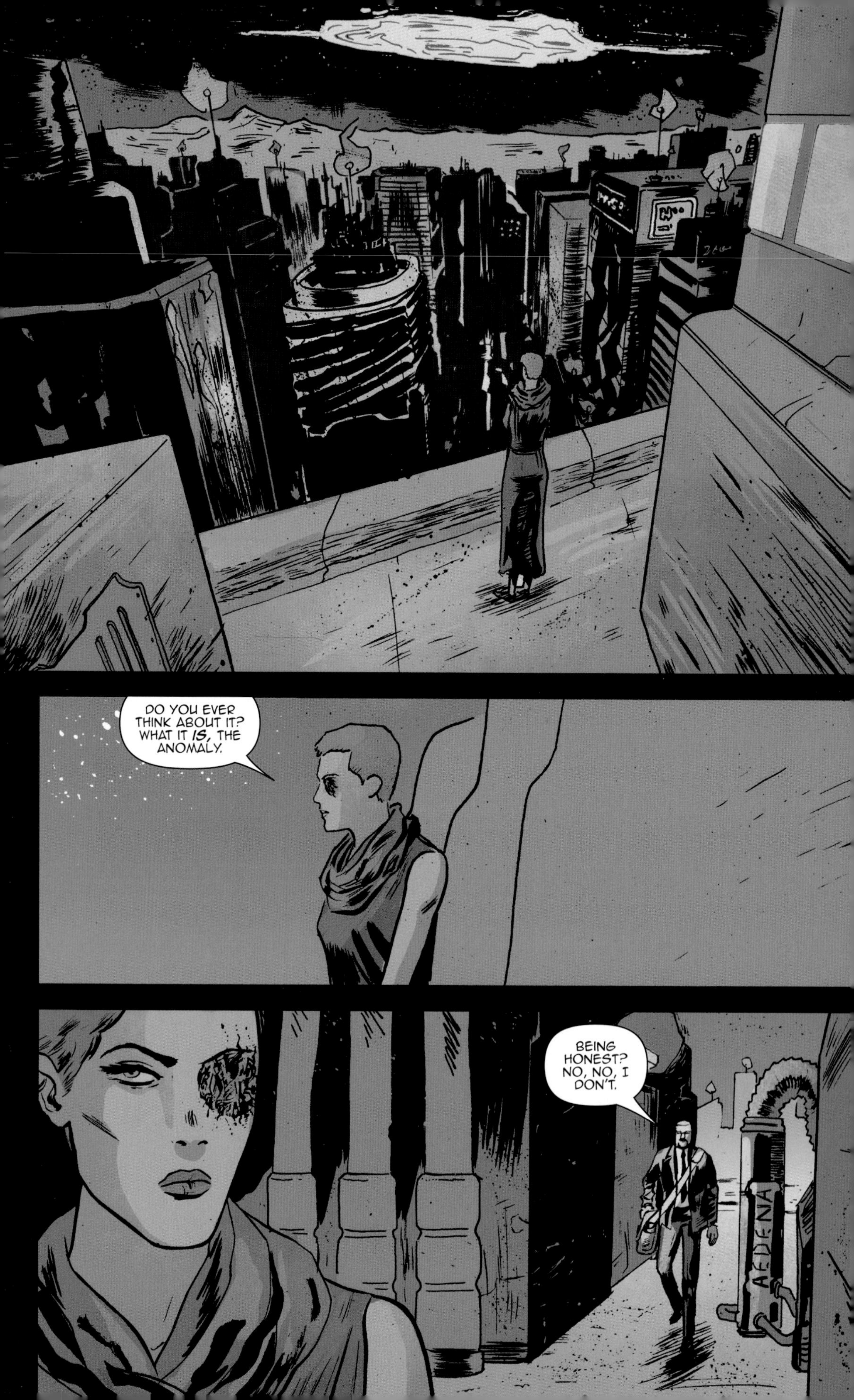

DO YOU EVER THINK ABOUT IT? WHAT IT *IS*, THE ANOMALY.
BEING HONEST? NO, NO, I DON'T.
AEDENA

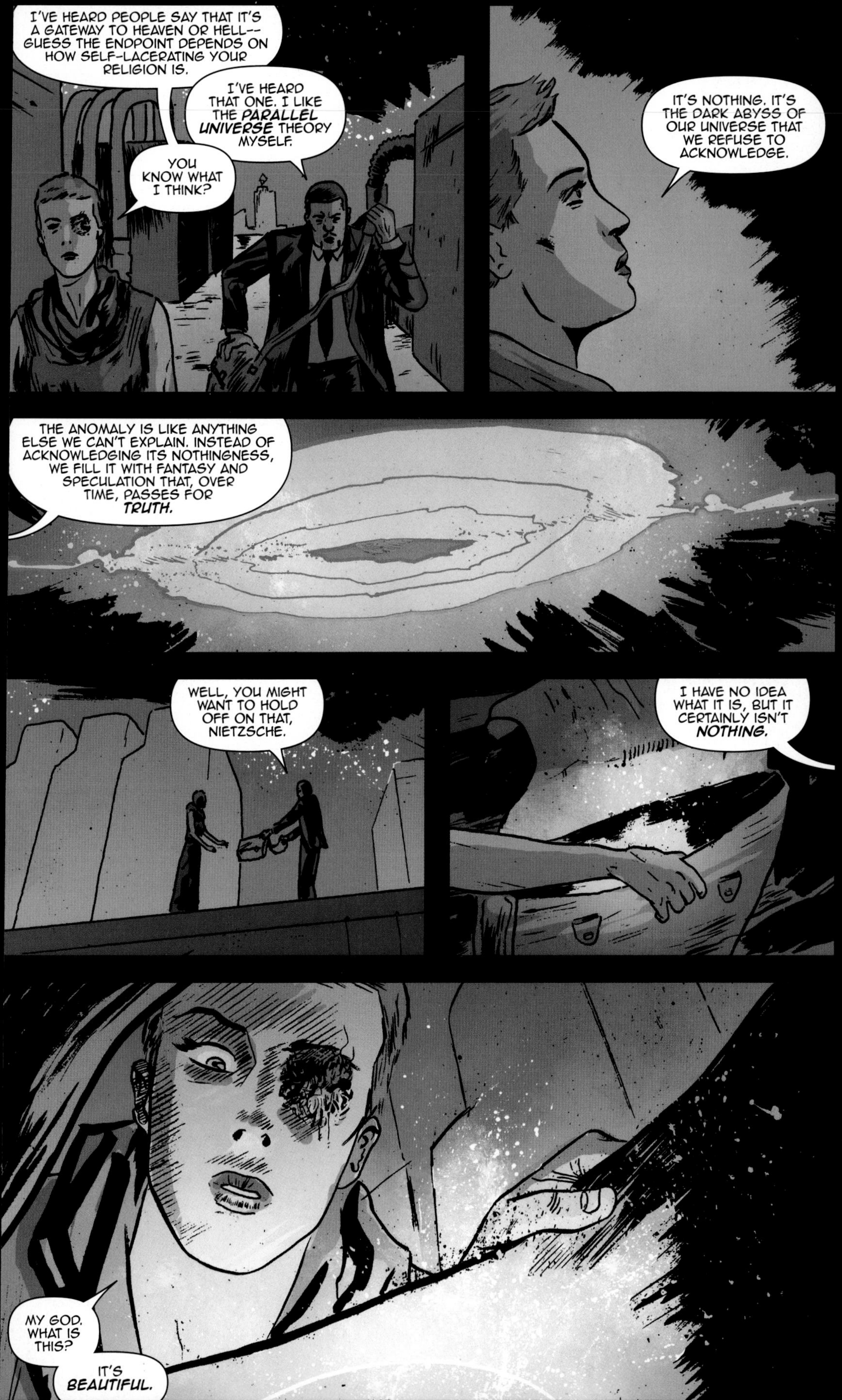
I'VE HEARD PEOPLE SAY THAT IT'S A GATEWAY TO HEAVEN OR HELL-- GUESS THE ENDPOINT DEPENDS ON HOW SELF-LACERATING YOUR RELIGION IS.
I'VE HEARD THAT ONE. I LIKE THE PARALLEL UNIVERSE THEORY MYSELF.
YOU KNOW WHAT I THINK?
IT'S NOTHING. IT'S THE DARK ABYSS OF OUR UNIVERSE THAT WE REFUSE TO ACKNOWLEDGE.
THE ANOMALY IS LIKE ANYTHING ELSE WE CAN'T EXPLAIN. INSTEAD OF ACKNOWLEDGING ITS NOTHINGNESS, WE FILL IT WITH FANTASY AND SPECULATION THAT, OVER TIME, PASSES FOR TRUTH.
WELL, YOU MIGHT WANT TO HOLD OFF ON THAT, NIETZSCHE.
I HAVE NO IDEA WHAT IT IS, BUT IT CERTAINLY ISN'T NOTHING.
MY GOD. WHAT IS THIS?
IT'S BEAUTIFUL.

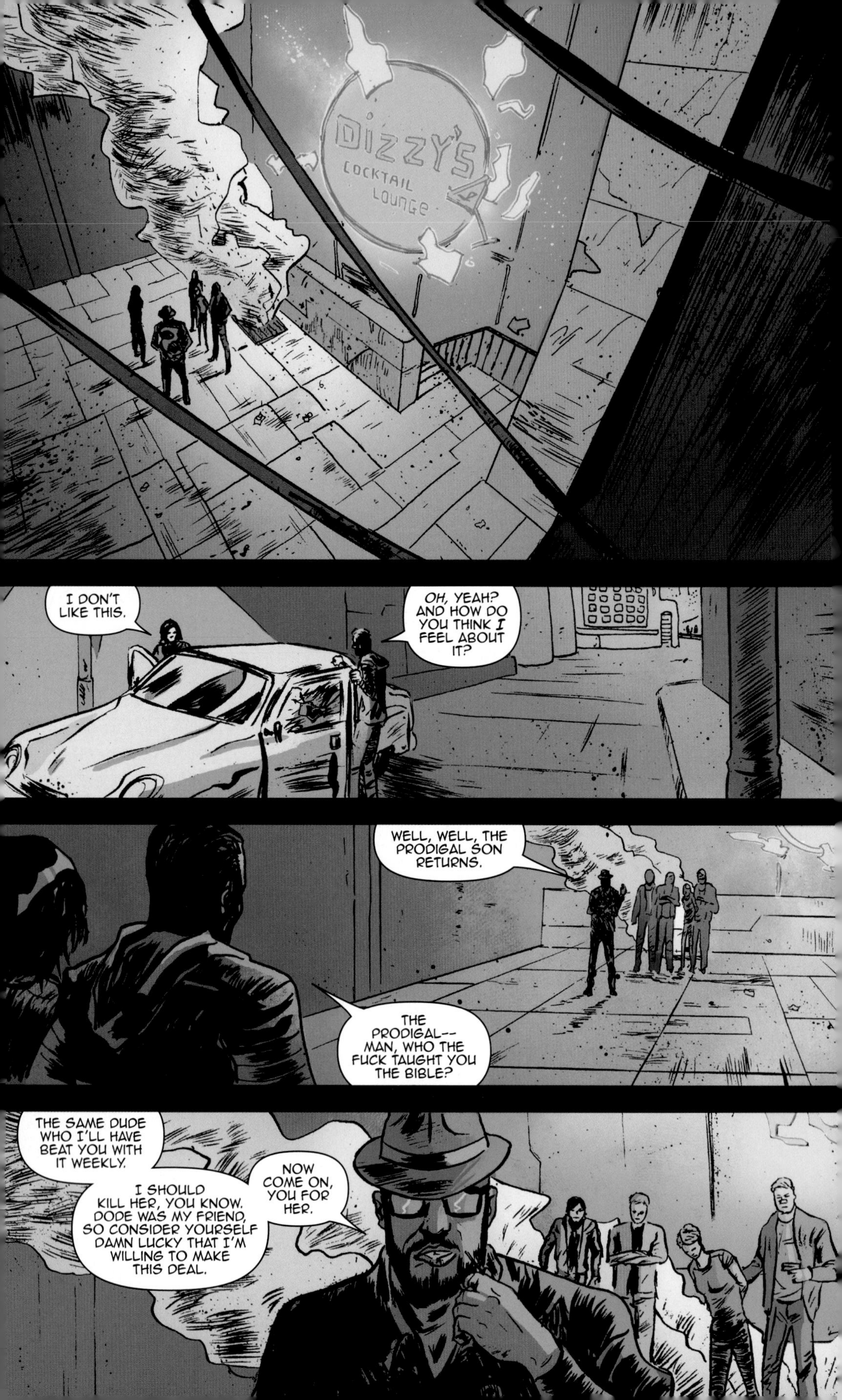
DIZZY'S
COCKTAIL
LOUNGE
I DON'T LIKE THIS.
OH, YEAH? AND HOW DO YOU THINK ***I*** FEEL ABOUT IT?
WELL, WELL, THE PRODIGAL SON RETURNS.
THE PRODIGAL-- MAN, WHO THE FUCK TAUGHT YOU THE BIBLE?
THE SAME DUDE WHO I'LL HAVE BEAT YOU WITH IT WEEKLY.
NOW COME ON, YOU FOR HER.
I SHOULD KILL HER, YOU KNOW. DODE WAS MY FRIEND, SO CONSIDER YOURSELF DAMN LUCKY THAT I'M WILLING TO MAKE THIS DEAL.

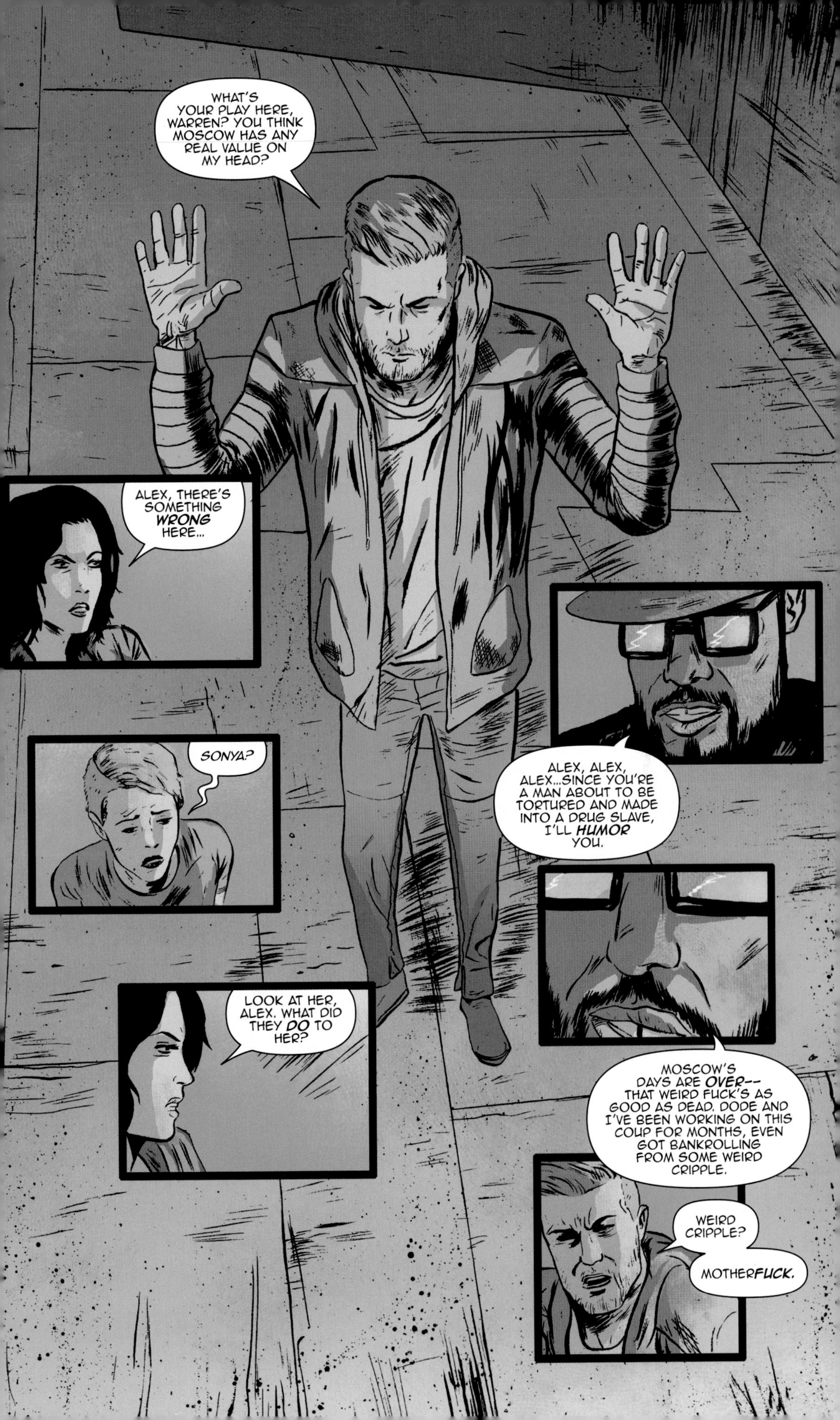
WHAT'S YOUR PLAY HERE, WARREN? YOU THINK MOSCOW HAS ANY REAL VALUE ON MY HEAD?
ALEX, THERE'S SOMETHING *WRONG* HERE...
ALEX, ALEX, ALEX...SINCE YOU'RE A MAN ABOUT TO BE TORTURED AND MADE INTO A DRUG SLAVE, I'LL *HUMOR* YOU.
SONYA?
MOSCOW'S DAYS ARE *OVER*-- THAT WEIRD FUCK'S AS GOOD AS DEAD. DODE AND I'VE BEEN WORKING ON THIS COUP FOR MONTHS, EVEN GOT BANKROLLING FROM SOME WEIRD CRIPPLE.
LOOK AT HER, ALEX. WHAT DID THEY *DO* TO HER?
WEIRD CRIPPLE?
MOTHER*FUCK.*

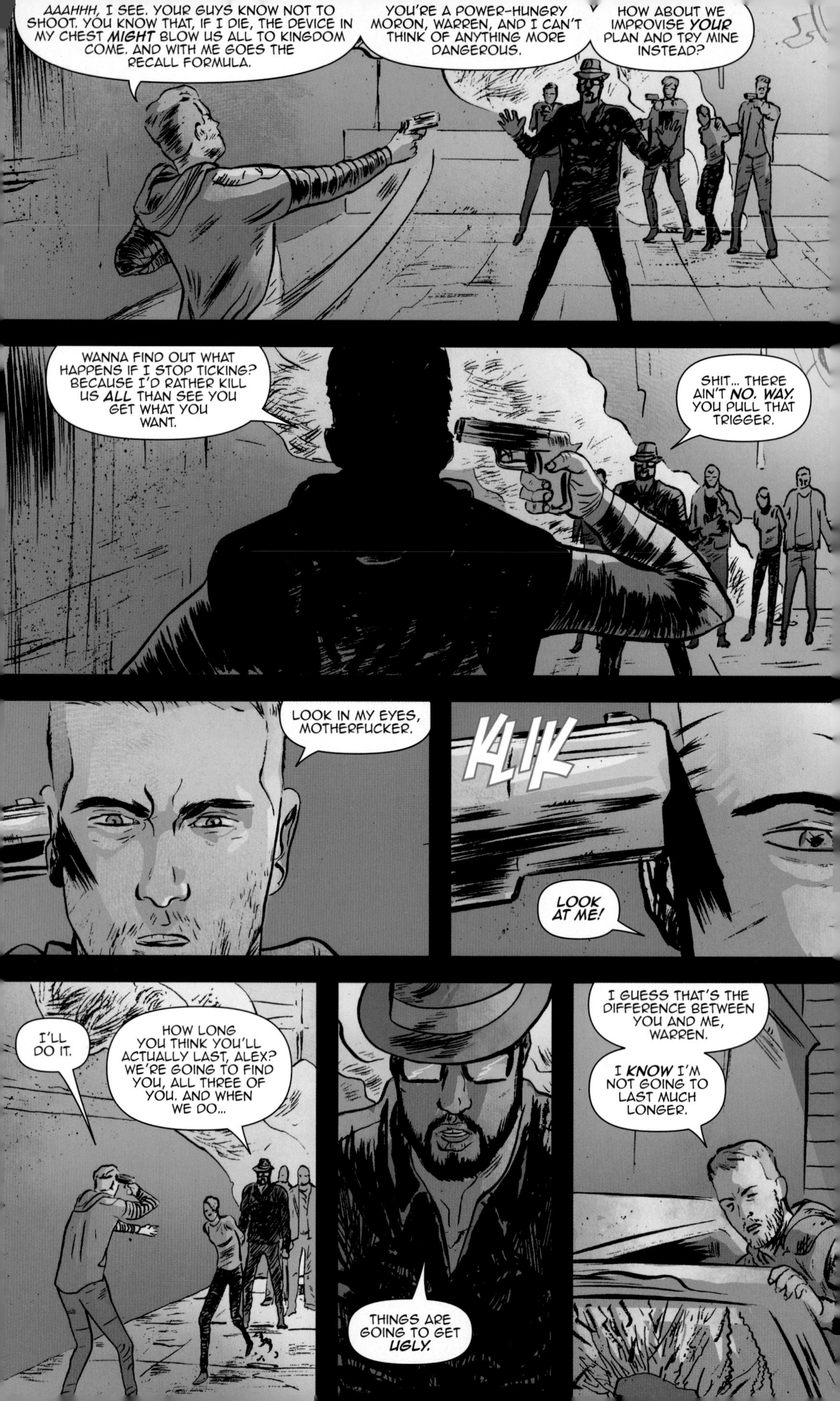
AAAHHH, I SEE. YOUR GUYS KNOW NOT TO SHOOT. YOU KNOW THAT, IF I DIE, THE DEVICE IN MY CHEST MIGHT BLOW US ALL TO KINGDOM COME. AND WITH ME GOES THE RECALL FORMULA.
YOU'RE A POWER-HUNGRY MORON, WARREN, AND I CAN'T THINK OF ANYTHING MORE DANGEROUS.
HOW ABOUT WE IMPROVISE YOUR PLAN AND TRY MINE INSTEAD?
WANNA FIND OUT WHAT HAPPENS IF I STOP TICKING? BECAUSE I'D RATHER KILL US ALL THAN SEE YOU GET WHAT YOU WANT.
SHIT... THERE AIN'T NO. WAY. YOU PULL THAT TRIGGER.
LOOK IN MY EYES, MOTHERFUCKER.
KLIK
LOOK AT ME!
I'LL DO IT.
HOW LONG YOU THINK YOU'LL ACTUALLY LAST, ALEX? WE'RE GOING TO FIND YOU, ALL THREE OF YOU. AND WHEN WE DO...
THINGS ARE GOING TO GET UGLY.
I GUESS THAT'S THE DIFFERENCE BETWEEN YOU AND ME, WARREN.
I KNOW I'M NOT GOING TO LAST MUCH LONGER.

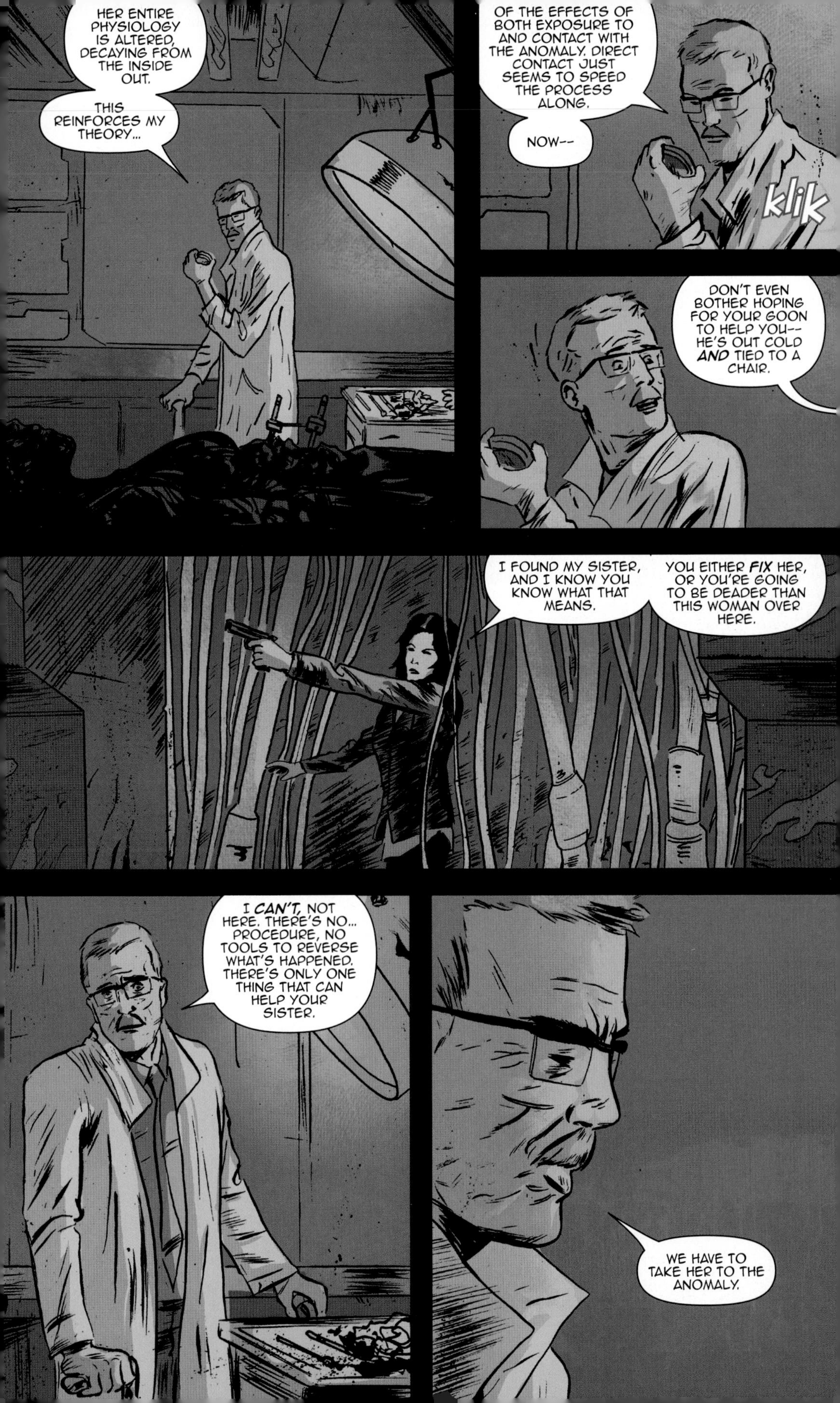
HER ENTIRE PHYSIOLOGY IS ALTERED, DECAYING FROM THE INSIDE OUT.
THIS REINFORCES MY THEORY...
OF THE EFFECTS OF BOTH EXPOSURE TO AND CONTACT WITH THE ANOMALY. DIRECT CONTACT JUST SEEMS TO SPEED THE PROCESS ALONG.
NOW--
klik
DON'T EVEN BOTHER HOPING FOR YOUR GOON TO HELP YOU-- HE'S OUT COLD AND TIED TO A CHAIR.
I FOUND MY SISTER, AND I KNOW YOU KNOW WHAT THAT MEANS.
YOU EITHER FIX HER, OR YOU'RE GOING TO BE DEADER THAN THIS WOMAN OVER HERE.
I CAN'T, NOT HERE. THERE'S NO... PROCEDURE, NO TOOLS TO REVERSE WHAT'S HAPPENED. THERE'S ONLY ONE THING THAT CAN HELP YOUR SISTER.
WE HAVE TO TAKE HER TO THE ANOMALY.

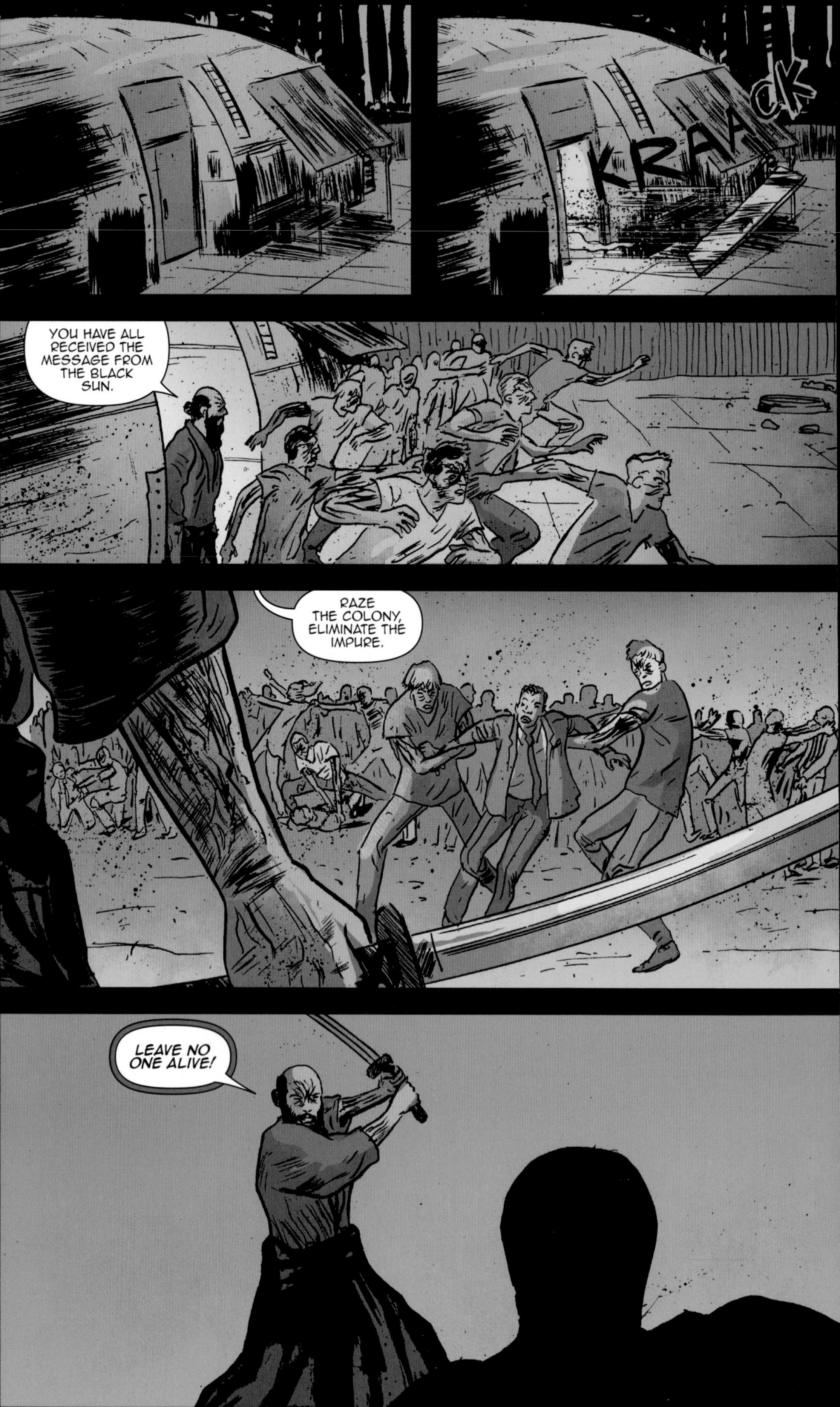

KRAACK
YOU HAVE ALL RECEIVED THE MESSAGE FROM THE BLACK SUN.
RAZE THE COLONY, ELIMINATE THE IMPURE.
LEAVE NO ONE ALIVE!

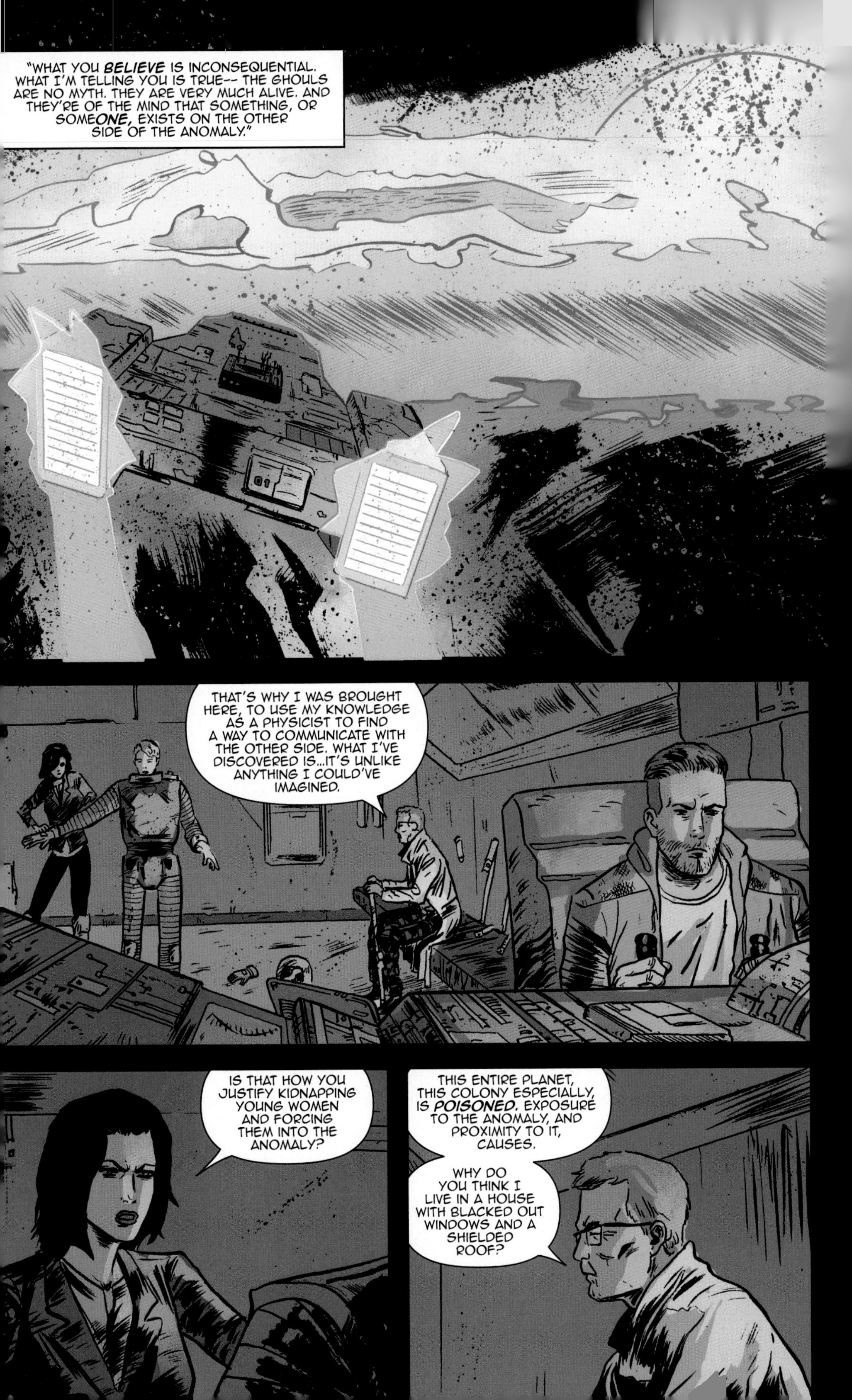
"WHAT YOU BELIEVE IS INCONSEQUENTIAL. WHAT I'M TELLING YOU IS TRUE-- THE GHOULS ARE NO MYTH. THEY ARE VERY MUCH ALIVE. AND THEY'RE OF THE MIND THAT SOMETHING, OR SOMEONE, EXISTS ON THE OTHER SIDE OF THE ANOMALY."
THAT'S WHY I WAS BROUGHT HERE, TO USE MY KNOWLEDGE AS A PHYSICIST TO FIND A WAY TO COMMUNICATE WITH THE OTHER SIDE. WHAT I'VE DISCOVERED IS...IT'S UNLIKE ANYTHING I COULD'VE IMAGINED.
IS THAT HOW YOU JUSTIFY KIDNAPPING YOUNG WOMEN AND FORCING THEM INTO THE ANOMALY?
THIS ENTIRE PLANET, THIS COLONY ESPECIALLY, IS POISONED. EXPOSURE TO THE ANOMALY, AND PROXIMITY TO IT, CAUSES.
WHY DO YOU THINK I LIVE IN A HOUSE WITH BLACKED OUT WINDOWS AND A SHIELDED ROOF?

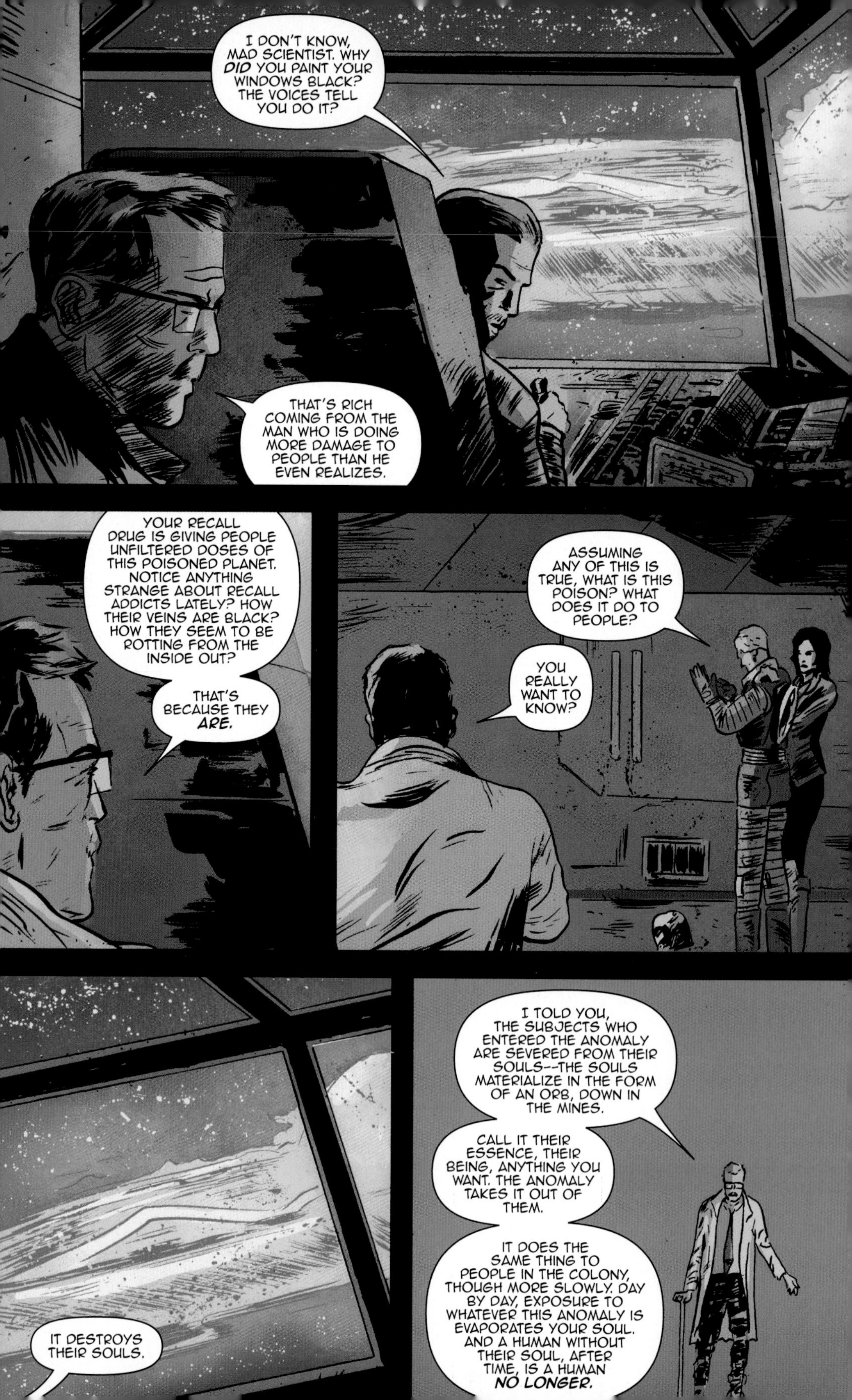
I DON'T KNOW, MAD SCIENTIST. WHY DID YOU PAINT YOUR WINDOWS BLACK? THE VOICES TELL YOU DO IT?
THAT'S RICH COMING FROM THE MAN WHO IS DOING MORE DAMAGE TO PEOPLE THAN HE EVEN REALIZES.
YOUR RECALL DRUG IS GIVING PEOPLE UNFILTERED DOSES OF THIS POISONED PLANET. NOTICE ANYTHING STRANGE ABOUT RECALL ADDICTS LATELY? HOW THEIR VEINS ARE BLACK? HOW THEY SEEM TO BE ROTTING FROM THE INSIDE OUT?
THAT'S BECAUSE THEY ARE.
ASSUMING ANY OF THIS IS TRUE, WHAT IS THIS POISON? WHAT DOES IT DO TO PEOPLE?
YOU REALLY WANT TO KNOW?
IT DESTROYS THEIR SOULS.
I TOLD YOU, THE SUBJECTS WHO ENTERED THE ANOMALY ARE SEVERED FROM THEIR SOULS--THE SOULS MATERIALIZE IN THE FORM OF AN ORB, DOWN IN THE MINES.
CALL IT THEIR ESSENCE, THEIR BEING, ANYTHING YOU WANT. THE ANOMALY TAKES IT OUT OF THEM.
IT DOES THE SAME THING TO PEOPLE IN THE COLONY, THOUGH MORE SLOWLY. DAY BY DAY, EXPOSURE TO WHATEVER THIS ANOMALY IS EVAPORATES YOUR SOUL. AND A HUMAN WITHOUT THEIR SOUL, AFTER TIME, IS A HUMAN NO LONGER.

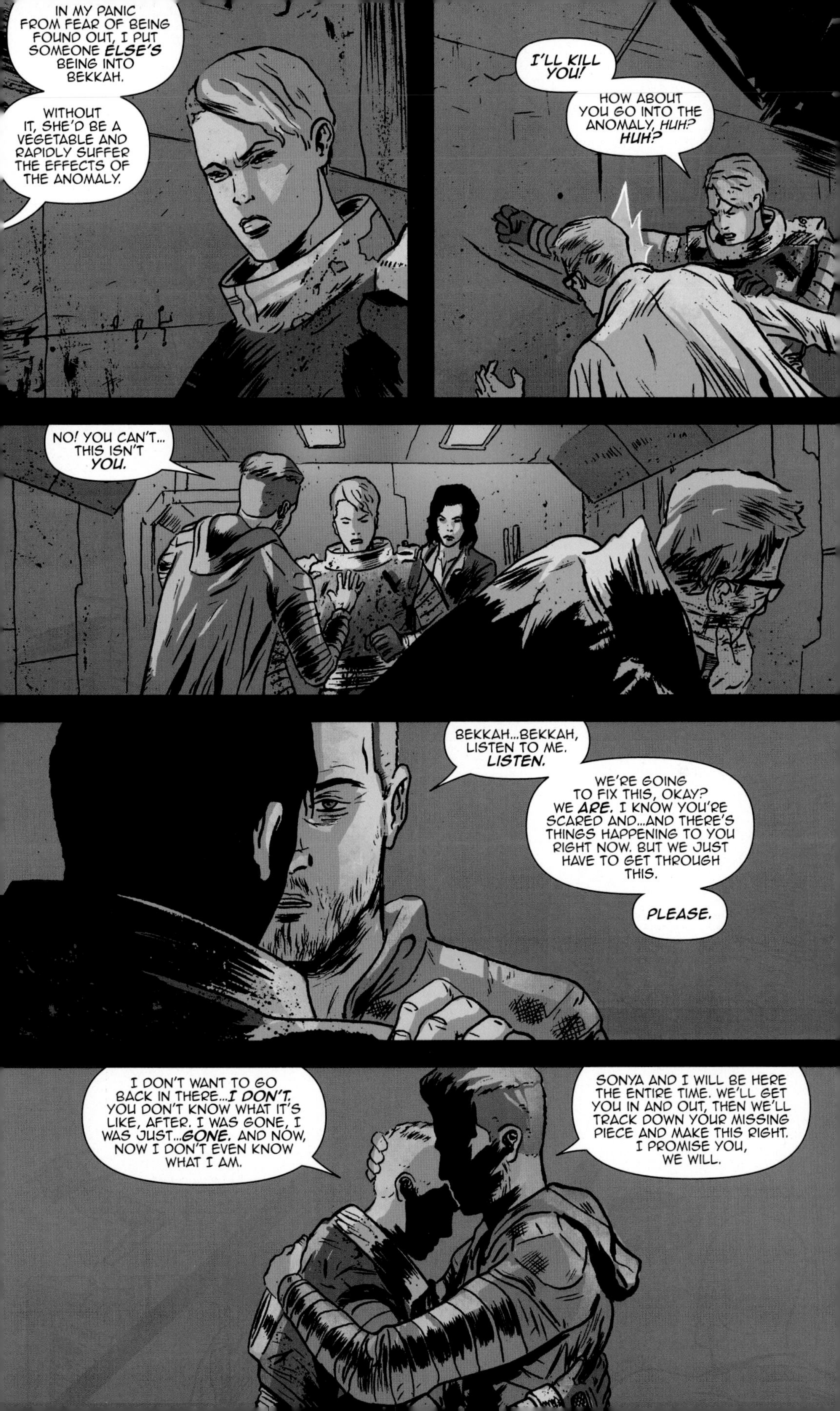
IN MY PANIC FROM FEAR OF BEING FOUND OUT, I PUT SOMEONE ELSE'S BEING INTO BEKKAH.
WITHOUT IT, SHE'D BE A VEGETABLE AND RAPIDLY SUFFER THE EFFECTS OF THE ANOMALY.
I'LL KILL YOU!
HOW ABOUT YOU GO INTO THE ANOMALY, HUH? HUH?
NO! YOU CAN'T... THIS ISN'T YOU.
BEKKAH...BEKKAH, LISTEN TO ME. LISTEN.
WE'RE GOING TO FIX THIS, OKAY? WE ARE. I KNOW YOU'RE SCARED AND...AND THERE'S THINGS HAPPENING TO YOU RIGHT NOW. BUT WE JUST HAVE TO GET THROUGH THIS.
PLEASE.
I DON'T WANT TO GO BACK IN THERE...I DON'T. YOU DON'T KNOW WHAT IT'S LIKE, AFTER. I WAS GONE, I WAS JUST...GONE. AND NOW, NOW I DON'T EVEN KNOW WHAT I AM.
SONYA AND I WILL BE HERE THE ENTIRE TIME. WE'LL GET YOU IN AND OUT, THEN WE'LL TRACK DOWN YOUR MISSING PIECE AND MAKE THIS RIGHT. I PROMISE YOU, WE WILL.

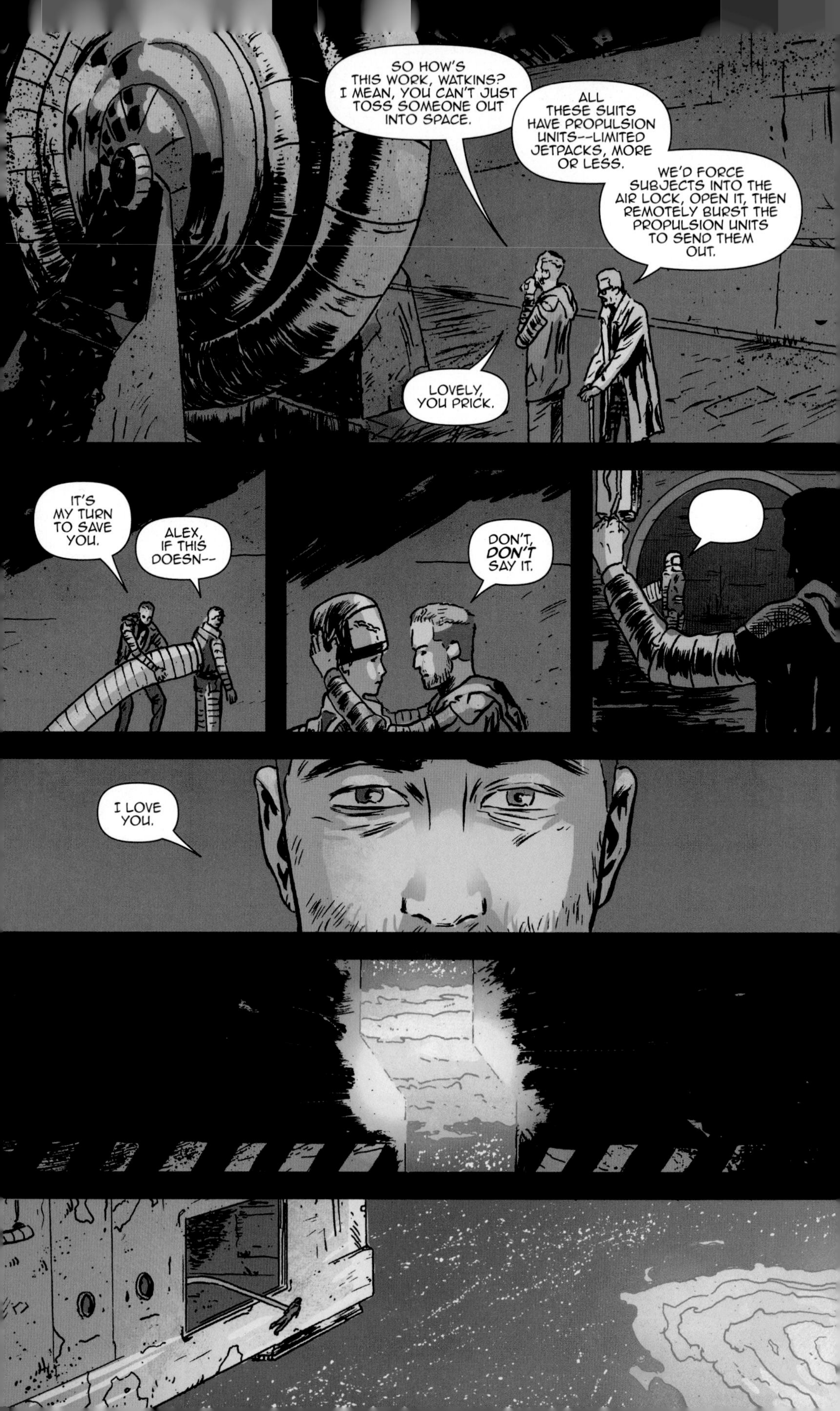
SO HOW'S THIS WORK, WATKINS? I MEAN, YOU CAN'T JUST TOSS SOMEONE OUT INTO SPACE.
ALL THESE SUITS HAVE PROPULSION UNITS--LIMITED JETPACKS, MORE OR LESS.
WE'D FORCE SUBJECTS INTO THE AIR LOCK, OPEN IT, THEN REMOTELY BURST THE PROPULSION UNITS TO SEND THEM OUT.
LOVELY, YOU PRICK.
IT'S MY TURN TO SAVE YOU.
ALEX, IF THIS DOESN--
DON'T, *DON'T* SAY IT.
I LOVE YOU.

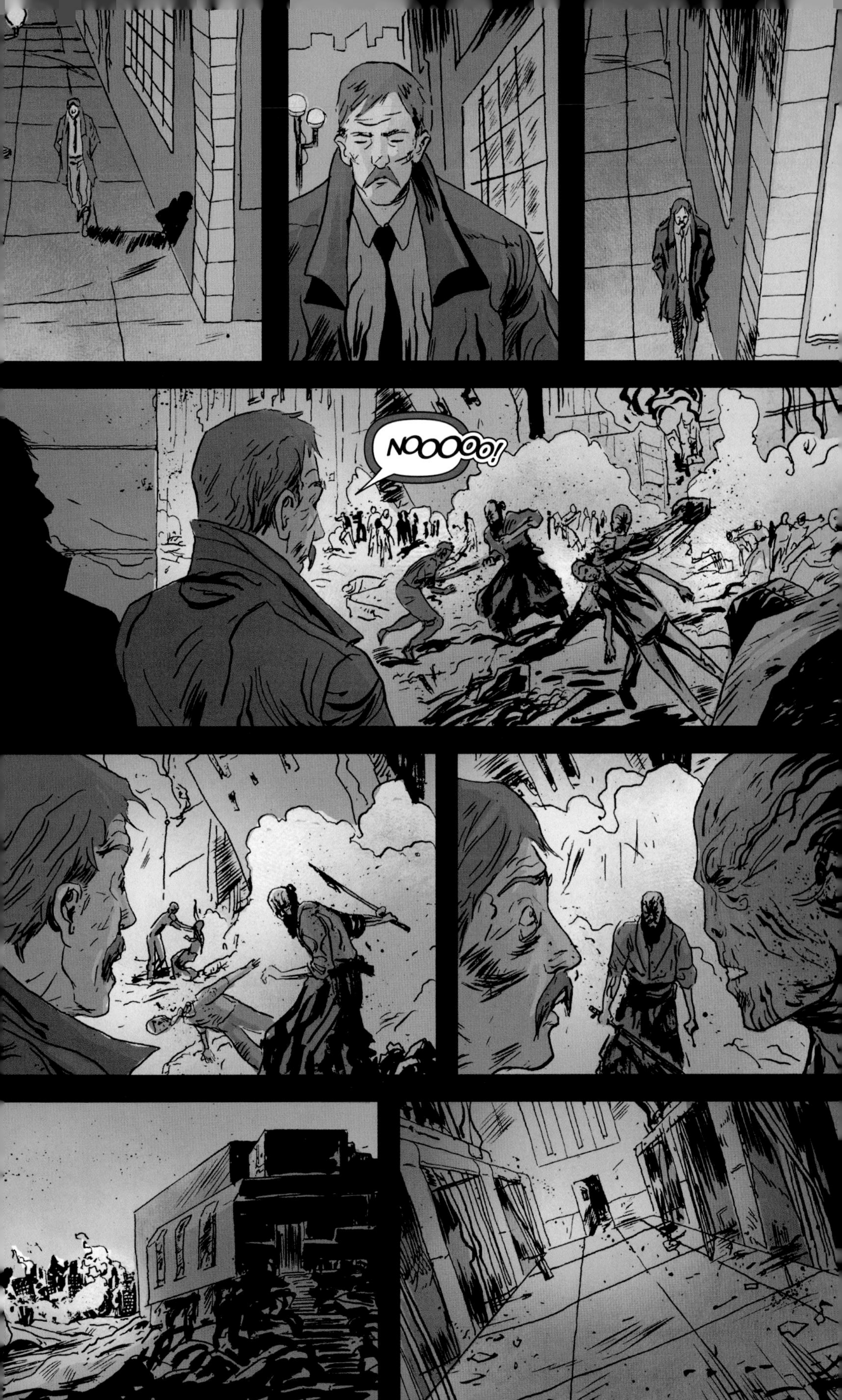
NOOOOO!

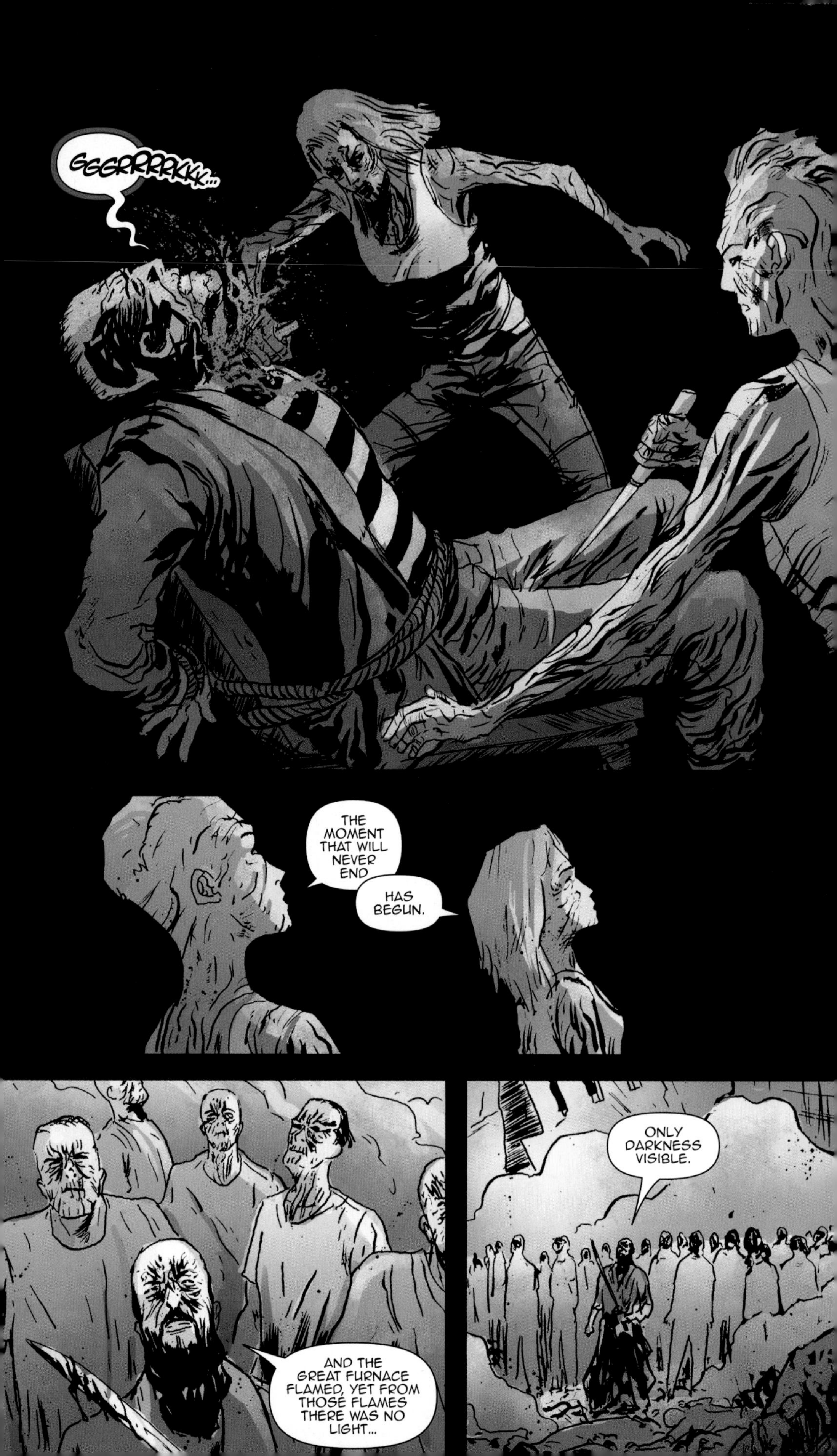
GGGRRRRRKKK...
THE MOMENT THAT WILL NEVER END
HAS BEGUN.
AND THE GREAT FURNACE FLAMED, YET FROM THOSE FLAMES THERE WAS NO LIGHT...
ONLY DARKNESS VISIBLE.

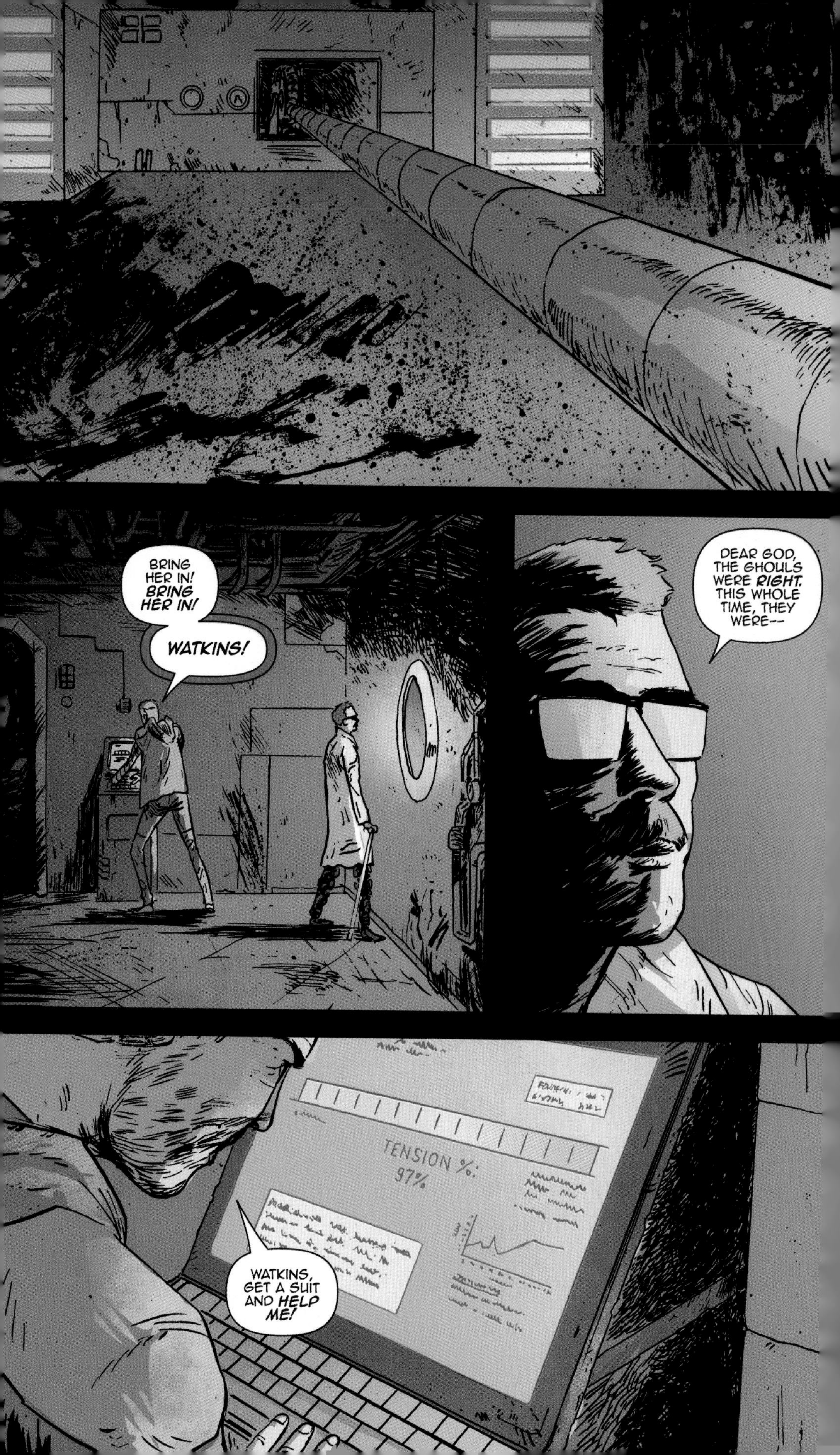
BRING HER IN! BRING HER IN!
WATKINS!
DEAR GOD, THE GHOULS WERE RIGHT. THIS WHOLE TIME, THEY WERE--
TENSION %: 97%
WATKINS, GET A SUIT AND HELP ME!

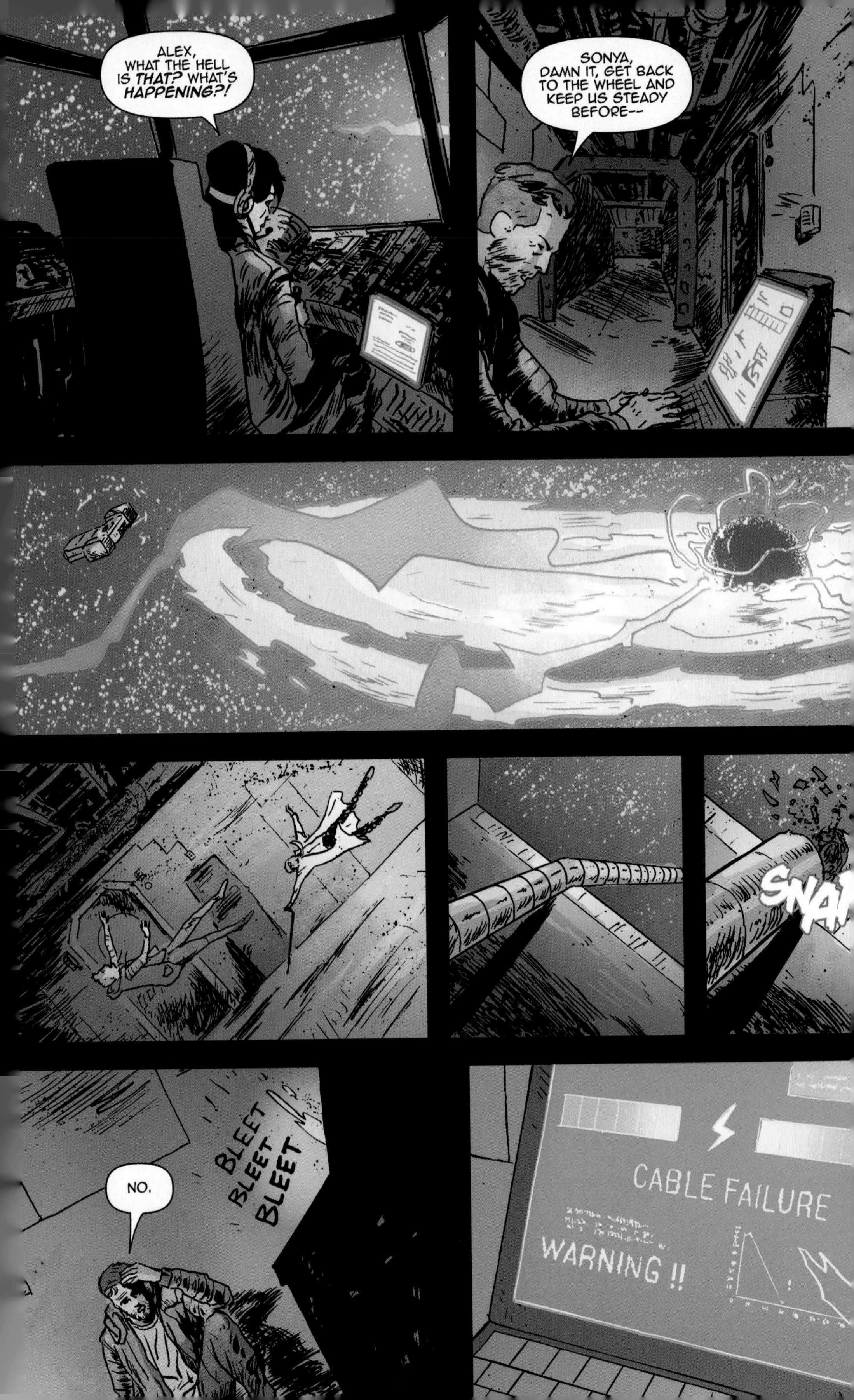
ALEX, WHAT THE HELL IS THAT? WHAT'S HAPPENING?!
SONYA, DAMN IT, GET BACK TO THE WHEEL AND KEEP US STEADY BEFORE--
SNA
BLEET
BLEET
BLEET
NO.
CABLE FAILURE
WARNING !!

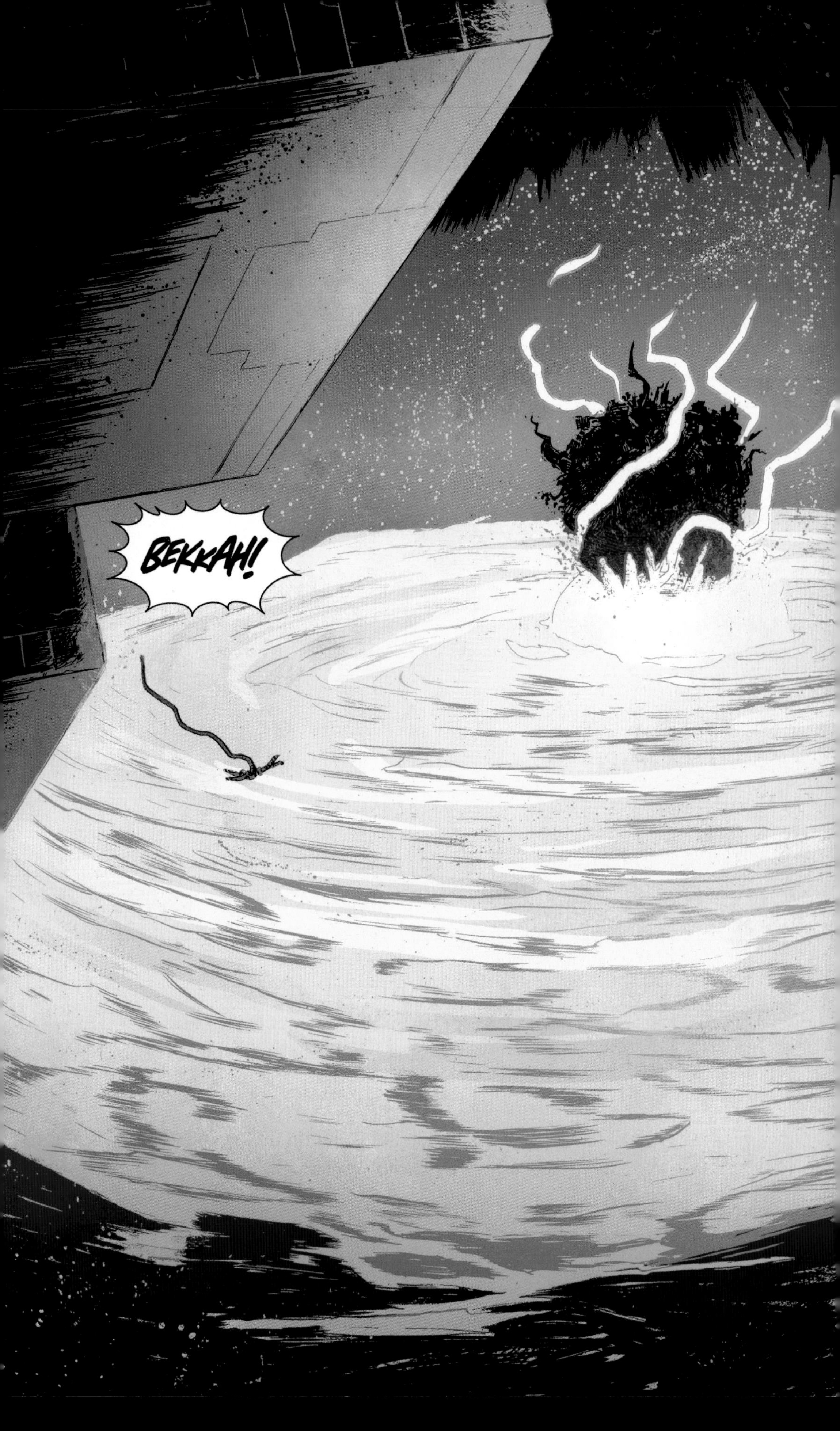
BEKKAH!

PHILLIP CURIONE ON REVISITING KUBRICK'S GENIUS

THE RESERVE

THE RESERVE MAGAZINE/$19.

VANISHING POINT

How to Lose a Planet: *The Failure of Roche Limit*

By Sammy Kannan

ARGO NOT

Did a Mysterious Satellite Land on the Argo Comet?

By Lucius Andrews

CROSSPATHS

Fiction

By E.Lauryn Daniel

Also: *Jackson Noah, Olivia Vienne*

ntinued from page 18)

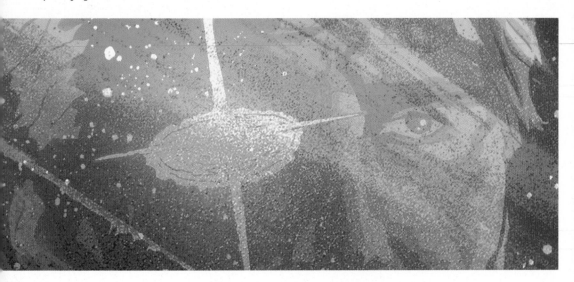

eams are only as good as the usefulness they
vide."

says Sana Fiedler, CEO of MoiraTech, on her
olvement with Langford Skaargred. Fiedler, along
a MoiraTech co-founders Don Lexington and
ndall Fife, are known to have bailed out Skaargred
r he poured his considerable wealth into building a
ony on Dispater—a decision many call the blunder of
century.

ngford had vision and the soul of a pioneer," Fife
, "but he never once considered the practical gain of
undertaking."

argred's mission, as most understand it, was to build
pace colony that would serve as a waypoint for
nkind's next step in space exploration. It was the stuff
paperback sci-fi novels from the mid-20th century:
overing new worlds, bumping into little green men,
be even a brush with time travel. The reality
argred faced, though, was far less fantastical.

lenges mounted for Skaargred. Terraforming the
ace required more work than expected, which
uired more workers, and that meant more costly
el from Earth to Dispater. Water from below the
ace was harder to obtain than originally planned.
tragic crash of Orbital flight 942, which burned up
route to the Roche Limit Colony, took with it
ions of dollars of supplies and materials, a lot of
ch was worth more than any insurance policy could
ount for. And through it all, there was Skaargred on
distant world, losing everything—his fortune, his
ims, and, according to some, his mind.

then, as most people were forgetting about
argred and his ill-fated voyage in space, Dispater
nd a new lease on life.

Fiedler, Lexington, and Fife gave Dispater the life
support it needed, providing resources, a committed
team of scientists straight from the award-winning
MoiraTech labs, and a spirit of innovation that was still
rooted in pragmatism. They bought out Skaargred's
Galactic Enterprises and quickly invested in initiatives
that would make Dispater, if nothing else, useful in some
way. With a focus on mining Dispater for energy
resources, Fiedler, Lexington, and Fife set out to discover
something, anything, that would make this distant dwarf
planet useful to the home Skaargred had all but
forgotten—Earth.

"We need a purpose for the endeavor," Lexington said.
"There's time to pursue Skaargred's vision, but not at the
sake of abandoning all the potential that Dispater
holds."

And so began the massive—and expensive—operation of
drilling into Dispater and shifting from one man's
singular vision to one corporation's drive for discoveries
and, ultimately, profit. Somewhere in these diametrically
opposed ambitions is where the entire endeavor came
undone for everyone involved. Any good that could have
been seems, now, like a faded memory that exists on the
fringes of your mind, waiting to be forgotten.

The undertaking required for MoiraTech's mission
required a significant uptick in workers, housing, and
resources. The Roche Limit Colony became an
intergalactic Pullman District, attracting all the wrong
kinds of people to meet its need for the task at hand.
One glance at the employment records of the individuals
MoiraTech hired and brought to Roche Limit paints the
entire picture; in the first wave alone, the percentage of
ex-convicts transported to Roche Limit was a staggering
71%. The remaining 29%, you can argue, were desperate
enough to take employment on another planet, leading
to serious questions about their mindset.

Cultural anthropologist Farrah Lang pointed out a key element of taking a job on Dispater at this time:

"Keep in mind—there was no guarantee of coming back. Space travel was still somewhat perilous and the conditions on Roche Limit, for the most part, were completely unknown. The men and women who traveled there for MoiraTech in those early days literally had no idea what they were getting into or if they'd ever return to Earth."

But MoiraTech wasn't thinking about the powder keg they were creating right under its nose. In an internal document that was leaked last year, Fife notes that the goal was to not only keep costs down in employing the largely unemployable, but to shield the company from the unknown risks that the planet might hold by hiring individuals who, more or less, wouldn't be missed.

Resultant, the rogues gallery that MoiraTech populated Roche Limit with soon stumbled into their usual habits of vice, crime, and other unsavory habits. Construction came to a halt—the very idea of discovering an essential resource (other than the mineral used to make, appropriately, the drug known as Recall) ran a distant second to, somehow, maintaining order on the colony.

And that is when things began to get strange.

As law officials on Earth turned a blind eye to R Limit—with its ills contained neatly in another ga why wouldn't they?—strange reports began circulati to what was happening in this distant world. Fact fiction began to blend, it still does, weaving a tapes unlivable conditions and strange occurrences. Lang went missing, presumed dead. The same fate rumored to capture Fiedler, Lexington, and Fife—the with a strange twist.

Urban legend calls them ghouls—the former Moira heads, who haven't been seen or heard from in mo are now the ghastly myth of Roche Limit. While tragic ends seems far more likely—most presume MoiraTech compound was invaded by denizens—stories still persist that all three of them very much alive, though much different than they were. Witnesses—their credibility assumed with a ma grain of salt—claim Fiedler, Lexington, and Fife are h of their former selves, their skin gray and decayed zombies, their minds existing on some sort of c plane. While no evidence has been produced to such claims, the bizarre legend that has manufactured only deepens the mysteries of R Limit.

Currently, Dispater and the colony it houses are a fa that most people on Earth would rather soon fo From the dreams of an eccentric billionaire to ambitions of an international corporation, Roche I has engendered nothing but

(continued on page

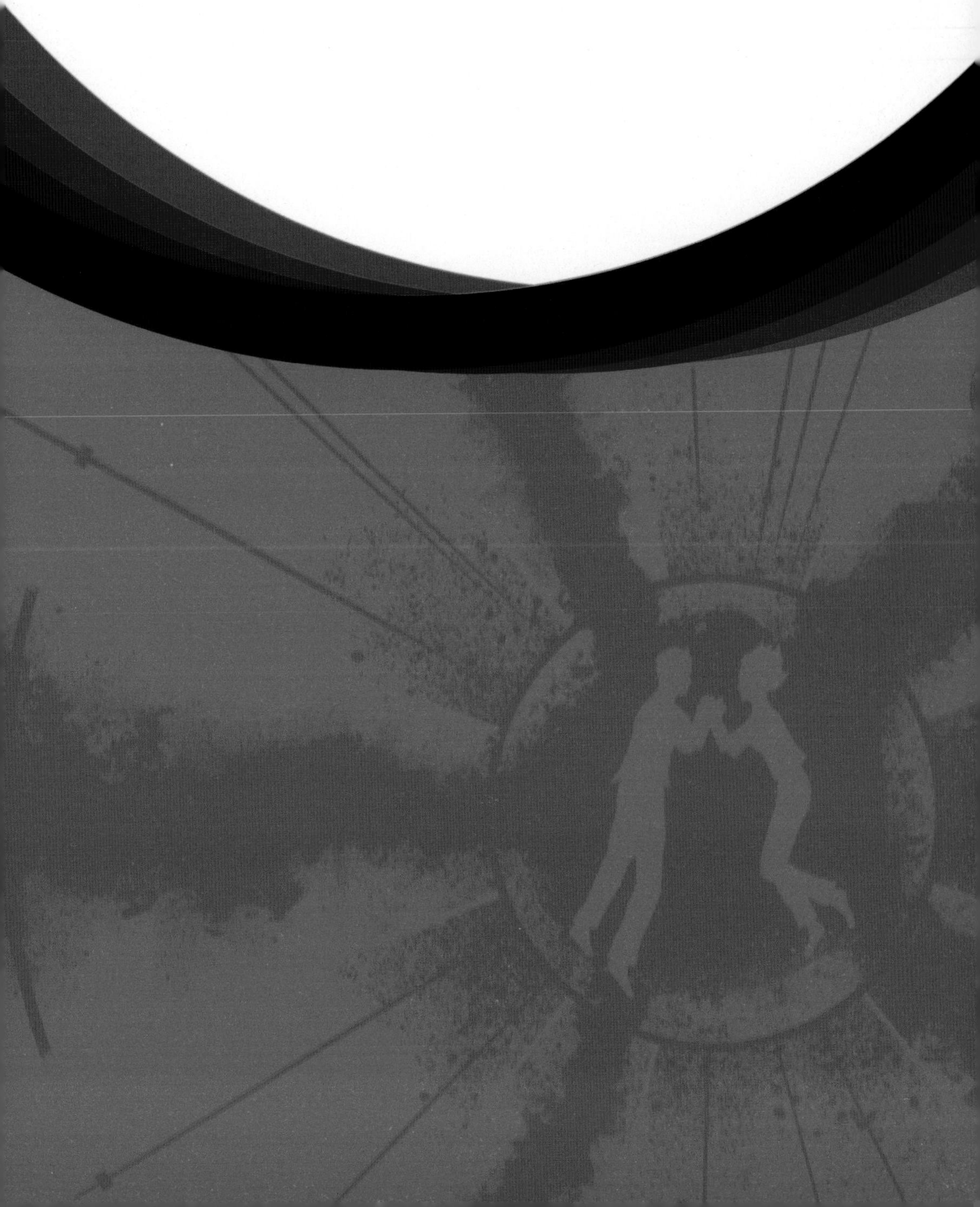

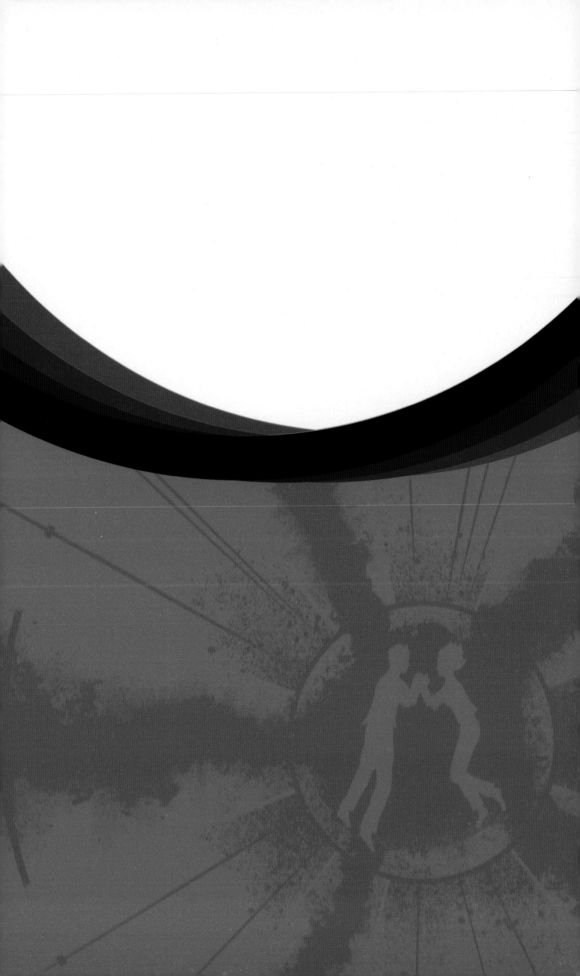

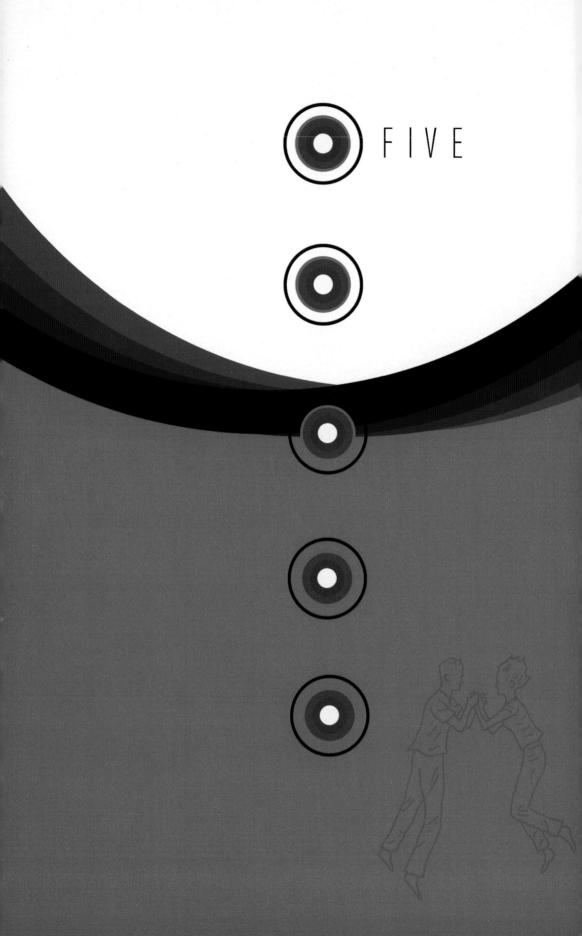

FIVE

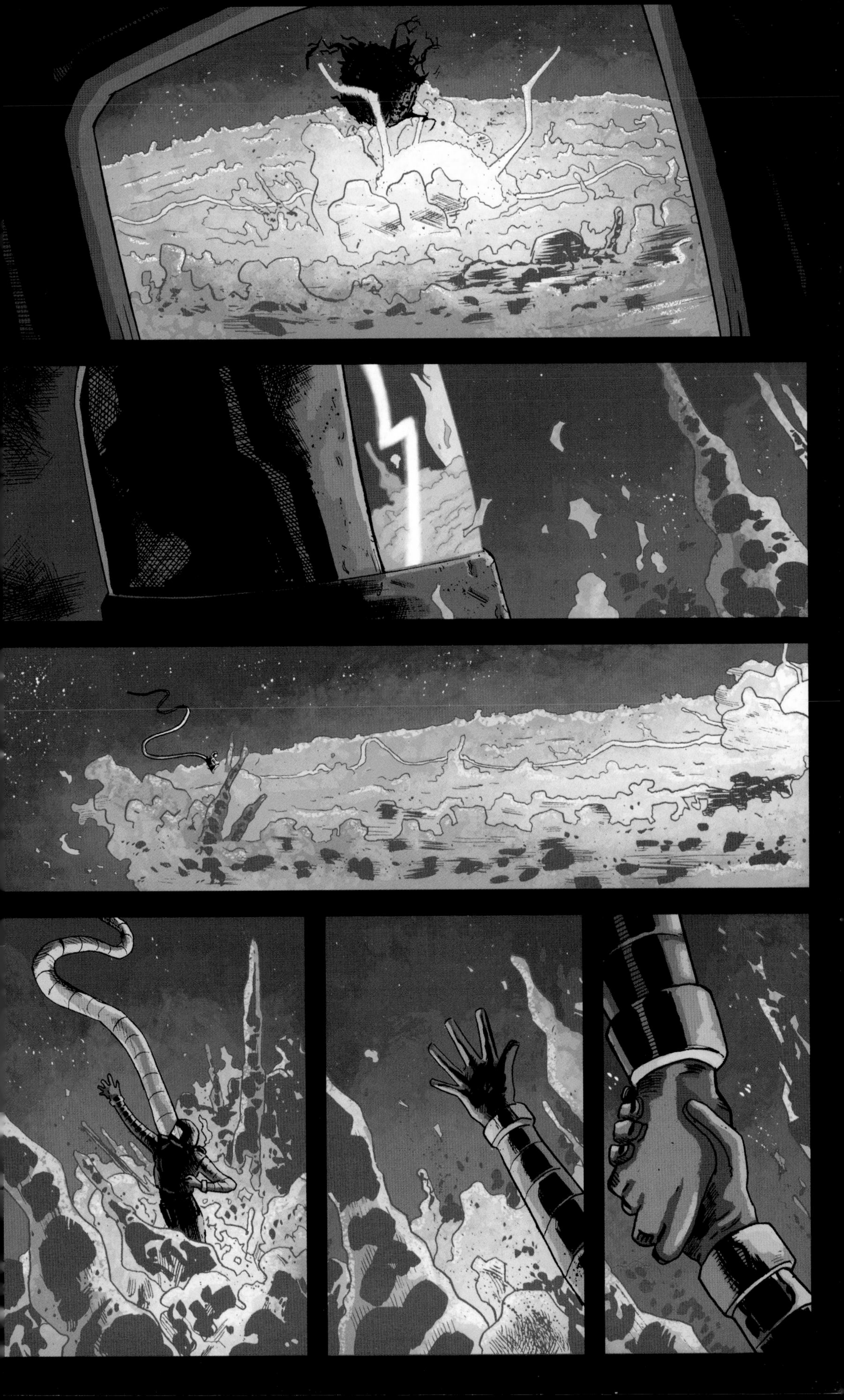

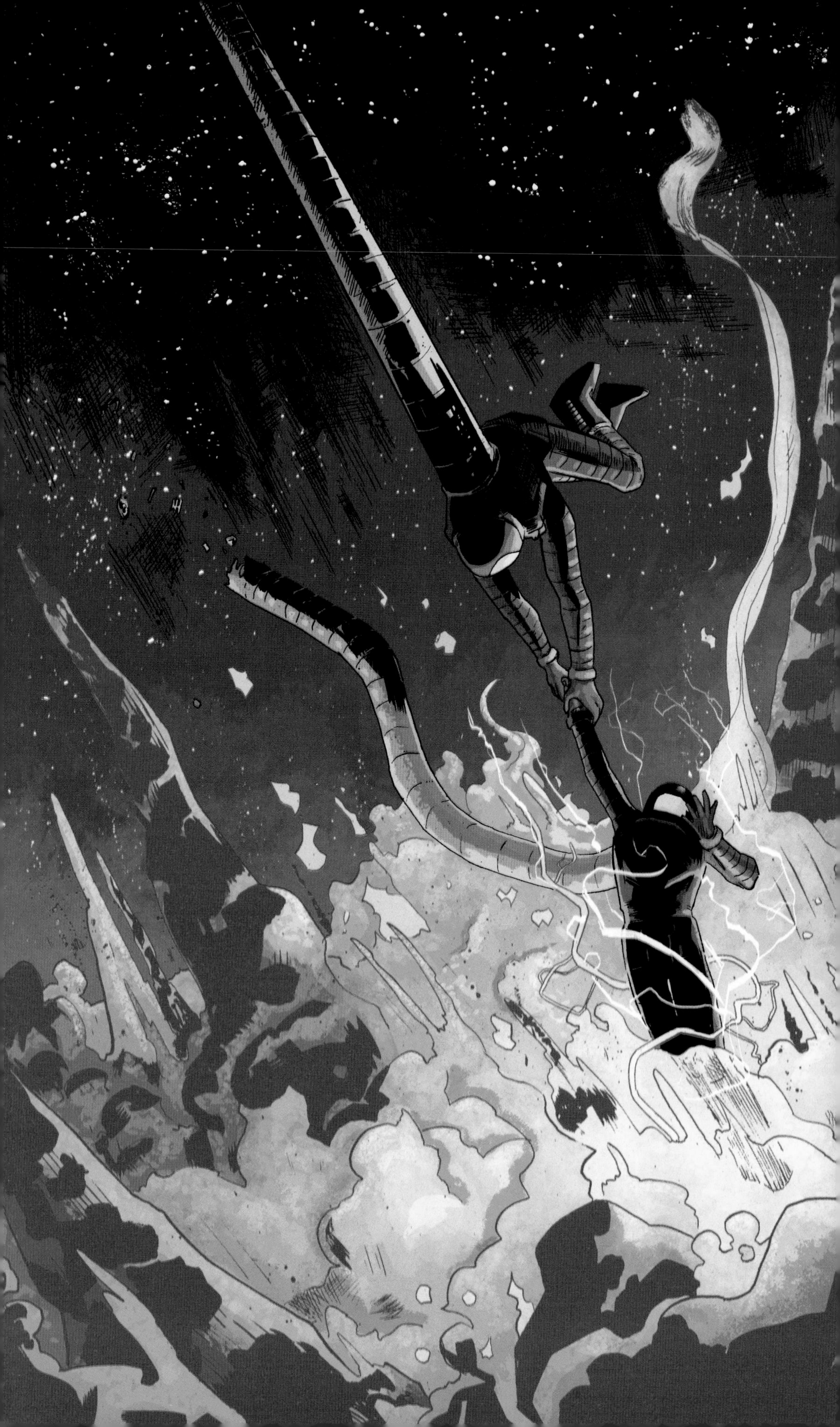

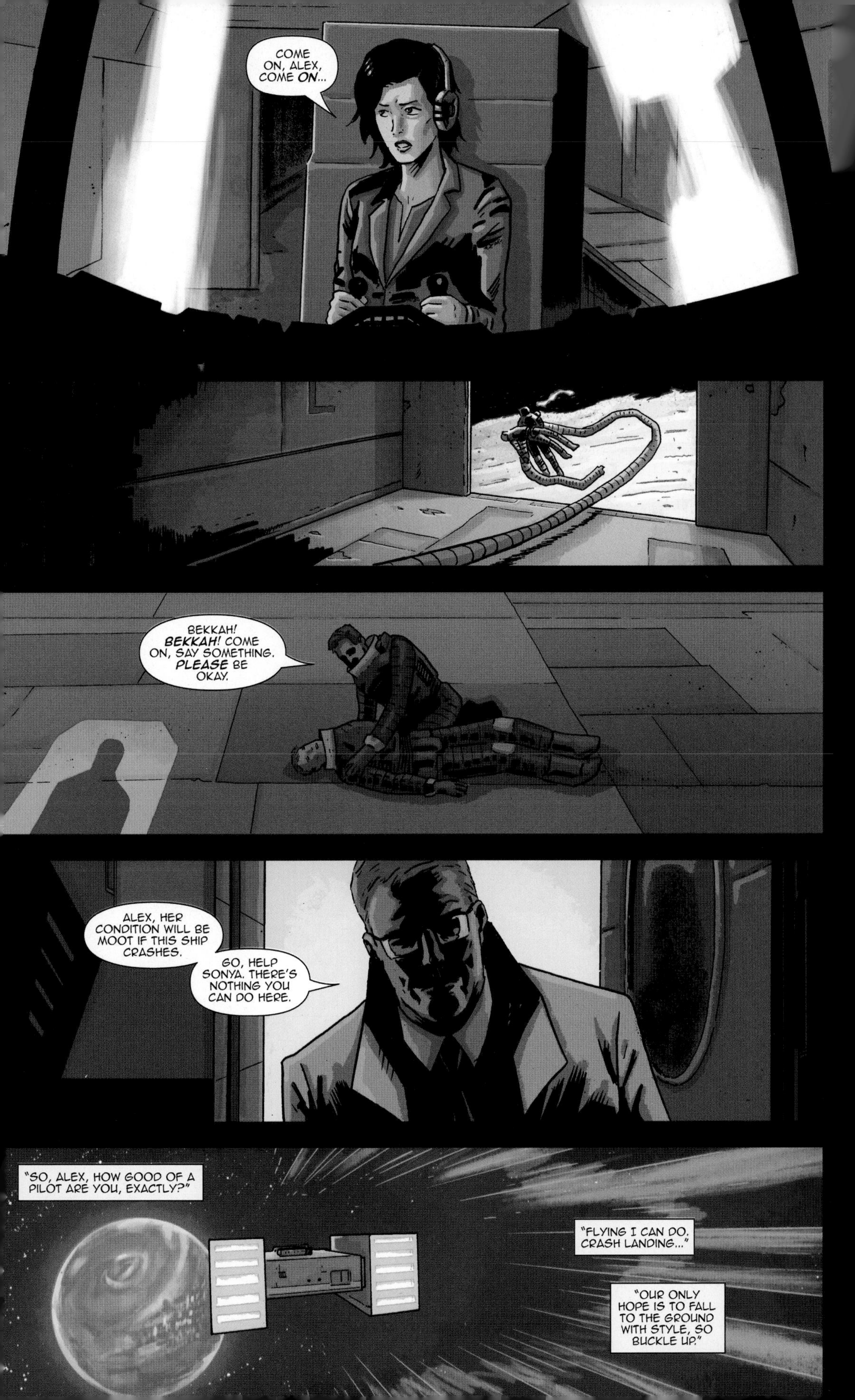
COME ON, ALEX, COME ON...
BEKKAH! BEKKAH! COME ON, SAY SOMETHING. PLEASE BE OKAY.
ALEX, HER CONDITION WILL BE MOOT IF THIS SHIP CRASHES.
GO, HELP SONYA. THERE'S NOTHING YOU CAN DO HERE.
"SO, ALEX, HOW GOOD OF A PILOT ARE YOU, EXACTLY?"
"FLYING I CAN DO. CRASH LANDING..."
"OUR ONLY HOPE IS TO FALL TO THE GROUND WITH STYLE, SO BUCKLE UP."

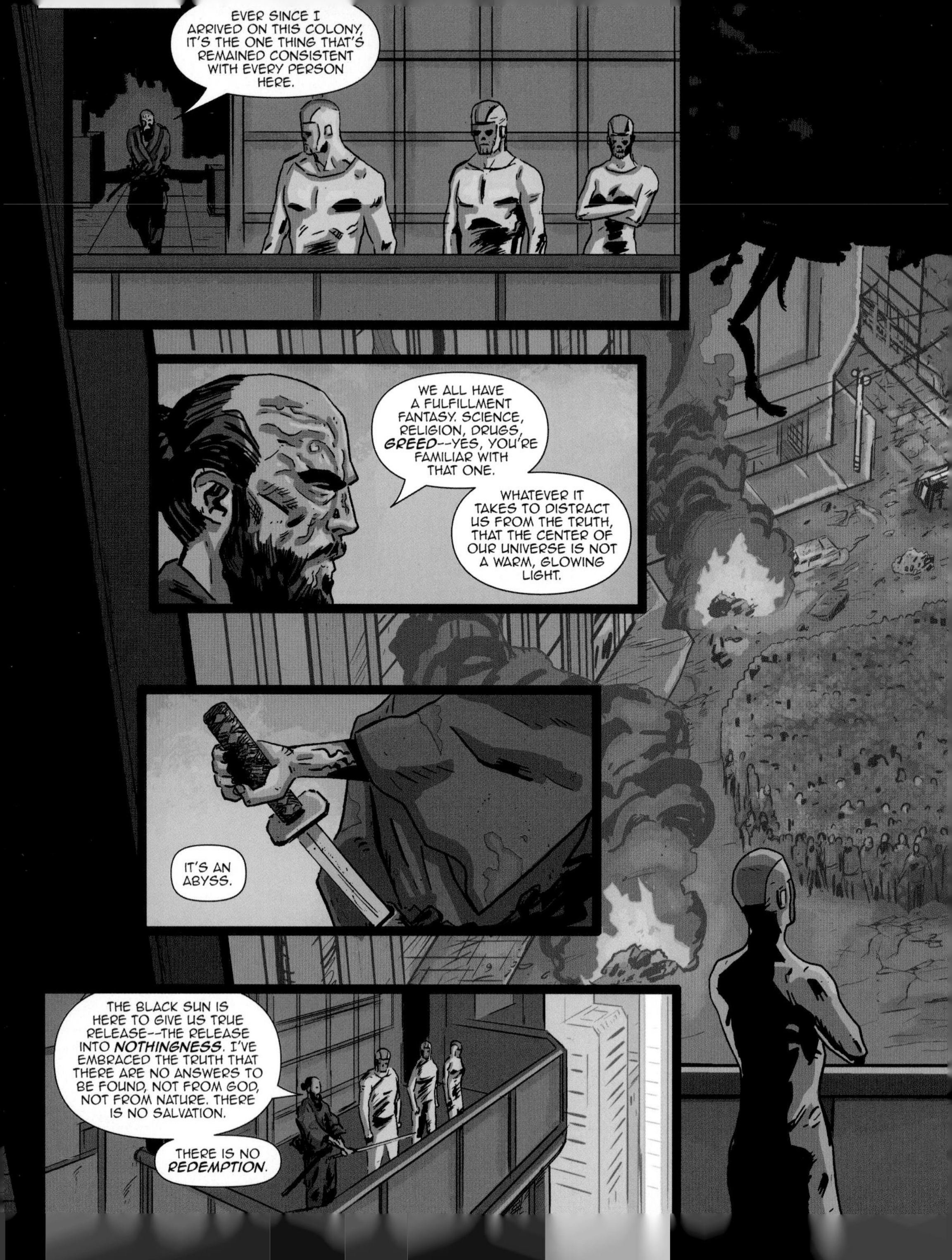
EVER SINCE I ARRIVED ON THIS COLONY, IT'S THE ONE THING THAT'S REMAINED CONSISTENT WITH EVERY PERSON HERE.
WE ALL HAVE A FULFILLMENT FANTASY. SCIENCE, RELIGION, DRUGS, GREED--YES, YOU'RE FAMILIAR WITH THAT ONE.
WHATEVER IT TAKES TO DISTRACT US FROM THE TRUTH, THAT THE CENTER OF OUR UNIVERSE IS NOT A WARM, GLOWING LIGHT.
IT'S AN ABYSS.
THE BLACK SUN IS HERE TO GIVE US TRUE RELEASE--THE RELEASE INTO NOTHINGNESS. I'VE EMBRACED THE TRUTH THAT THERE ARE NO ANSWERS TO BE FOUND, NOT FROM GOD, NOT FROM NATURE. THERE IS NO SALVATION.
THERE IS NO REDEMPTION.

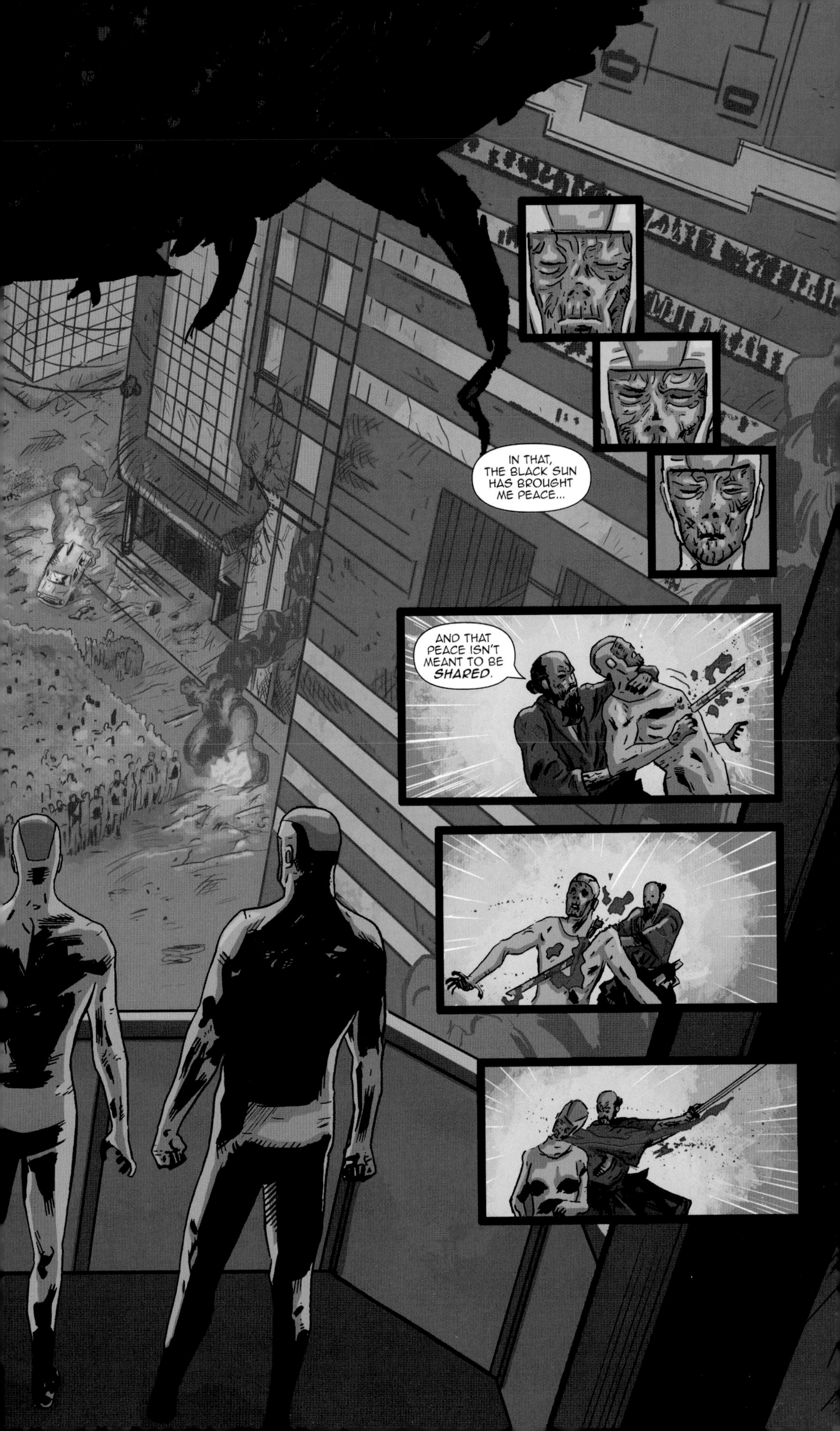
IN THAT, THE BLACK SUN HAS BROUGHT ME PEACE...
AND THAT PEACE ISN'T MEANT TO BE *SHARED*.

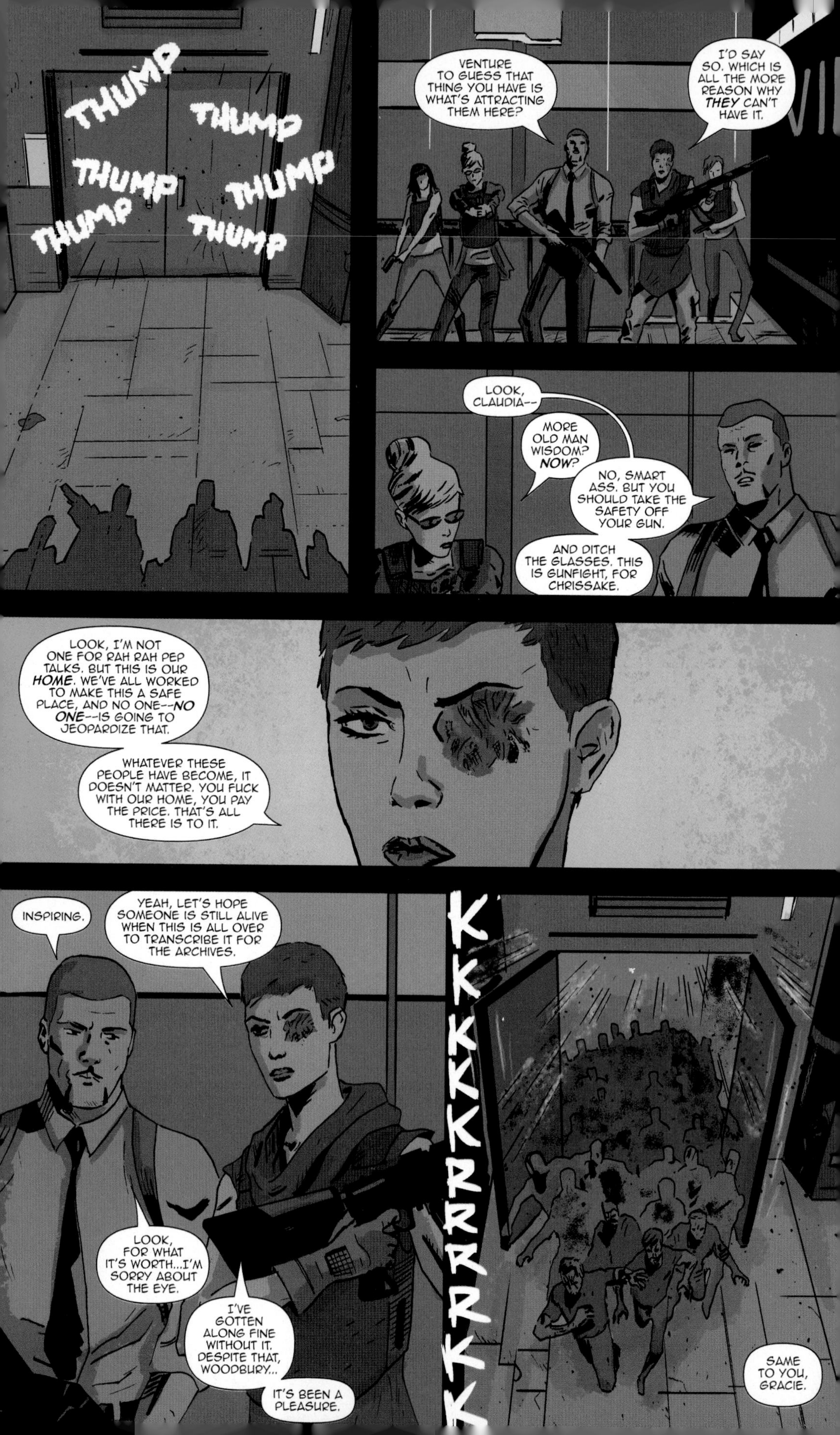
THUMP THUMP THUMP THUMP THUMP THUMP
VENTURE TO GUESS THAT THING YOU HAVE IS WHAT'S ATTRACTING THEM HERE?
I'D SAY SO. WHICH IS ALL THE MORE REASON WHY THEY CAN'T HAVE IT.
LOOK, CLAUDIA--
MORE OLD MAN WISDOM? NOW?
NO, SMART ASS. BUT YOU SHOULD TAKE THE SAFETY OFF YOUR GUN.
AND DITCH THE GLASSES. THIS IS GUNFIGHT, FOR CHRISSAKE.
LOOK, I'M NOT ONE FOR RAH RAH PEP TALKS. BUT THIS IS OUR HOME. WE'VE ALL WORKED TO MAKE THIS A SAFE PLACE, AND NO ONE--NO ONE--IS GOING TO JEOPARDIZE THAT.
WHATEVER THESE PEOPLE HAVE BECOME, IT DOESN'T MATTER. YOU FUCK WITH OUR HOME, YOU PAY THE PRICE. THAT'S ALL THERE IS TO IT.
INSPIRING.
YEAH, LET'S HOPE SOMEONE IS STILL ALIVE WHEN THIS IS ALL OVER TO TRANSCRIBE IT FOR THE ARCHIVES.
LOOK, FOR WHAT IT'S WORTH...I'M SORRY ABOUT THE EYE.
I'VE GOTTEN ALONG FINE WITHOUT IT. DESPITE THAT, WOODBURY...
IT'S BEEN A PLEASURE.
KKKKKRRRRKK
SAME TO YOU, GRACIE.

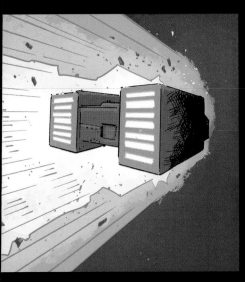

JED's SCRAPYARD
YOUR #1 STOP FOR ALL YOUR SCRAP NEEDS

CCCCCRRRSSSSHHHH

COME ON, WE HAVE TO MOVE.

HOW IS SHE?

STILL NON-RESPONSIVE. BUT PHYSICALLY... I THINK SHE'S OKAY.

ALEX, HOW ARE WE GOING TO PULL THIS OFF? WE HAVE TO FIND HER SOUL AND, SOMEHOW, GET THE HELL OFF OF THIS PLANET BEFORE GOD KNOWS *WHAT* HAPPENS.

YOU JUST GET BEKKAH TO THE DOCKS. GRAB A SHIP BEFORE THEY'RE ALL GONE AND HOLD IT. I'LL TAKE WATKINS AND--

OH SHIT...

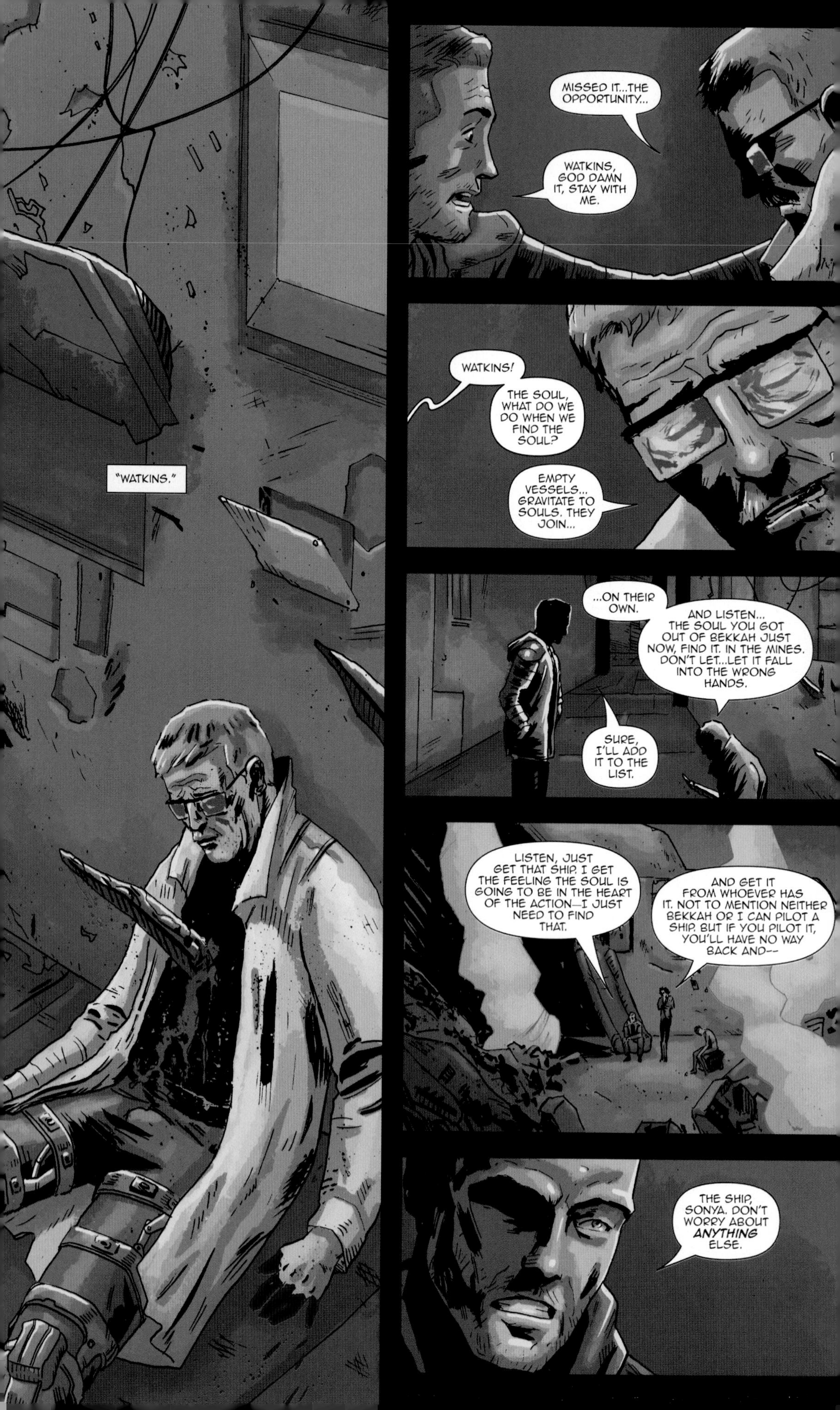
"WATKINS."
MISSED IT...THE OPPORTUNITY...
WATKINS, GOD DAMN IT, STAY WITH ME.
WATKINS!
THE SOUL, WHAT DO WE DO WHEN WE FIND THE SOUL?
EMPTY VESSELS... GRAVITATE TO SOULS. THEY JOIN...
...ON THEIR OWN.
AND LISTEN... THE SOUL YOU GOT OUT OF BEKKAH JUST NOW, FIND IT. IN THE MINES. DON'T LET...LET IT FALL INTO THE WRONG HANDS.
SURE, I'LL ADD IT TO THE LIST.
LISTEN, JUST GET THAT SHIP. I GET THE FEELING THE SOUL IS GOING TO BE IN THE HEART OF THE ACTION—I JUST NEED TO FIND THAT.
AND GET IT FROM WHOEVER HAS IT. NOT TO MENTION NEITHER BEKKAH OR I CAN PILOT A SHIP. BUT IF YOU PILOT IT, YOU'LL HAVE NO WAY BACK AND--
THE SHIP, SONYA. DON'T WORRY ABOUT *ANYTHING* ELSE.

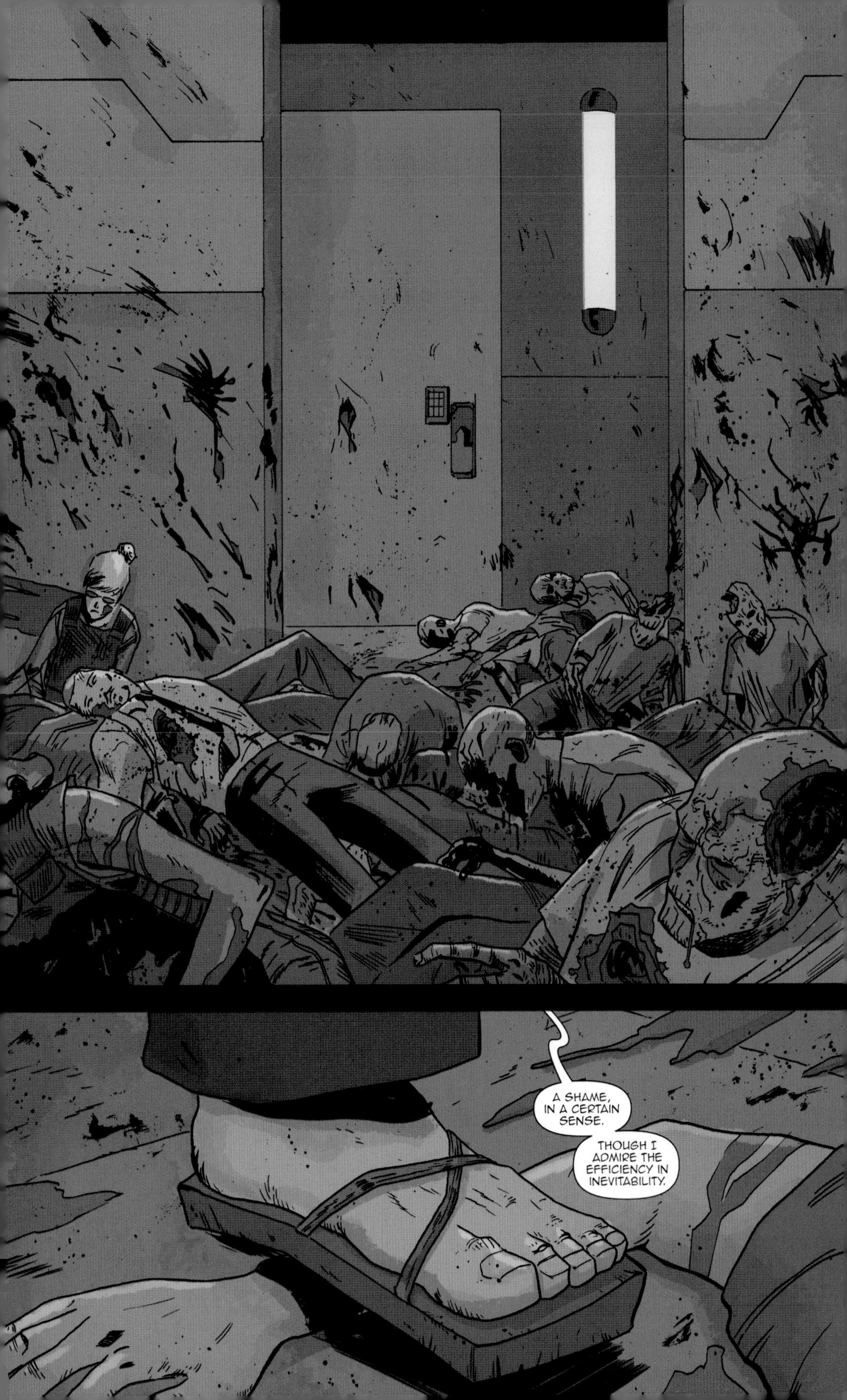
A SHAME, IN A CERTAIN SENSE.
THOUGH I ADMIRE THE EFFICIENCY IN INEVITABILITY.

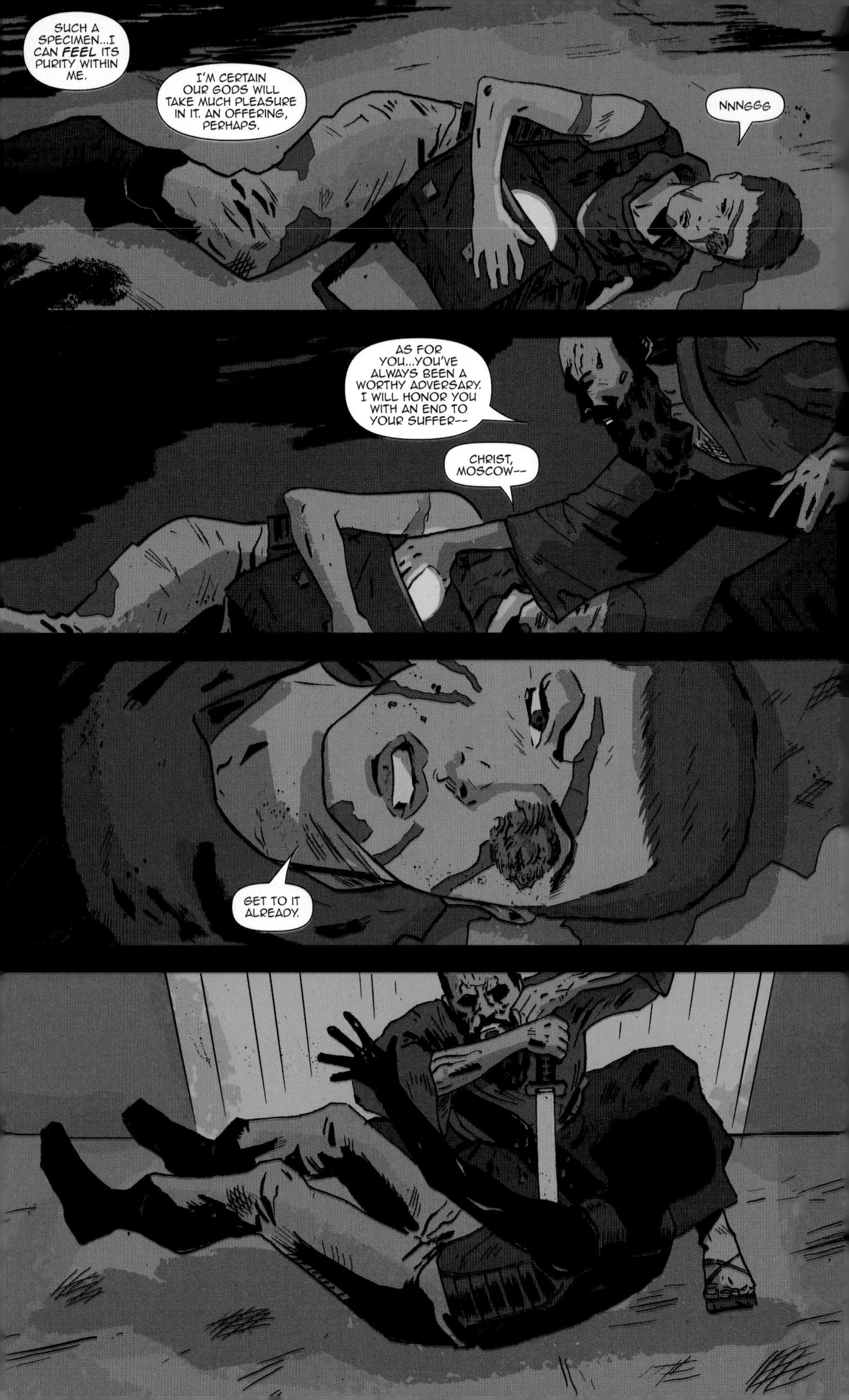
SUCH A SPECIMEN...I CAN FEEL ITS PURITY WITHIN ME.
I'M CERTAIN OUR GODS WILL TAKE MUCH PLEASURE IN IT. AN OFFERING, PERHAPS.
NNNGGG
AS FOR YOU...YOU'VE ALWAYS BEEN A WORTHY ADVERSARY. I WILL HONOR YOU WITH AN END TO YOUR SUFFER--
CHRIST, MOSCOW--
GET TO IT ALREADY.

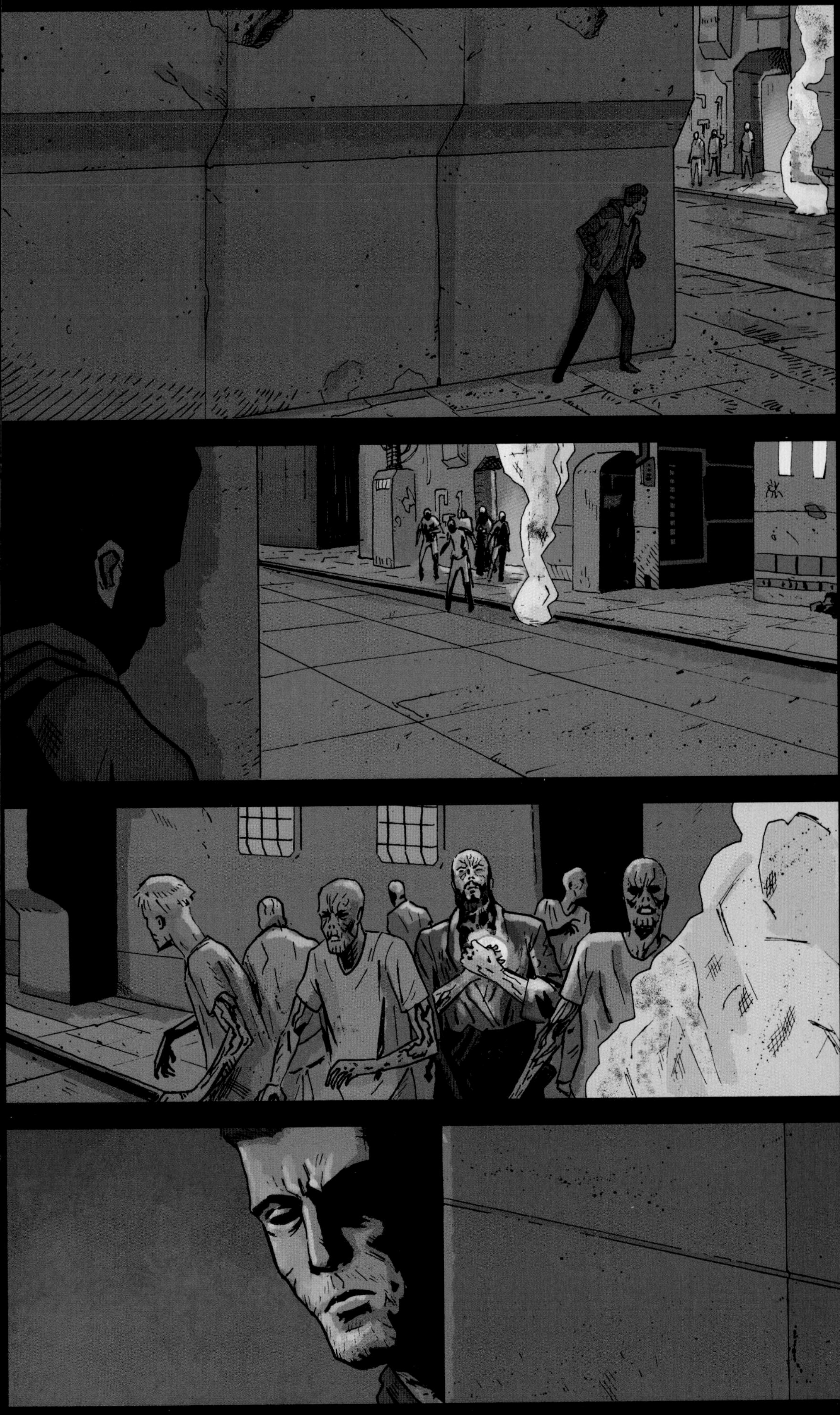

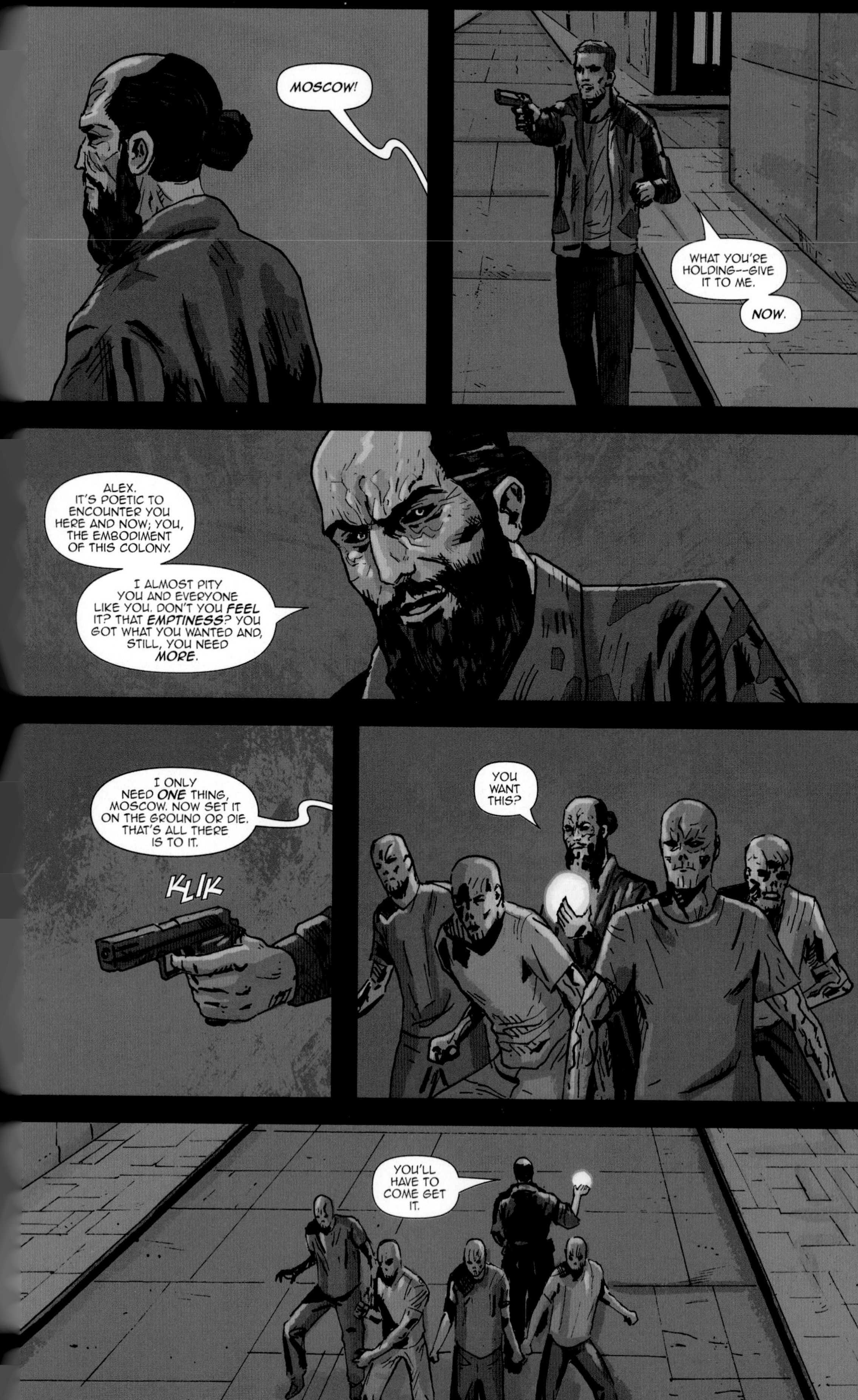
MOSCOW!
WHAT YOU'RE HOLDING--GIVE IT TO ME.
NOW.
ALEX. IT'S POETIC TO ENCOUNTER YOU HERE AND NOW; YOU, THE EMBODIMENT OF THIS COLONY.
I ALMOST PITY YOU AND EVERYONE LIKE YOU. DON'T YOU FEEL IT? THAT EMPTINESS? YOU GOT WHAT YOU WANTED AND, STILL, YOU NEED MORE.
I ONLY NEED ONE THING, MOSCOW. NOW SET IT ON THE GROUND OR DIE. THAT'S ALL THERE IS TO IT.
KLIK
YOU WANT THIS?
YOU'LL HAVE TO COME GET IT.

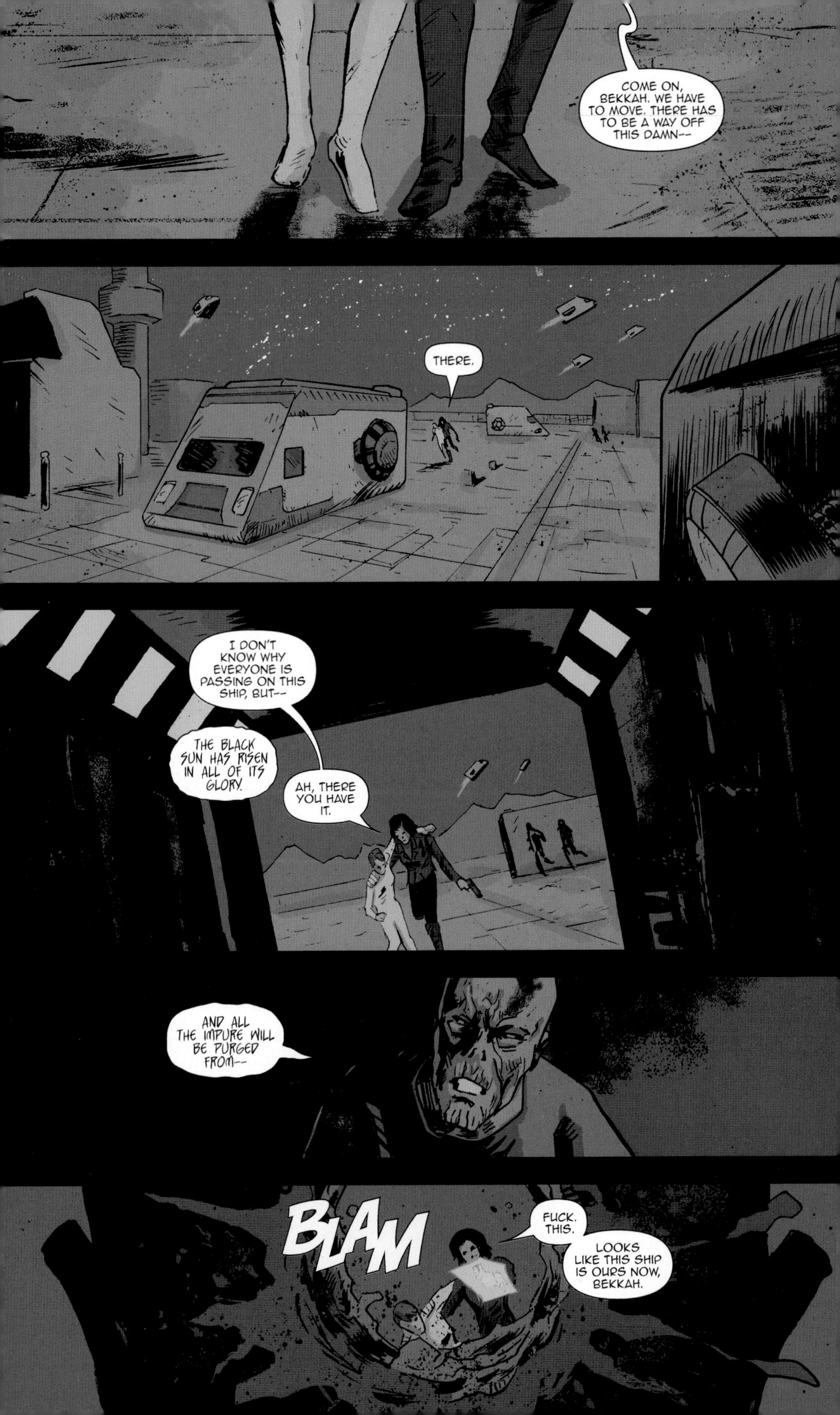

COME ON, BEKKAH. WE HAVE TO MOVE. THERE HAS TO BE A WAY OFF THIS DAMN--
THERE.
I DON'T KNOW WHY EVERYONE IS PASSING ON THIS SHIP, BUT--
THE BLACK SUN HAS RISEN IN ALL OF ITS GLORY.
AH, THERE YOU HAVE IT.
AND ALL THE IMPURE WILL BE PURGED FROM--
BLAM
FUCK. THIS.
LOOKS LIKE THIS SHIP IS OURS NOW, BEKKAH.

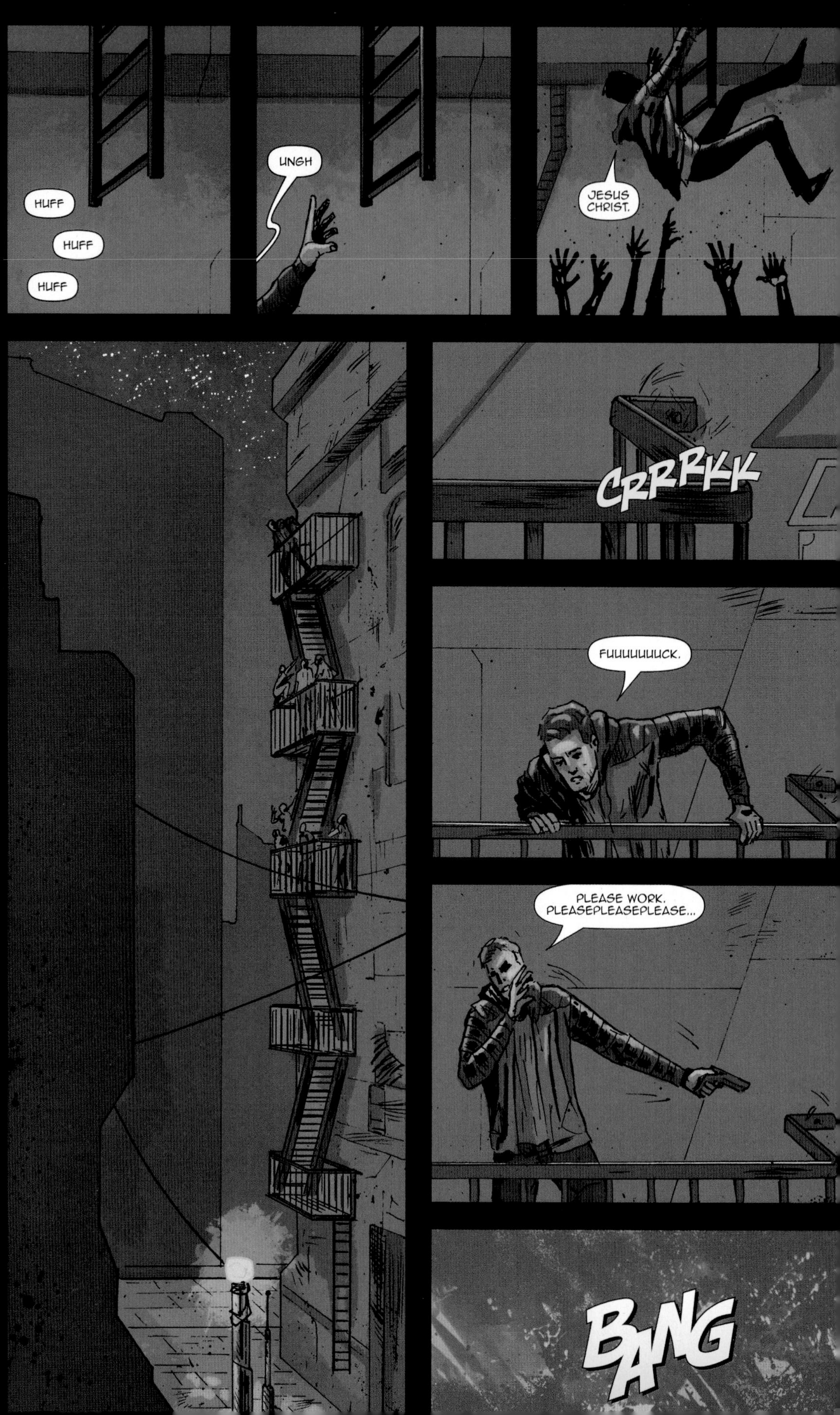
HUFF
HUFF
HUFF
UNGH
JESUS CHRIST.
CRRRKK
FUUUUUUUCK.
PLEASE WORK. PLEASEPLEASEPLEASE...
BANG

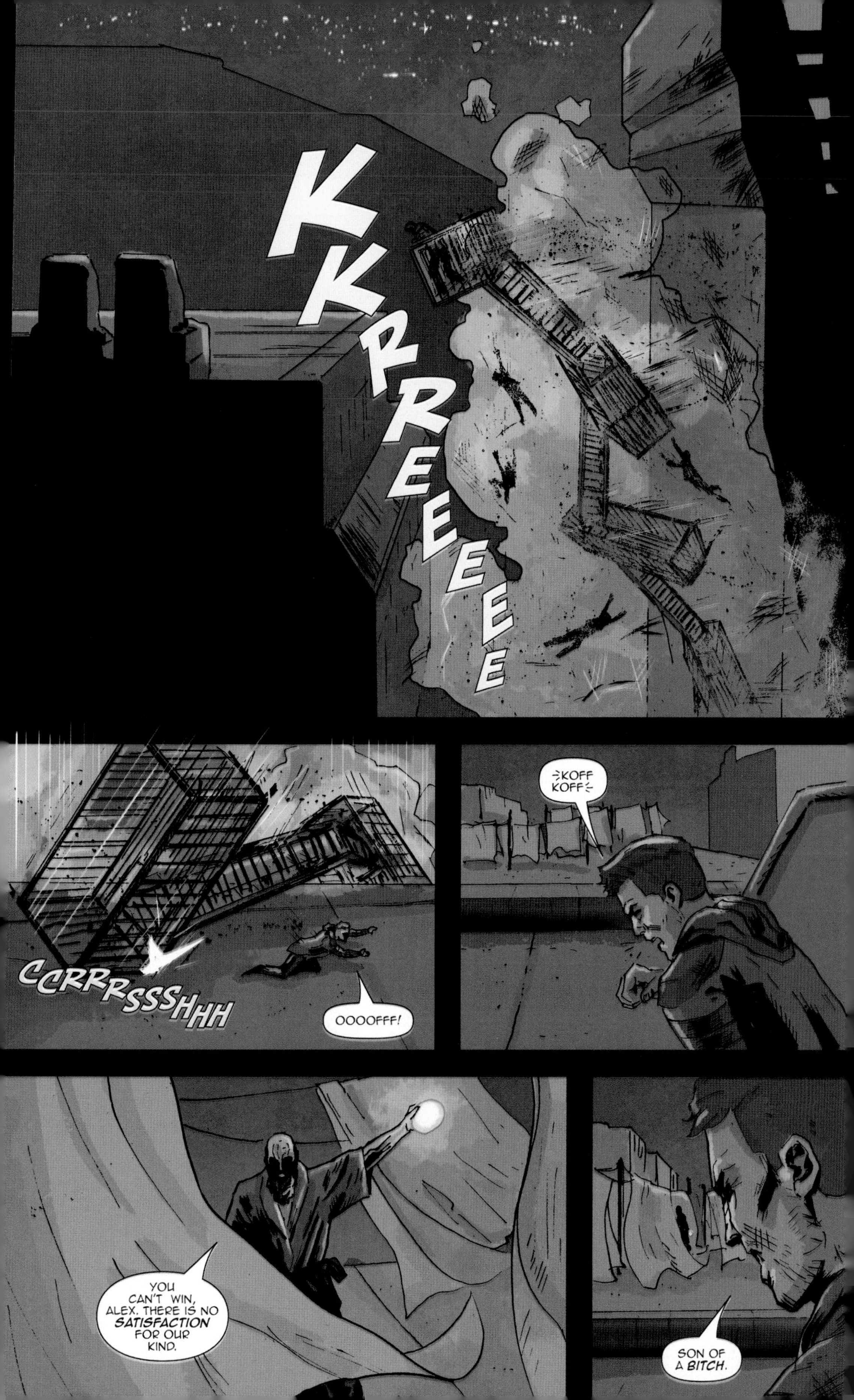
KKRREEEEEE
CCRRRSSSHHH
OOOOFFF!
KOFF KOFF
YOU CAN'T WIN, ALEX. THERE IS NO SATISFACTION FOR OUR KIND.
SON OF A BITCH.

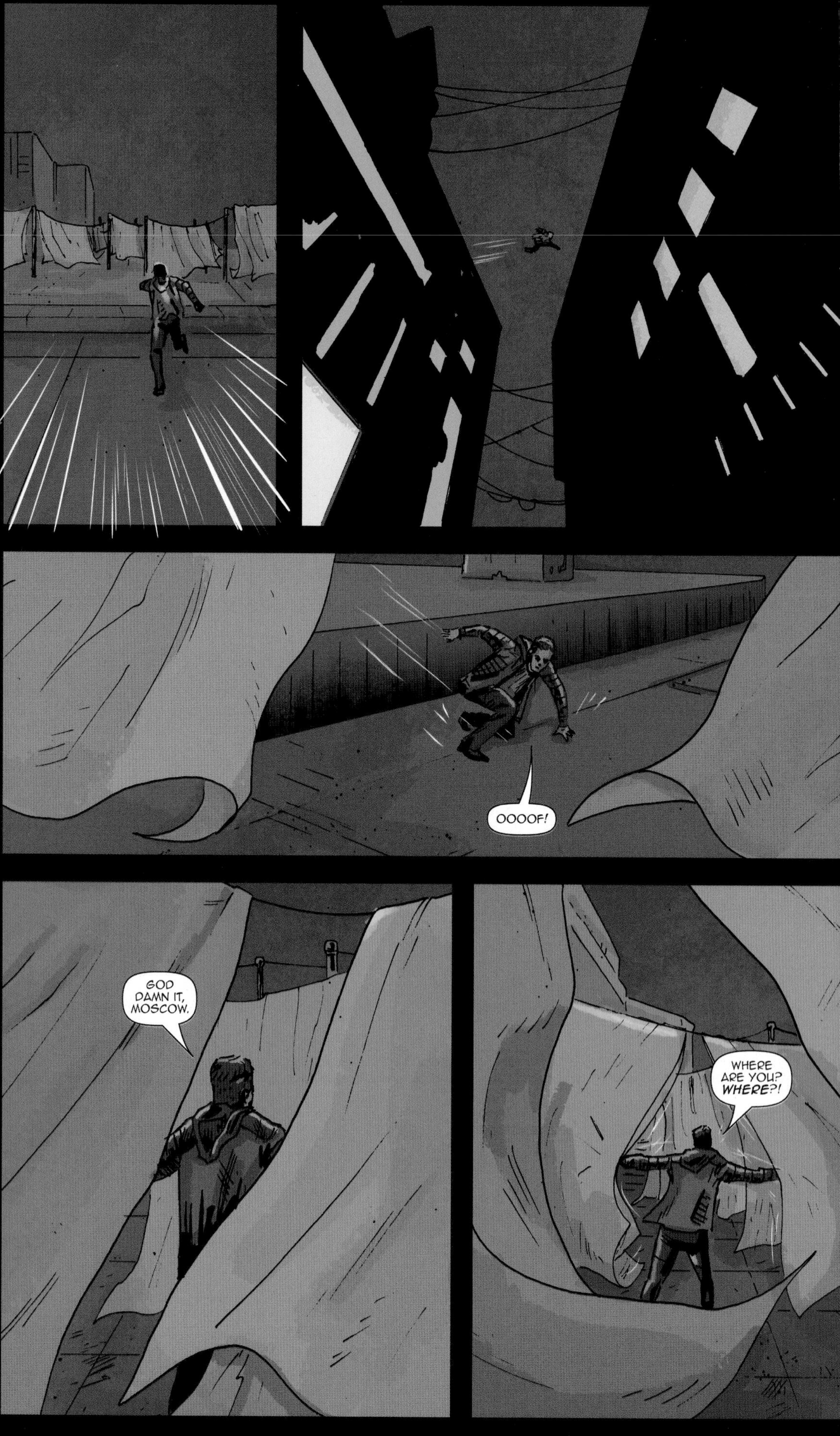
OOOOF!
GOD DAMN IT, MOSCOW.
WHERE ARE YOU? *WHERE?!*

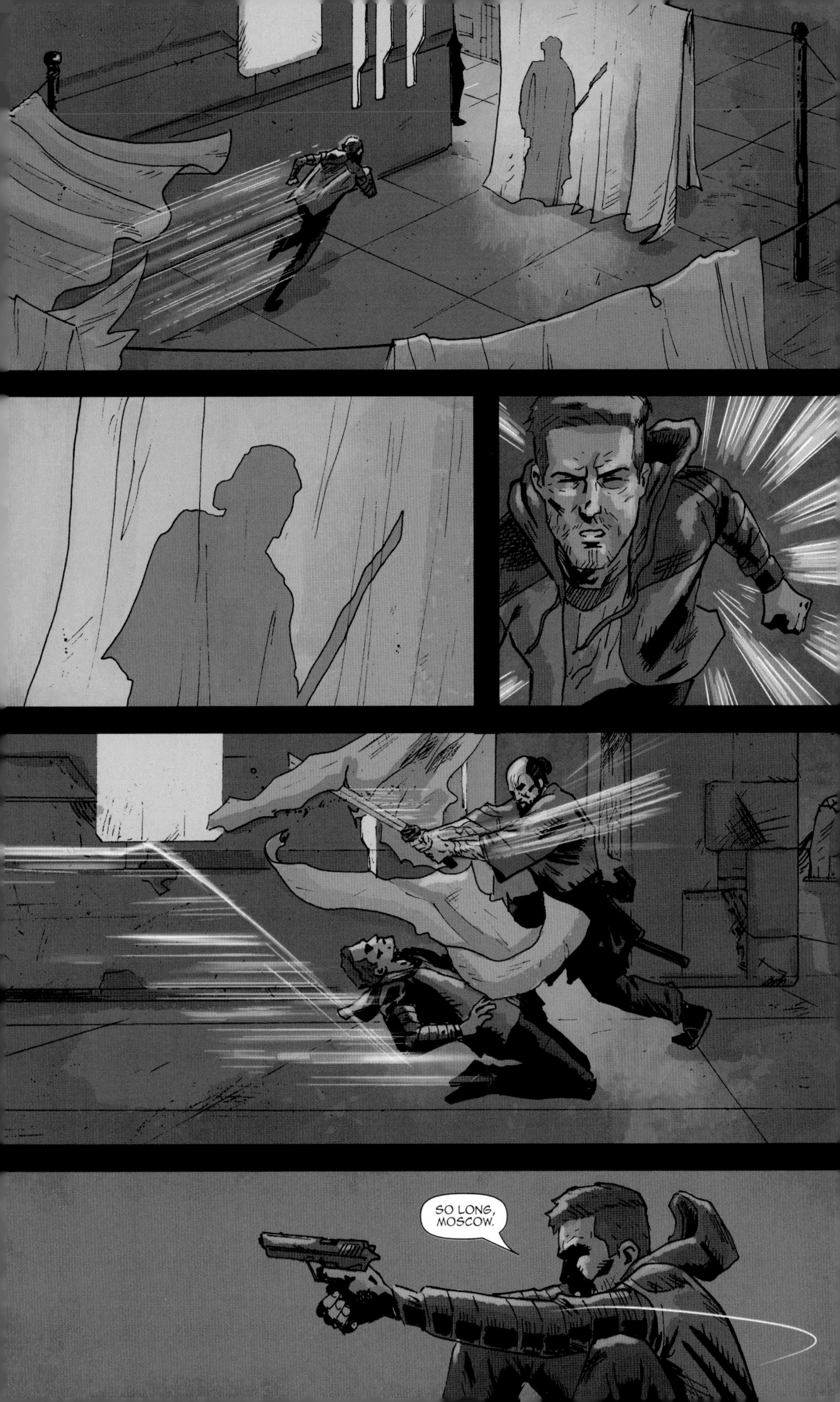
SO LONG,
MOSCOW.

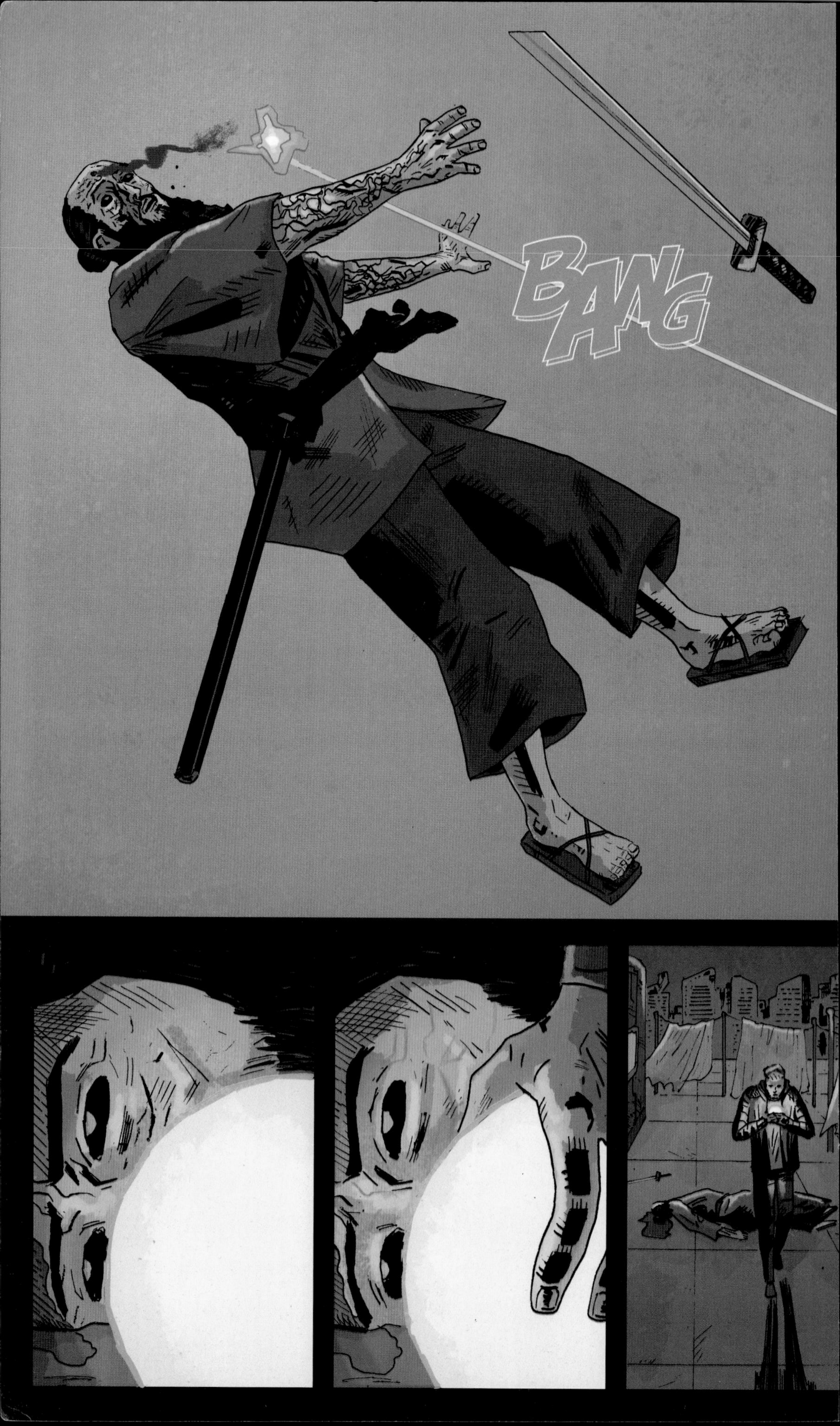
BANG

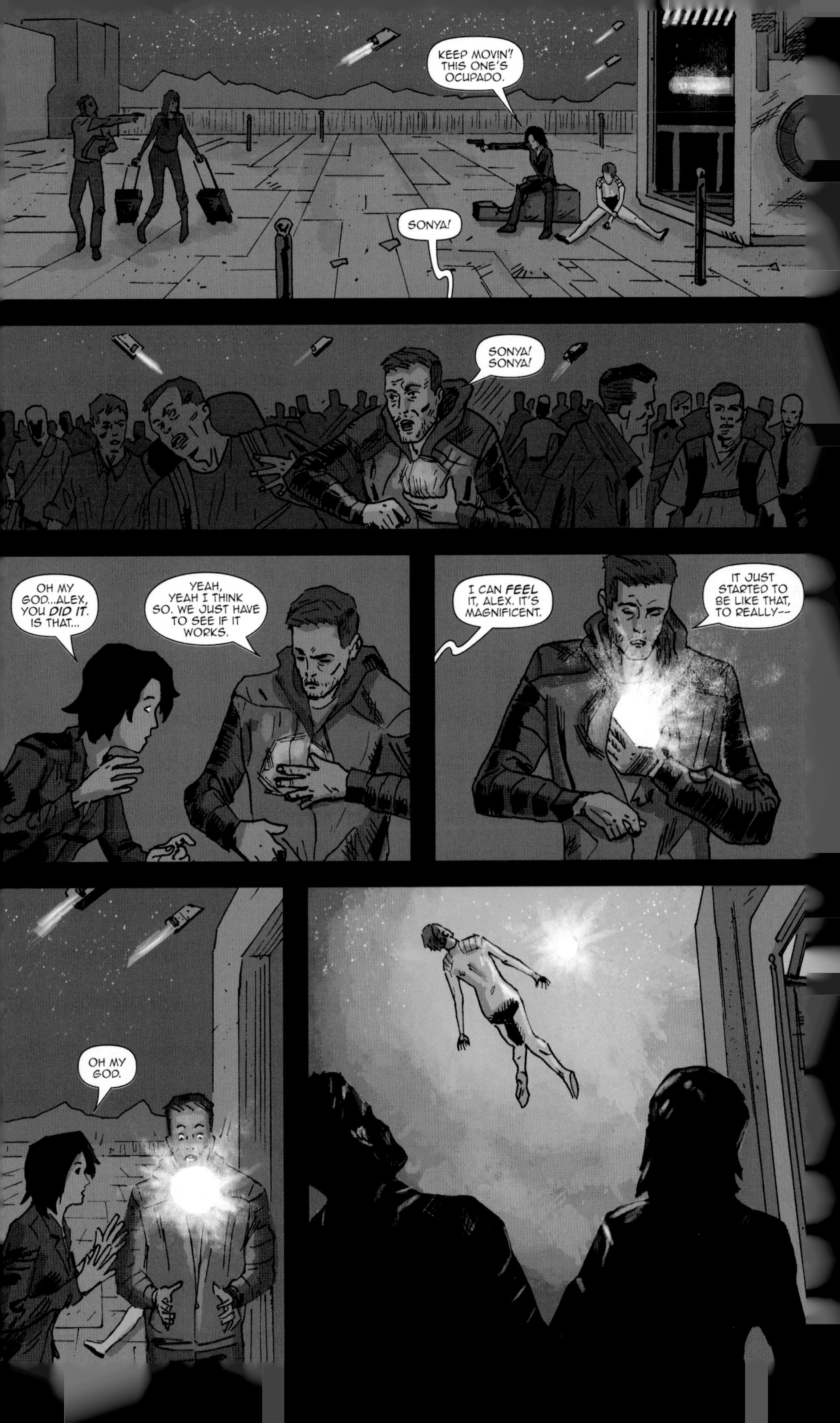
KEEP MOVIN'! THIS ONE'S OCUPADO.
SONYA!
SONYA! SONYA!
OH MY GOD...ALEX, YOU *DID IT*. IS THAT...
YEAH, YEAH I THINK SO. WE JUST HAVE TO SEE IF IT WORKS.
I CAN *FEEL* IT, ALEX. IT'S MAGNIFICENT.
IT JUST STARTED TO BE LIKE THAT, TO REALLY--
OH MY GOD.

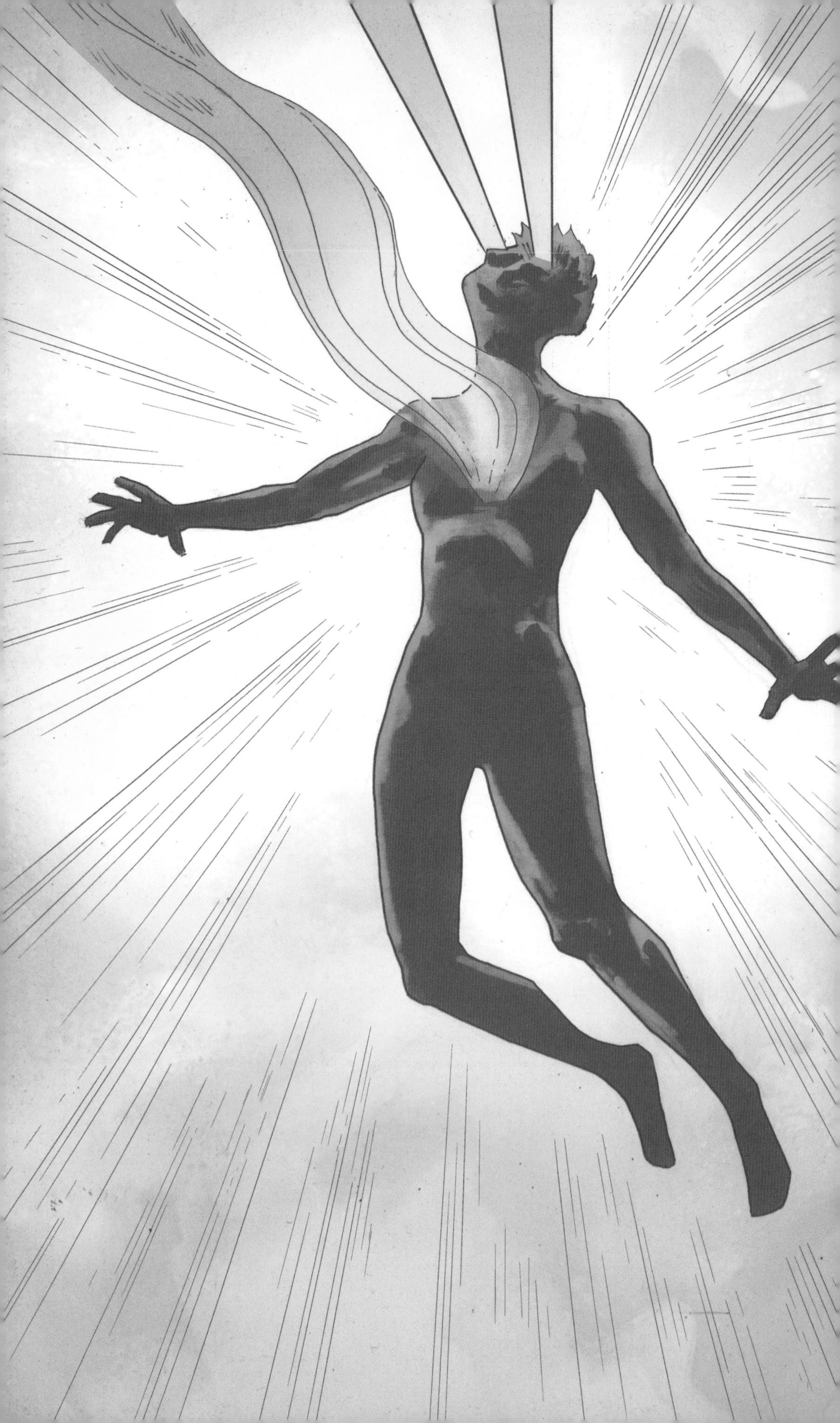

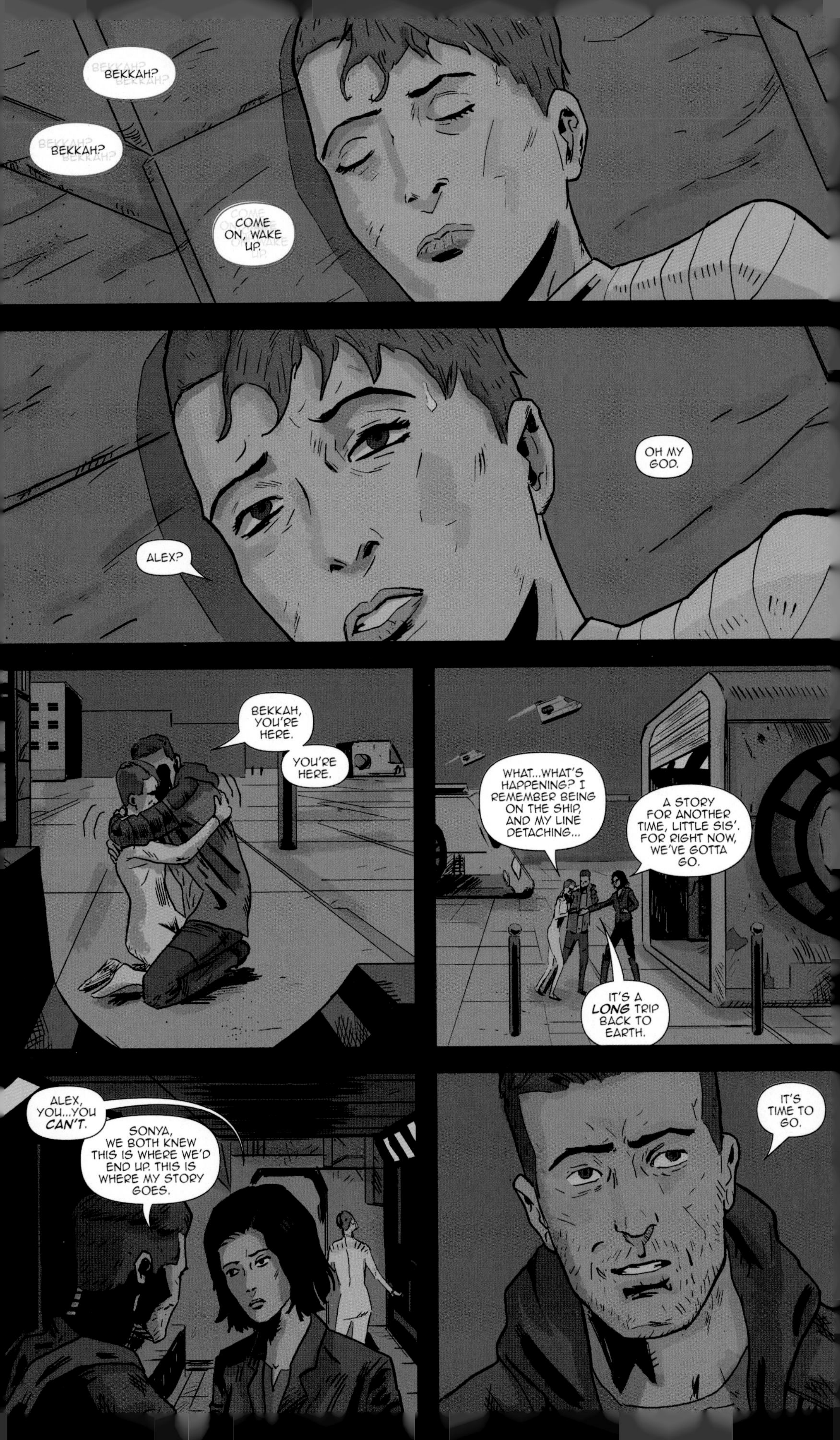
BEKKAH?
BEKKAH?
COME ON, WAKE UP.
OH MY GOD.
ALEX?
BEKKAH, YOU'RE HERE.
YOU'RE HERE.
WHAT...WHAT'S HAPPENING? I REMEMBER BEING ON THE SHIP, AND MY LINE DETACHING...
A STORY FOR ANOTHER TIME, LITTLE SIS'. FOR RIGHT NOW, WE'VE GOTTA GO.
IT'S A LONG TRIP BACK TO EARTH.
ALEX, YOU...YOU CAN'T.
SONYA, WE BOTH KNEW THIS IS WHERE WE'D END UP. THIS IS WHERE MY STORY GOES.
IT'S TIME TO GO.

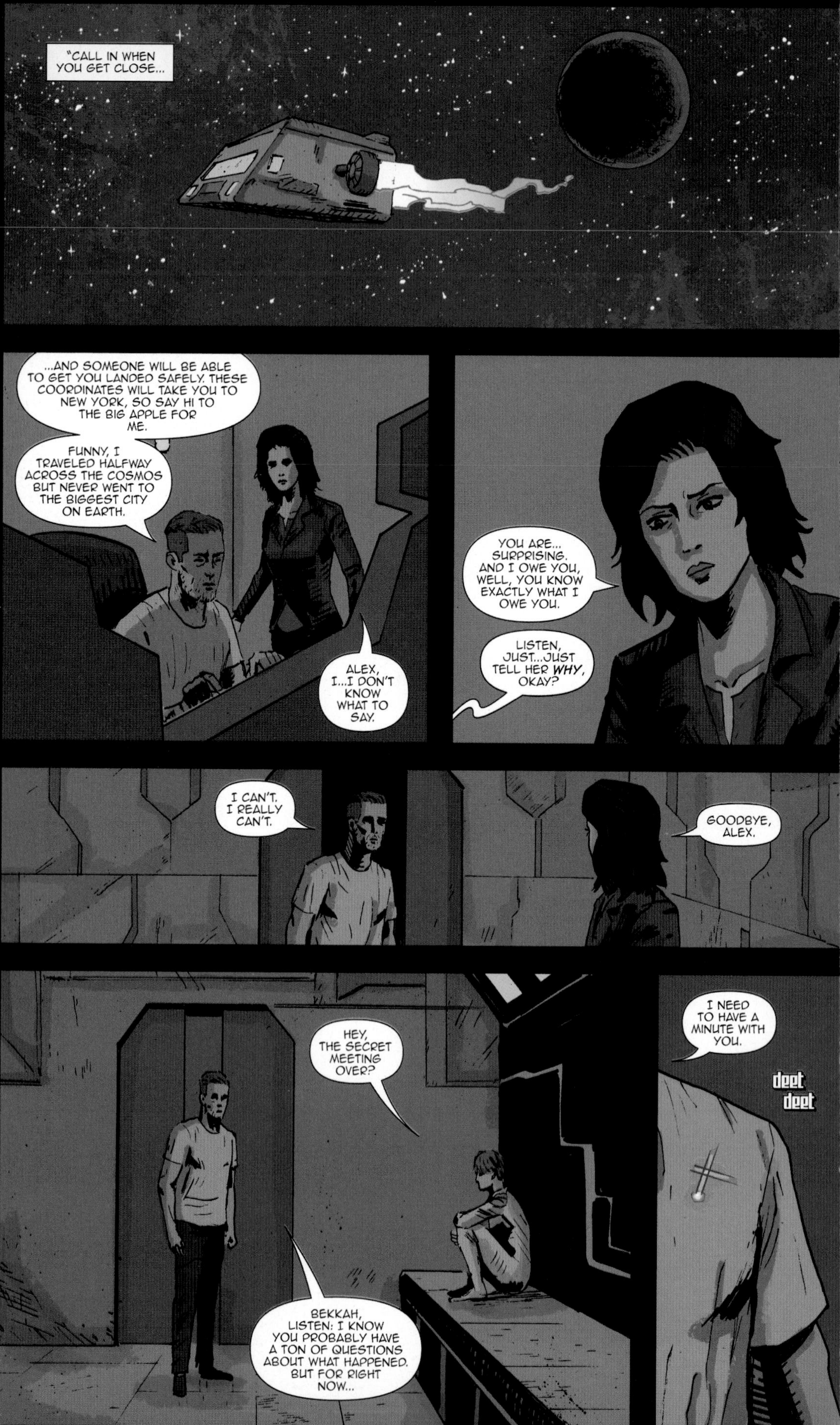
"CALL IN WHEN YOU GET CLOSE...
...AND SOMEONE WILL BE ABLE TO GET YOU LANDED SAFELY. THESE COORDINATES WILL TAKE YOU TO NEW YORK, SO SAY HI TO THE BIG APPLE FOR ME.
FUNNY, I TRAVELED HALFWAY ACROSS THE COSMOS BUT NEVER WENT TO THE BIGGEST CITY ON EARTH.
ALEX, I...I DON'T KNOW WHAT TO SAY.
YOU ARE... SURPRISING. AND I OWE YOU, WELL, YOU KNOW EXACTLY WHAT I OWE YOU.
LISTEN, JUST...JUST TELL HER *WHY*, OKAY?
I CAN'T. I REALLY CAN'T.
GOODBYE, ALEX.
HEY, THE SECRET MEETING OVER?
BEKKAH, LISTEN: I KNOW YOU PROBABLY HAVE A TON OF QUESTIONS ABOUT WHAT HAPPENED. BUT FOR RIGHT NOW...
I NEED TO HAVE A MINUTE WITH YOU.
deet deet

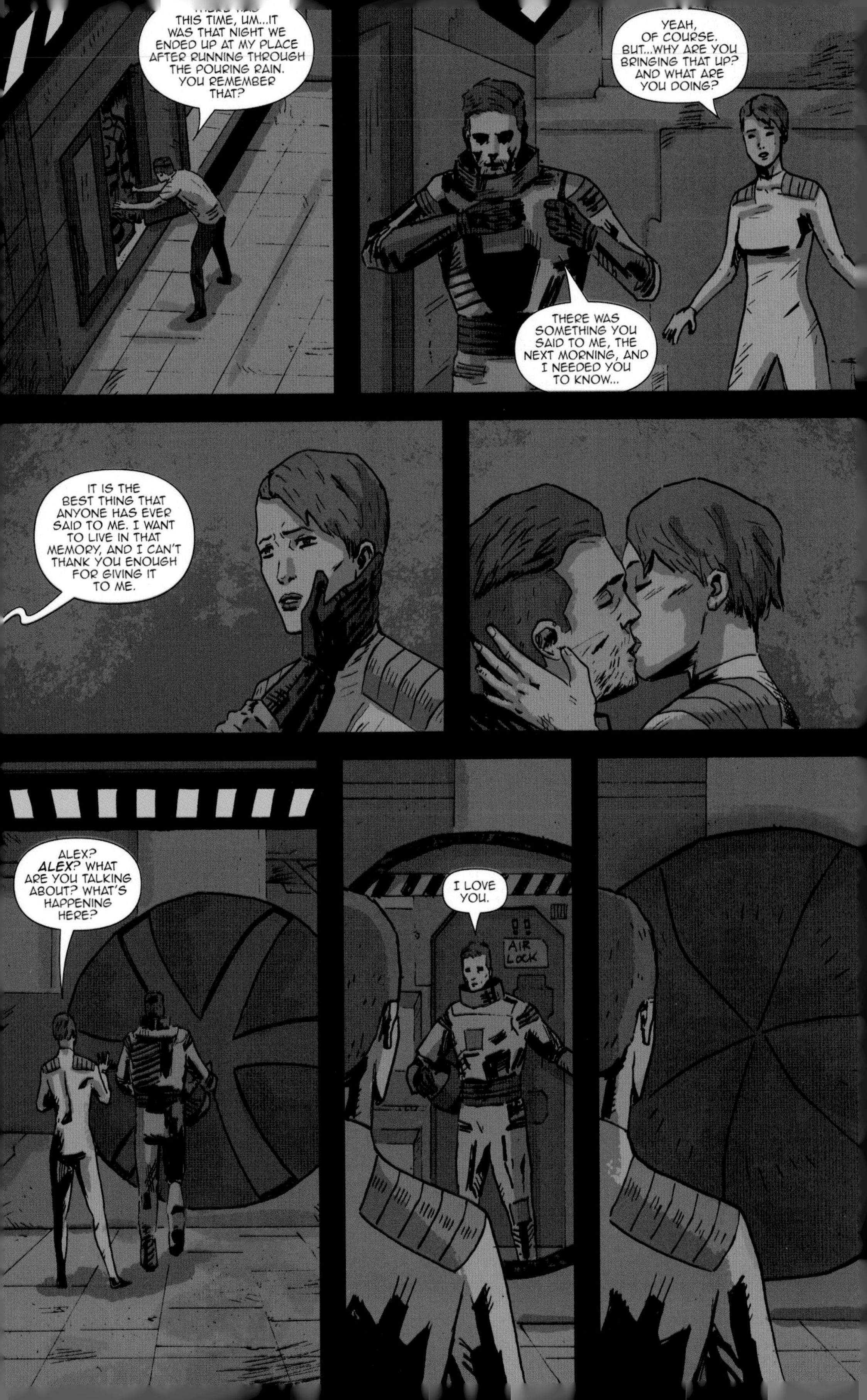
THIS TIME, UM...IT WAS THAT NIGHT WE ENDED UP AT MY PLACE AFTER RUNNING THROUGH THE POURING RAIN. YOU REMEMBER THAT?
YEAH, OF COURSE. BUT...WHY ARE YOU BRINGING THAT UP? AND WHAT ARE YOU DOING?
THERE WAS SOMETHING YOU SAID TO ME, THE NEXT MORNING, AND I NEEDED YOU TO KNOW...
IT IS THE BEST THING THAT ANYONE HAS EVER SAID TO ME. I WANT TO LIVE IN THAT MEMORY, AND I CAN'T THANK YOU ENOUGH FOR GIVING IT TO ME.
ALEX? ***ALEX?*** WHAT ARE YOU TALKING ABOUT? WHAT'S HAPPENING HERE?
I LOVE YOU.
AIR LOCK

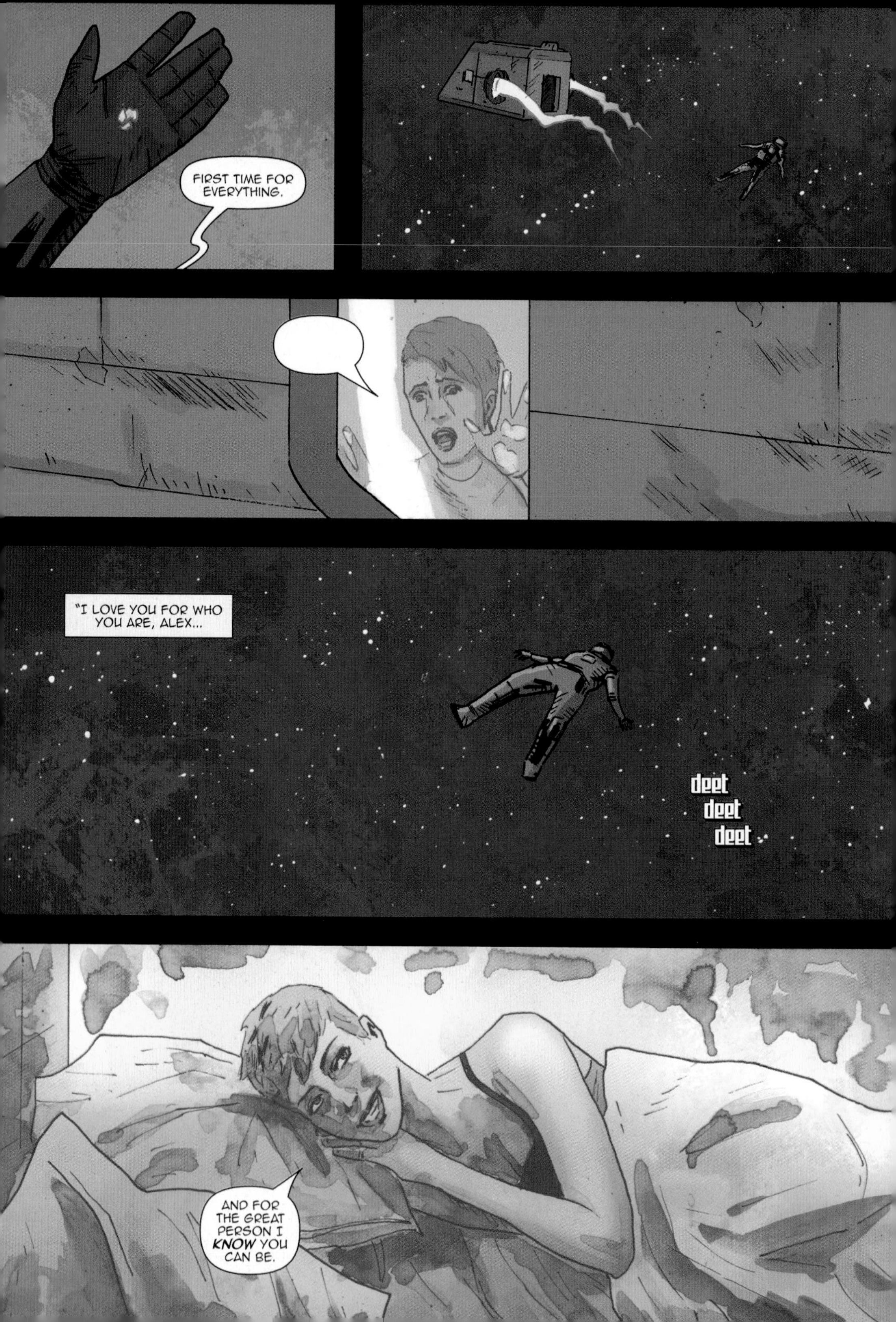
FIRST TIME FOR EVERYTHING.
"I LOVE YOU FOR WHO YOU ARE, ALEX...
deet
deet
deet
AND FOR THE GREAT PERSON I *KNOW* YOU CAN BE.

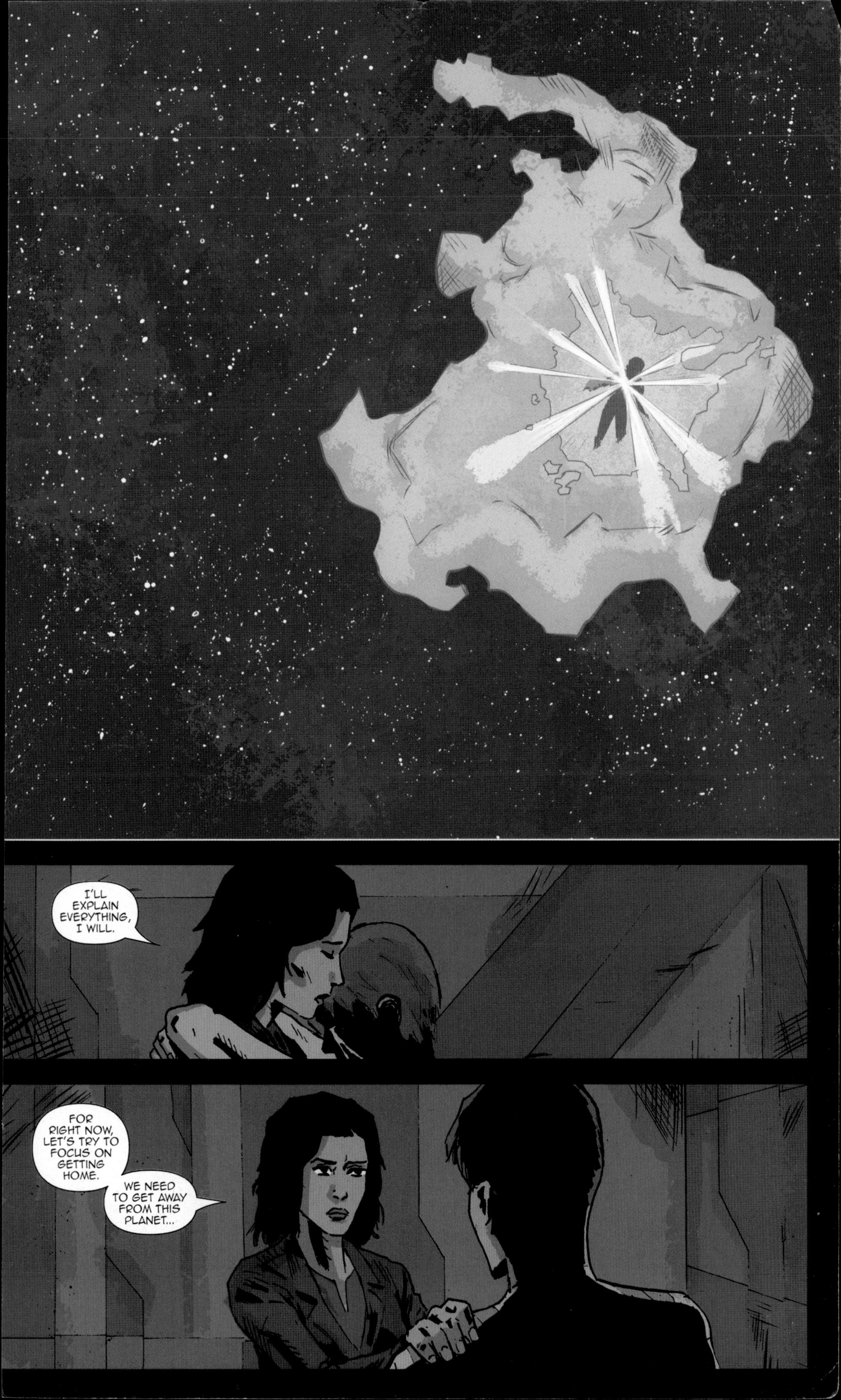
I'LL EXPLAIN EVERYTHING, I WILL.
FOR RIGHT NOW, LET'S TRY TO FOCUS ON GETTING HOME.
WE NEED TO GET AWAY FROM THIS PLANET...

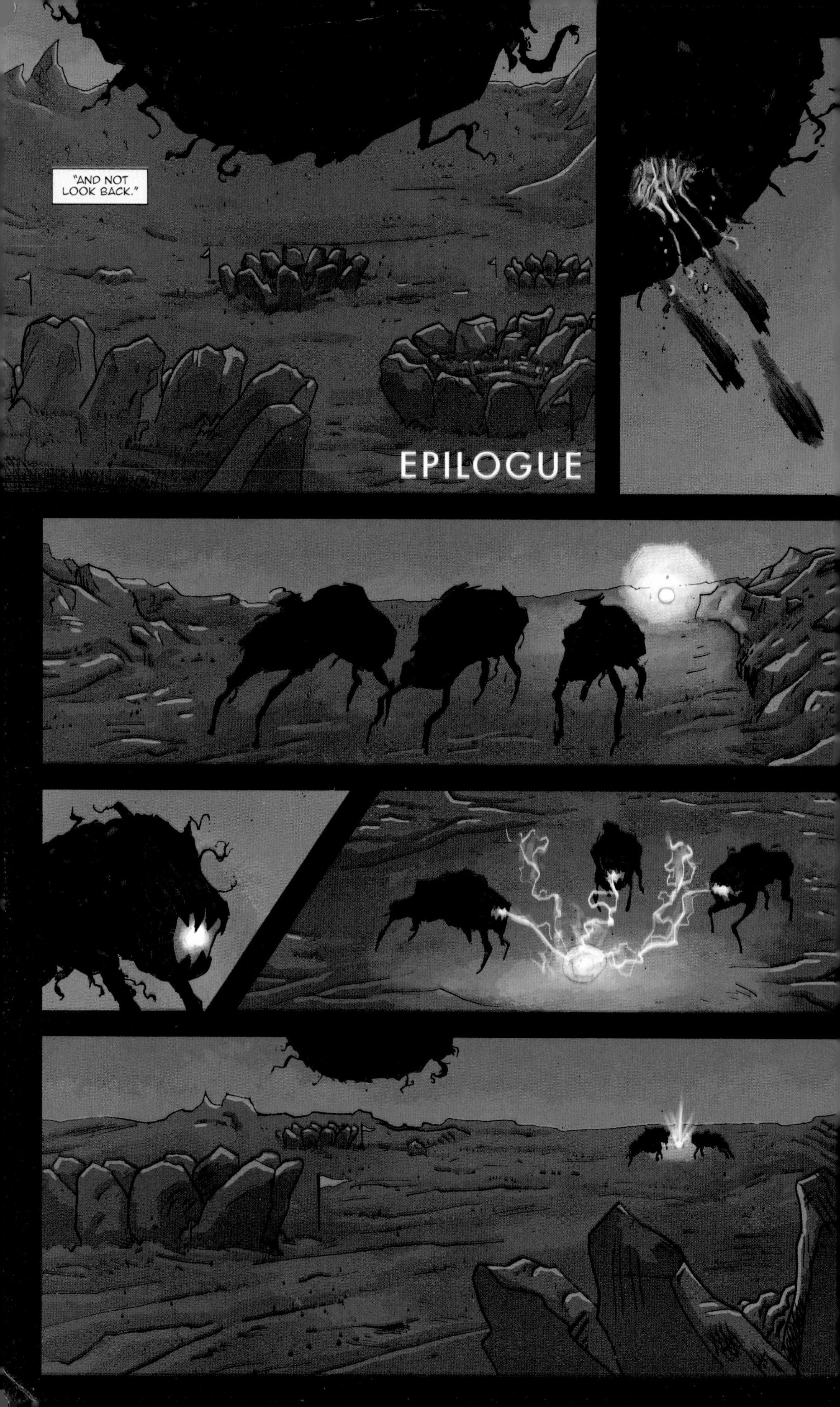
"AND NOT LOOK BACK."
EPILOGUE

WRITTEN BY  MICHAEL
MORECI

ART BY  VIC
MALHOTRA

ART ASSISTS

 KYLE CHARLES + BEN HOLLIDAY
(ISSUE THREE)   (ISSUE FIVE)

COLORS

 JUSTIN BOYD + LAUREN AFFE
(ISSUE FOUR)
COLOR ASSISTS BY MARISSA LOUISE
(ISSUE FIVE)

LETTERS

 RYAN FERRIER + JIM CAMPBELL
(ISSUE FOUR)

DESIGN

 TIM DANIEL

CO-CREATED BY MICHAEL MORECI, VIC MALHOTRA + STEVE SEELEY

75 YEARS
AFTER THE ROCHE LIMIT COLONY
WAS LEFT IN FLAMES.

A CREW OF MILITARY AND SCIENCE PERSONNEL
ARE SENT TO THE FORGOTTEN AND DESOLATE PLANET
ON A MYSTERIOUS EXPEDITION,
THEY QUICKLY LEARN ITS DARK SECRETS.

THEIR MISSION IS NOT WHAT THEY THOUGHT IT TO BE.

DANGER LURKS ALL AROUND,
THE CREW MEMBERS FIGHT TO FIND
A WAY OFF THE PLANET
AND TRY TO RESIST

A MYSTERIOUS PRESENCE
THAT HAUNTS THEM ALL.

CLANDESTINY